NERUDA'S SINS

Neruda's Sins

Hernán Loyola

TRANSLATED BY

Greg Dawes

Raleigh, North Carolina

Copyright © 2022
All rights reserved for this edition copyright © 2022 Editorial A Contracorriente

Originally published as *Los pecados de Neruda* in 2019
by Penguin Random House in Santiago

Library of Congress Cataloging-in-Publication Data
Names: Loyola, Hernán, author. | Dawes, Greg, translator.
Title: Neruda's sins / Hernán Loyola ; translated by Greg Dawes.
Other titles: Pecados de Neruda. English
Description: [Raleigh, North Carolina] : Editorial A Contracorriente, Department of Foreign Languages and Literatures at North Carolina State University, 2022. | Originally published as: Los pecados de Neruda in 2019. | Includes bibliographical references. | In English, translated from Spanish.
Identifiers: LCCN 2022004978 | ISBN 9781469672007 (paperback) | ISBN 9781469672014 (ebook)
Subjects: LCSH: Neruda, Pablo, 1904–1973—Criticism and interpretation. | Neruda, Pablo, 1904–1973. | Poets, Chilean—Biography.
Classification: LCC PQ8097.N4 Z6849 2022 | DDC 861/.62—dc23/eng/20220421
LC record available at https://lccn.loc.gov/2022004978

This is a publication of the Department of Foreign Languages and Literatures at North Carolina State University. For more information visit http://go.ncsu.edu/editorialacc.

Distributed by the University of North Carolina Press
www.uncpress.org

CONTENTS

Translator's Note, Greg Dawes vii

Preamble ix

The Original Sin:
Useless 1

The First Sin:
Sexist 14

The Second Sin:
Fable-Spinner 25

The Third Sin:
Rapist 36

The Fourth Sin:
Bad Husband 47

The Fifth Sin:
Bad Father 68

The Sixth Sin:
Plagiarist 86

The Seventh Sin:
Insolent 100

The Eighth Sin:
Abandoner 107

A Mortal Sin:
Stalinist 130

An Additional Sin:
Bourgeois 170

'Archives' on Josie Bliss 171

More 'Archives' on Josie Bliss 196

Bibliography 205
Author Bio 209

TRANSLATOR'S / EDITOR'S NOTE

IN THE MIDST of the COVID pandemic this year (2021), I approached the great Neruda critic and personal friend Hernán Loyola about translating his book *Los pecados de Neruda* (Santiago: PenguinRandomHouse / Lumen, 2019) into English. After agreeing to it, I set to work. When the translation was ready several months later, Hernán and I began reviewing it over Skype together. We spent hours upon hours going over the translation of the book, Neruda's poetry, expressions, vocabulary, and the like. Many times, we would get off topic and talk about Neruda, his life and works, politics, jazz and many other things, which made it all worth while.

I would like to let the reader know some of the decisions I made as a translator along the way. All of the translations in the book except the quotes from Antony Beevor's *The Spanish Civil War* (New York / London: Penguin Books, 1982) are mine. I also included "translator's notes" throughout the text regarding well-known cultural and political figures known in Spain and Latin America, unusual expressions Neruda used, references to Chilean culture, clarifications, and consultations with the author. In addition, I made some important decisions as a translator. For instance, I decided to use the past tense throughout and thereby changed the future that refers to the past that is so often used in publications in Spanish. I debated whether to use contractions or not and decided not to use them. I also provided both the Spanish original poems and their translations into English, but not so in the case, say, of Neruda's correspondence or passages from his memoirs. Finally, I furnished translations into English of books in Spanish wherever possible in the bibliography.

As General Editor of Editorial A Contracorriente I am proud to add this book to our collection.

Greg Dawes

PREAMBLE

The essayist Adriana Valdés, Director of the Chilean Academy of the Language, warns of a noticeable shortcoming regarding the image of Neruda in feminist circles, given the profound cultural changes which have taken place with respect to the situation of women in society:
"This deterioration does not refer to his poetry but rather to his personal behavior, but, like any type of condemnation, it extends to his entire public persona. [Indeed], if irreproachable personal behavior were a prerequisite to read and admire writers and thinkers, we would have to manage without people like Rimbaud, Céline, Sartre, Lope de Vega, Verlaine, and, it goes without saying, Oscar Wilde, Baudelaire, Rousseau, Nietzsche, Heidegger...those are the ones that I think of off the top of my head, and I have not named any Chileans."
Interview in *El Mercurio*, Santiago, 11/18/2018

THE APRIL 14TH 2018 issue of the Santiago newspaper *La Tercera* dedicated two pages to comment on the recent publication of a "Brief Decalogue of Ideas for a Feminist School" published in the magazine of the [female] Union Workers Commission of Spain [Sindicato Comisiones Obreras de España], in which its seventh point read thusly: "Eliminate writings by sexist and misogynist authors among the required reading for students." Among the writers and books worthy of being condemned in the *Decalogue* were "Pablo Neruda (*Veinte poemas de amor y una canción desesperada* [Twenty Love Poems and a Song of Despair], Arturo Pérez Reverte and Javier Marías (any of his books)." Additionally, it recommended that the instructors talk with their students "about the misogynist side of authors considered to be canonical."

I find it difficult to imagine *Twenty Love Poems*—close to turning one hundred years of age serving as an aid for lovers who have trouble communicating their feelings—in the defendant's chair. A worldwide poetry best seller in the

20th century and even today, thanks to the thousands of young readers (male and female) who adopted it with devotion in Chile in 1924, the condemnation of this book seems incomprehensible to me unless it is tied to fanaticism or ignorance. Besides the millions of copies published to this point, in practically all conceivable languages (and we are a few years away from the centennial of the first edition published by Nascimento), I testify that I witnessed how young and older couples—especially foreign couples (I saw Japanese, French and North American ones)—would go to Isla Negra asking for ten minutes of Neruda's time to thank him for writing those *Twenty Love Poems* which had fused their love and conjugal life. "As you see, I am still a matchmaking poet," he would tell me later with his proud smile.

I do not know the details of the arguments raised in the book by the severe feminist prosecutor as proof of his sexism, but I imagine it must include the first line in Poem 15: "Me gustas cuando callas porque estás como ausente" [I like you when you are silent because it as though you were absent], which to the Spanish feminists in the *Decalogue* must sound sexist, much as certain American feminists must take offense with the title of Raymond Carver's renowned short story "Will You Please Be Quiet, Please?" In both cases, it is due to the lack of understanding or ignorance of the true meaning or role of the phrases in context in each composition.

The denunciation of Neruda's 'sins,' at least since the beginning of the 1930s, was always abundant, tenacious and ferocious. The bard himself was used to them. But this latest denunciation motivated me to undo the wrongs: not jump in the ring like a defense lawyer for the poet, who, incidentally, needs no defense, but rather to clear up the incidents and events while dotting the i's and crossing the t's. In other words, to review and discuss—with the greatest amount of intellectual honesty that I can humanly muster as an admiring literary critic and with deep sympathy for my unforgettable friend—the most tenacious and disseminated accusations regarding evil intentions, defects, vices, guilt, errors, infractions, cruelty, crimes and malice which have been attributed to Pablo Neruda. Accusations that up to this day—forty-eight years after the death of the poet—circulate and have increased in richness of detail, as we have seen.

Before beginning, let me remind the attentive reader that this endless process of criticizing Neruda, some of whose chapters I intend to recount or analyze, is a type of sport in Chile that, as far as I know, is only practiced enthusiastically and continually with regards to Neruda. I have not seen essays or articles, interviews or reports in the media with pre-meditated and microscopic headlines like "Has the public image of so and so deteriorated...?" or denouncing ignominies other poets have committed. Neither have I seen nor become aware of denigrating films, nor stories by "professional" detractors about Vicente Huidobro, Pablo de Rokha, Gonzalo Rojas, Nicanor Parra, Enrique Lihn, Jorge Teiller, Óscar Hahn, Pedro Lastra or Waldo Rojas.[1] Certainly, their human sins and little sins are of interest to nobody, they simply are not news. Neruda's are—who knows why. I think only Gabriela Mistral has endured as much malicious gossip and rumors.

---

[1] Translator's note: these are names of some of Chile's major poets.

The Original Sin

Useless

"¿De dónde lo copiaste?"
["Where did you copy it from?"]
Confieso que he vivido [Memoirs]

I

"De un paisaje de áureas regiones
yo escogí
para darle querida mamá
esta humilde postal. *Neftalí*"

[From a scenery of golden regions
I chose
to give you my dear mother
this humble postcard. *Neftalí*]

NEFTALÍ REYES BASOALTO HAD NOT quite turned eleven when he wrote these lines on a postcard, dating them June 30th, 1915 in Temuco, to celebrate the day his stepmother Trinidad turned 46. It is the first poem written by Pablo Neruda. He alludes to it in his memoirs:

> I have been asked many times when I wrote my first poem, when poetry was born in me.
> I'll try to remember. Early in my childhood and having barely learned to write, I once felt very intense emotions and I traced several words that rhymed somewhat, but they were strange to me, different from everyday language. Prisoner of a profound anxiety, of an unknown feeling, a mix of anguish and sadness, I wrote them out clearly on paper. It was poem dedicated to my mother, that is, the woman I recognized as such, to my

angelical stepmother whose soft shadow protected me during my childhood. Completely unable to judge my first composition, I took it to my parents. They were in the dining room, lost in one of those conversations in hushed voices which divide, more than a river could, the world of children from the world of adults. I handed them the paper with the lines, trembling still from my first visit to inspiration. My father, distractedly, took it in his hands, distractedly read it, distractedly gave it back to me, and said:

"Where did you copy it from?"

And he continued talking in a low voice with my mother about his important and remote matters.

I seem to remember that that was how my first poem was born and that that was the first time I received the first, distracted glance of literary criticism.[1]

His recollection is not faithful to all the details, but in an ironic tone it evokes his first encounter with José del Carmen Reyes' hostility towards his son's poetic writing. The reasons for this rough rail worker's reaction to artistic activity arise from a nineteenth century pragmatic notion of progress, although, unconsciously, the energic method with which he applied the reasons essentially reproduced, in a layman's form, his father's religious authoritarianism. He was reacting against his own father, José Ángel.

Neftalí's father did not want the lazy poet his son was becoming in his house, much as he cruelly and violently opposed his eldest son Rodolfo accepting a scholarship to develop his considerable skills as a lyrical singer in the Conservatory in the capital. He would not have idle artists in his family. His sons should choose more productive careers which were denied to him and attain a higher standard of living than his. All of this according to the pragmatic mentality promoted by Chilean public education during the first few decades of the twentieth century. José del Carmen took this on with clear determination. How else to explain the conviction and zeal with which he tried to push Neftalí, who was not harmoniously in agreement with that effort?

El Liceo, el Liceo! Toda mi pobre vida
en una jaula triste... Mi juventud perdida!

---

1 Pablo Neruda, *Confieso que he vivido* [Memoirs], pp. 32–33.

Pero no importa, vamos! Pues mañana o pasado
seré burgués lo mismo que cualquier abogado,
que cualquier doctorcito que usa lentes y lleva
cerrados los caminos hacia la luna nueva...
Qué diablos, y en la vida como en una revista
un poeta se tiene que graduar de dentista!²

[High school, high school! All of my poor life / in a sad cell... My youth, lost! / But it matters not, after all! Tomorrow or the day after / I will be bourgeois much as any other lawyer, /and any little doctor who wears glasses and has /closed off the roads to the new moon... / What the hell, and in life as in magazines / the poet needs to graduate as a dentist!]

The conflict with his father was one of the most potent driving forces behind Neftalí's poetic growth. The first thing the young man had to face was to learn how to overcome his fear of José del Carmen. In his poem "El padre" [The Father] (1962), and in other places, Neruda remembered how *doña*³ Trinidad and he recognized the whistle of the cargo train perforating the rain, and how a short time later the gusts of wind would penetrate the house with its wooden planks once the railroad worker arrived, and from that moment on there was door slamming, heavy footsteps and loud scolding, orders and threats.

Neftalí was raised fearing that figure with rough gestures and angry expressions. But he also grew to love his father, which he showed until the death of that *caballero* (gentleman: that was what he called him in letters he sent to his sister Laura) after failed attempts to show him the *productivity* of his poetry and his activities as a Consul. He even failed in his attempt—announced in Buenos Aires in 1934—to make him a grandfather. José del Carmen Reyes died in 1938, when his son was just beginning to become renowned poetically and politically in Chile.

---

2 Pablo Neruda, "El liceo", 1920.
3 Translator's note: *Doña* is a term of endearment and respect in Spanish which cannot really be translated into English. Some examples would be Rómulo Gallegos' *Doña Bárbara* [Doña Barbara, 1929] and Federico García Lorca's *Doña Rosita la soltera* [Doña Rosita the Single Woman, 1935].

2

In a symmetrical way, José del Carmen's efforts to block Neftalí's poetic vocation and channel his interests also failed. All strategies that he put into play to achieve that outcome had the exact opposite effect than those he pursued.

Ironically, José del Carmen was the first and most important promoter of his son's literary future, beginning with the fact that he had taken him from Parral to Temuco. The frontier: can we imagine the bard Pablo Neruda being raised in any other place? Under these circumstances it is vital to not overlook the principal merit of the American citizen Charles Sumner Mason, born in Portland, Maine in 1829, and a resident of Parral since approximately 1865. With a pioneer's spirit he did not cease until he had moved his family (including his sister-in-law Trinidad Candia) to the recently established city of Temuco, where he lived until his death in 1914. Perhaps Neftalí Reyes would have been born in Parral anyway, but Pablo Neruda would not have emerged if his father, thanks to Mason's support, would not have found stable work on the frontier's railway and would not have married Trinidad in 1905.

Thus, starting out with the prejudice that writing poems was not only a useless activity but also the road to becoming effeminate and weak of character, José del Carmen decided to educate the young man austerely so that, in providing some daylight between him and his writing, he would "learn to be a man." He began to oblige him to wake up at dawn and to climb on the cargo train while he shivered from the cold and lack of sleep. Requiring Neftalí to accompany him on his work excursions was a surefire way to strengthen him physically and personally, since his son was notoriously weak and sickly.

Taking off from the station in Temuco, after a few kilometers the cargo train switched from the longitudinal tracks (North-South) to the branch line heading toward the woods near Boroa, Pitrufquén or Carahue. But once in a while it continued straight toward the South. There is a manuscript of the sonnet "Esta iglesia no tiene..." [This church does not have...], dated 1920 and written by Lake Llanquihue, hundreds of kilometers from Temuco. Therein the reference to Puerto Varas, a small and beautiful city which rises above the lake's bank, in this eneasyllable poem penned in 1958:

> Aunque murió hace tantos años
> por allí debe andar mi padre
> con el poncho lleno de gotas
> y la barba color de cuero.

La barba color de cebada
que recorría los ramales,
el corazón de aguacero,
y que alguien se mida conmigo
a tener padre tan errante,
a tener padre tan llovido:
su tren iba desesperado
entre las piedras de Carahue,
por los rieles de Collipulli,
en las lluvias de Puerto Varas.[4]

[Although he died many years ago / somewhere my father must be walking / with his poncho covered with water drops / and his leather-colored beard. //His barley-colored beard / that traveled the rail lines, / the heart of a rainstorm, / and I dare anyone / to find a more errant father, / to find a father more rained on: / his train ran desperately / among the rocks of Carahue, / along the tracks of Collipulli, /in the rain in Puerto Varas.]

The rude rail worker never knew that it was his own locomotive that led Neftalí to the foundational nucleus of his poetic imaginary: the Southern forests. When the train stopped beside quarries, as a child he walked among the trees while the workers broke up the stones to reinforce the railways threatened by the frequent rains in the region. The forests revealed to Neftalí fascinating, enormous trees, birds, beetles, partridge's eggs. Straying far from the train at times he would find himself alone and lost in the midst of the dense woods, oscillating between dread and curiosity and discovering a world populated by confusing forms, colors and aromas. This sensorial and aesthetic rite of passage was joined by an earthly initiation: the lessons provided by matter. The Chilean forests introduced Neftalí to the mystery of biodegradation ("Un tronco podrido: qué tesoro!" [A rotten tree trunk: what a treasure!], that is, the interdependence of life and death, which would later always be present in his best works ("Galope muerto", "Entrada a la madera", "Alturas de Macchu Picchu" ["Dead Gallop", "Opening to Wood", "Heights of Machu Picchu"].

---

4 Pablo Neruda, "Carta para que me manden madera" [Letter so you will send me Wood], *Estravagario* [Extravagaria], 1958.

3

Along with that house with wooden planks, where his *mamadre*[5] Trinidad reigned supreme, for Neftalí the Southern forests were a feminine, maternal space, profound darkness to which he arrived on the cargo train. But he did not perceive it fully as a Romantic haven, but rather as energy, like a hot spring of forms, colors, and dynamic action. The forests were a space of active absorption, a fountain of *knowledge*. But it was immobile space. In a complementary way, Neftalí found *action* in February of 1920: in the midst of summer and his first—much yearned—trip to the sea.

The rail worker José del Carmen Reyes decided that the powerful, southern ocean provided another useful opportunity to make Neftalí a man... and not a poet. With his customary willfulness his father was able to have his friend and buddy Horacio Pacheco lend him a house in Puerto Saavedra (formerly Bajo Imperial), 80 kilometers west of Temuco, which could be reached via the Imperial river. There were no other access roads; only the fluvial route from docks at Carahue.

Under this name and in humble condition the city-fortress La Imperial has arisen from the ashes, founded in 1552 by Pedro de Valdivia. It was the conquistadors' most important military enclave during the centuries when they were at war with the Araucanian natives, whom they were never able to submit to their rule. La Imperial was the capital of that *American Flanders*. There, the poet and soldier Alonso de Ercilla[6]—later known as the author of *La Araucana* [The Araucaniad]—was about to be executed on orders from the young governor García Hurtado de Mendoza, in whose presence don Alonso had extracted his sword to duel with Juan de Pineda. The Araucanians attacked and destroyed La Imperial in 1600, and it was left abandoned and forgotten until the end of the nineteenth century, when it was christened with another name: Carahue, a small fluvial port of certain significance as a point of embarkment to Puerto Saavedra and other places not far away.

The train with José del Carmen and the family aboard arrived in Carahue filling the station with clouds of smoke, with the engine's loud noise and bells.

---

5 Translator's note: This is an affectionate term Neruda used for his stepmother. He considered her to be his mother.

6 Translator's note: Alonso de Ercilla y Zúñiga (1533–1594). Born in Madrid, he was nobleman, soldier and epic poet who fought against the Araucanians (Mapuche) natives in Chile (1556–63) and wrote the renowned *La Araucana* (1569/1578/1589).

Unloading the countless pieces of luggage, getting the small family organized and making our way in the oxcart to the steam engine that would take us down the Imperial river, was quite a production, directed, of course, by my father's blue eyes and rail worker's whistle. We squeezed both the luggage and ourselves into the small riverboat that would take us to the sea. There were no sleeping quarters. I sat near the bow. The wheels churned the fluvial currents with their paddles, the vessel's engines ground and huffed and puffed...[7]

There were two small boats: the *Cautín*—in which the Reyes clan traveled—and the *Saturno*.[8]

In his memoirs Neruda only dedicated—in 1972—a few lines to this second part of the trip: "An acordeon broke into its romantic plea, its love call. Nothing can flood a fifteen-year-old's heart with feeling like a voyage down a strange, wide river, between steep banks, on the way to the mysterious sea."[9] But ten years before he had made it the focus of the important poem "The First Sea" [El primer mar] in *Memorial de Isla Negra* [*Isla Negra*], where he summed up the meaning the trip had for him in an unsurpassable way:

...yo, en la proa, pequeño
inhumano,
perdido,
aún sin razón ni canto,
ni alegría,
atado al movimiento de las aguas
que iban entre los montes apartando
para mí solo aquellas soledades,
para mí solo aquel camino puro,
para mí solo el universo.[10]

[...I, on the bow, small / inhumane, / lost, / still without reason or song, / nor joy, / tied to the movement of the waters / which meandered through the hills setting aside / that solitude only for me, / that pure route only for me, / the universe only for me.

---

7 Pablo Neruda, *Confieso que he vivido* [Memoirs], p. 27.
8 Translator's note: *Cautín* is the former name of the province whose capital is Temuco. It is also the name of a river in that province. *Saturno* means "Saturn."
9 Pablo Neruda, *Confieso que he vivido* [Memoirs], p. 28.
10 Pablo Neruda, *Obras completas* [Complete Works], II, 1999, p. 1149.

He evoked that river trip via an anaphora *para mí—only for me—*as the road to recognizing his own creative individuality. Subsequent lines in the same poem visualized with even greater precision the meaning of this spacial leap from the forests to the sea:

...y cuando el mar de entonces
se desplomó como una torre herida,
se incorporó encrespado de su furia,
salí de las raíces,
se me agrandó la patria,
se rompió la unidad de la madera:
la cárcel de los bosques
abrió una puerta verde
por donde entró con su trueno
y se extendió mi vida con un golpe de mar, en el espacio.

[...and when that sea / collapsed like a wounded tower, / rose curled in its fury, / I left the roots behind, / my view of my homeland grew, / the unity of the wood was shattered: / the forest's cell / opened the green door / through which a wave entered with its thunder / and my life was stretched out / with the blow of the sea, in the open space.]

That first encounter with the ocean in the South allowed Pablo to understand that the protection provided by the maternal cloisters (the southern forests) was a limitation resolved by the integration of the polar opposite: the coastal ocean in Puerto Saavedra—with its tireless and furious attack on the rocks—represented the masculine model, the paternal model that José del Carmen could not offer him. He glimpsed another way of transforming his knowledge into *action* thanks to the ocean. As a consequence, for Neftalí 1920 was the year of his great leap forward, which ended in October with an act of rebellion against José del Carmen: the invention of the name Pablo Neruda. The inner part of the back cover of the first of three notebooks that his sister Laura kept, included the stamp Neftalí Reyes, under which the high schooler wrote by hand and in blue ink: *Pablo Neruda since October 1920*.[11]

José del Carmen underlined the type of rite of passage that that experience near the sea in Southern Chile had on Neftalí. Neruda's memoirs

---

11 For more details on this matter, see Hernán Loyola, *El joven Neruda* [The Young Neruda] 1904–1935, pp. 58–62.

evoked—with affectionate irony—Neftalí's first immersion into the very cold waters of the ocean:

> What frighetened me was the apocalyptic moment in which my father ordered us to take our daily swim. Far from the giant waves, the water splashed my sister Laura and me with cold whiplashes. And, shivering, we thought that a wave's finger would drag us into the mountains of the sea. When my sister and I, holding hands, our teeth chattering and our ribs blue, were prepared to die, we would hear my father's railroad whistle as he ordered us to take of leave of our martyrdom.[12]

In this paragraph Neruda evoked his father's characteristic gestures and some obsessions for the first time in detail, which likely exasperated him, and which he had never dared reveal openly. Seen from the point of view of an old and dying man and without meaning to, Neruda's affectionate irony left us with an image of José del Carmen confirming yet again—completely against his own wishes—his son's poetic future. On this occasion, it was the trying swimming ritual among the many stages of initiation that awaited Neftalí in the course of 1920.

4

There were critical moments in the relationship, such as when his father, unleashed his fury when he discovered some early high school publication in *Corre-Vuela*, or when he caught Neftalí simply writing a poem. He picked up a box or bag of books, magazines and various other notebooks the poet had, and made a big fire with them on the patio. Neftalí broke down crying, but his sister Laura called him aside and told him in a soft voice that he need not worry because she had hidden his main notebooks, those in which he had written out the final versions of his poems.

In 1926 Pablo no longer went to classes at the university and his father cut off his monthly support. At the end of October he wrote to his sister: "...as of yesterday I am left without economic support. How can I fix this? The last resort would be Anita's, because there are too many people and I do not like it... I would be better off at Señora Petrona's, Bulnes 30, which you are familiar

---

12 Pablo Neruda, *Obras completas* [Complete Works], V, 2002, pp. 411–412.

with. She is Laurita Vega's friend and that is where Fidias is. Anyway, whatever they decide, let me know quickly because I am too old to not eat every day."[13]

On top of the miseries of daily life there were those associated with international travel, a trip to Italy in December ("and I do not have more money for the ticket. What will I eat in Genova? Smoke?") which did not materialize, and a position in the Consulate in Rangoon, Burma, which he would be offered a few months later—in the fall of 1927—thanks to the help of Manuel Bianchi Gundián. To Laurita, who asked him nicely to come home, he responded in March: "What am I going to do in Temuco? Rather than having run ins with my father, I prefer to stay here, at ease."[14] He would leave June 8th without bidding farewell to his mother and his father except through Laura.

But upon returning from Asia in April in 1932, his first stopping point would be the house made of wooden siding. Neruda disembarked from the *Forafric* in Puerto Montt, and immediately took the northbound train to Temuco. For José del Carmen as for Pablo seeing each other again was surely difficult, suggestive of a reticent, controlled love. The prodigal son returned without any money, without clear work prospects, without any visible signs of fame and with a book in progress; in sum, not exactly a successful homecoming. And besides with his wife Maruca in tow.[15] Nonetheless, she contributed significantly to making the situation—which she barely understood—more pleasurable during those days thanks to her smooth and educated manners and to her winning over Trinidad and Laura. In private, and with likely sarcastic comments and reproaches, José del Carmen ended up helping his 'useless' son settle in once again in Santiago.

From November 1932 on, Pablo received news of doña Trinidad's failing health, who in those days must have had a delicate operation: "I was immensely happy knowing that [my mom] made it through the operation. It was a real miracle, and I hope she is in good spirits. [...] Here it is terribly hot, and I hope to have permission shortly to take off for the South."[16]

At the end of March of the following year (1933), he traveled to Temuco to spend a few days there without Maruca (because of the cold weather and the

---

13 Pablo Neruda, *Obras completas* [Complete Works], V, 2002, p. 798.
14 Pablo Neruda, *Obras completas* [Complete Works], V, 2002, p. 801.
15 Translator's note: Maruca is the nickname Neruda gave to his first wife, María Antonieta Hagenaar, the daughter of a Dutch bank employee, whom he met and married in Batavia.
16 Pablo Neruda, *Obras completas* [Complete Works], V, 2002, p. 825; letter to Laura, 11/27/1932.

lack of money), to visit with doña Trinidad, still recovering from the effects of her operation. During the first half of May he traveled again, this time due to José del Carmen's sudden illness. He stayed for at least seven days on the Frontier, some of them in the longed-for Puerto Saavedra, which he had not been able to visit since his return from Asia. His reencounter with the ocean turned out to be decisive for the development of his new book (which did not yet have the title *Residence en la tierra 2* [Residence on Earth 2]). Once more his father, whose illness was the reason for the trip, became the unwilling promoter of the important poem "El Sur del océano" [The South of the Ocean].

5

Mi pobre padre duro
allí estaba, en el eje de la vida,
la viril amistad, la copa llena.
Su vida fue una rápida milicia
y entre madrugar y sus caminos,
entre llegar para salir corriendo,
un día con más lluvia que otros días
el conductor José del Carmen Reyes
subió al tren de la muerte y hasta ahora no ha vuelto.
"El padre", *Memorial de Isla Negra*

[My poor, hardened father / was there, at the axis of his life, /the virile friendship, the glasses / full. / His life was a rapid militia / and between rising at dawn and his roads, / between / arriving to leaving on the run, / one day when it was raining more than others / the conductor José del Carmen Reyes / boarded Death's train and has not been back since.]
"The Father", *Isla Negra*

On May 1st, 1938, having returned from Spain the year before, Neruda read a passionate speech along the lines of Popular Front politics in Temuco to a crowd at Casa del Pueblo [The People's House]. Its themes covered solidarity with Republican Spain, the exaltation of the tasks of the Alliance of Intellectuals in defense of a threatened culture in Chile, and, in particular, the condemnation of the simultaneous celebration of a pro-Nazi event at the German Club in the city, supported by a two-page tribute in *Diario*

Austral [The Southern Daily] on German Day. "This city, Temuco, should be," Neruda declared, "the center of the anti-Nazi, anti-German campaign, by which I mean not against peaceful Germans who do not have any imperialist or political intentions in our country, but rather those who helped by the disorder and the greediness of the governing class have taken hold of our land and blatantly walk past us with the swastika symbols of assassins."[17] At the end of his speech Neruda referred to a private matter:

> This is my message and I have not hedged in coming to talk with you having left for the moment the bedside of my overwhelmed father who is gravely ill and almost unconscious, because in coming here I also speak for his radical Popular Front ideas, I, his prodigal son from Temuco, to lay in my city's ears and heart these words by La Pasionaria,[18] written in blood and honor: *It is better to die standing that to live kneeling.*

This event in Temuco—the space of his childhood and adolescence—was Neruda's first political speech, his debut as public orator. But it was a happenstance because Pablo had come from Santiago a week before, not motivated by politics but by his father's worsening health. He was staying in an old friend's house—Dr. Manuel Marín, who was his father's physician (and the brother of the writer Juan Marín), where he wrote to Delia del Carril,[19] who was in Santiago:

> My dad is still bad off...he has been in an anguishing condition on a respirator...but he is responding. He has the strength of an ox, but I cannot believe this will end well. Here I spend the days and nights giving him what he asks for (he has been able to recall some words) and I miss you very much. María has been behaving like an angel, she comes every day, gets up at midnight, etc. My mother is bedridden [,] awaiting the blow

---

17 Pablo Neruda, *Obras completas* [Complete Works], V, 2002, p. 400–404. "Fuera de Chile los enemigos de la patria!" [Expel the Enemies of the Homeland!]. Originally published in *La Voz Radical* [The Radical Voice], Temuco, 7/2/1938.

18 Translator's note: "La Pasionaria" was the nickname of Isidora Dolores Ibárruri Gómez, a communist from the Basque country, who fought on the Republican side in the Spanish Civil War (1936–1939). She was the one who coined the famous cry "¡No Pasarán! [They will not pass]."

19 Translator's note: Delia del Carril, Neruda's second wife, was an Argentine painter and communist he met and with whom fell in love in Madrid. They stayed together for a little more than twenty years (1934–1955).

that will also kill her and Laura is a wreck under these circumstances, so everything falls on me.[20]

José del Carmen Reyes Morales, conductor of the cargo train, died on May 7th at 67 years of age, a rather early age because "he was a man of other climates."[21] In the last weeks of his life, he was then able to appreciate the love his rebellious son had for him, who, bedside, undoubtedly knew how to tell him he loved him, which alleviated his agony. Perhaps he passed away with the suspicion that his son the poet was not exactly useless.

---

20 For more details, see David Schidlowsky, *Neruda y su tiempo: las furias y las penas*. [Neruda and his Time: Furies and Suffering], Volume I, 1904–1939, 2008, p. 374.
21 Translator's note: José del Carmen Reyes was born and grew up in Parral, Chile, which has a dry and hot climate. He suffered greatly in Temuco due to its rainy and cold climate.

The First Sin

Sexist

"Me gustas cuando callas"
[I like you when you are silent]
Poema 15 [Poem 15]

I

THERE MAY BE SOME doubts harbored with regards to the muse in some of the poems in *Twenty Love Poems*, but not so in the case of Poem 15. "Me gustas cuando callas porque estás como ausente" [I like you when you are silent because it is as though you are absent] was written, without a doubt for Albertina Azócar, a student of French at the Instituto Pedagógico [The Pedagogical Institute] at the University of Chile, located then on the corner of Alameda and Cumming Avenue, next to the trade school Liceo de Aplicación. Neruda fell in love with Albertina in 1921, shortly after settling in in Santiago. In his letters he called her "mi Pequeña" [my Little One] or Netocha.[1]

Far from a sexist threat to be silent, this line, and all of Poem 15, converted Albertina's common characteristic into an act of praise for something that could have been unfavorable: her silence. Albertina, the silent one, was a young woman of few words, perhaps because of her timidity or because her repressive family made her grow accustomed to keeping quiet. We do not know. The first original draft of Poem 15 carried the title "Poema de su silencio" [Poem about her Silence]. Neruda would later remember how they would walk hand in hand in the Parque Forestal[2] without Albertina saying a word. But her silence was not a problem for Pablo, who was happy and at ease with her, especially in bed in the poet's modest room on Padura Street (today Club Hípico).

---

[1] Translator's note: This was a term of endearment that Neruda invented.
[2] Translator's note: The Parque Forestal is the Santiago equivalent of Central Park in New York.

In his biography about Neruda, Volodia Teitelboim asked what Pablo saw in Albertina.[3] The answer was simple: the young woman was the intense, slow and soft lover of whom he had dreamed, the incarnation of the sweetest skin yearned for in his fantasies. Sensuality, as the academic Alain Sicard loves to reiterate, is the key to understanding Neruda's poetry, not only in the sexual sphere but also in his delight with objects in the world. The powerful sexual attraction Albertina held was perhaps the only real sustenance of that love, but the enamored poet did not try to idealize that reality but rather verbalize sincerely that physical intensity which dictated his emotions and feelings (therein the success of the book). Their relationship lasted until mid 1923, when Albertina returned for good to Lota after having had urgent surgery in Santiago, obliged by her parents to return to the family home and continue her studies of French in the recently created program at the University of Concepción. She was not able or she did not know how to stand up for the love that united her with her poet.

But the sexual fascination continued to haunt Neruda, who did not cease writing to Albertina—asking and pleading in vain for them to be reunited—until mid 1927, when, with his friend Álvaro Hinojosa, he boarded the trans-Andean train to Buenos Aires in order to take the passenger ship *Baden* to Rangoon. The proof of the sway she held over him are numerous letters (more than one hundred) in which her wordsmith frenetically tried to convince her from 1923 to 1927 to act, to overcome any barriers, to reunite with him and thus recover the erotic intimacy that they had shared for nearly two years. No other woman was the recipient of so many avid letters—so pathetic at times—from our poor poet than the young woman from Lota. To no other woman, before Matilde Urrutia, did he invent and propose so many plans to at the very least spend another night with her. This included a possible rendezvous at the end of 1925 in Ancud (on the island of Chiloé), where Pablo had traveled to accompany Albertina's brother, Rubén Azócar—a friend and teacher at the local high school—where he dreamed of his lover's parallel trip from Lota. She did not board the train to reunite with her poet, not then and not even when Pablo was about to embark on his trip to Rangoon in 1927: that was the form her silence took. Although Pablo never lacked consoling lovers in those years, none would top the sincerity and force of his sentiments for Albertina.

---

3 Volodia Teitelboim, *Neruda*, 1996, p. 80.

2

That sexual attraction was the driving force that inspired many—and especially the expressive atmosphere—of the *Twenty Love Poems* and the letters and Pablo's anxious interventions until 1927. It had then a heightened effect on his poetic authenticity that paid off so well for the lover-author and has until this day. But that same erotic fascination granted Albertina another type of negative power. To overcome his intimate crisis of 1923, the poet's egocentric ambition, along with his fear and insecurity, allowed his passion for Albertina to become the false figure of an all-powerful cosmic poetic and energetic source, capable of stirring in him the poems that should have saved him from his defeat and frustration in *Crepusculario* [The Book of Twilights] in 1923:

> It has to do with a cycle of poems which had many titles until it took on the title *El hondero entusiasta* [The Ardent Slingsman]. That book, inspired by an intense passionate love, was my first cyclical attempt in poetry: to encompass man, nature, passions and events themselves which were developed in it, in a single unity of purpose. In writing those poems I considered them deeply, feverishly and wildly mine.[4]

If the feminists who criticized him today would have read that book, they would have found in it much more material for their inquisitorial mission than in *Twenty Love Poems*. The poet, in a state of crisis, had conceived a rescue plan in which he called aloud for the erotic help of his lover:

> Sumérgeme en tu nido de vértigo y caricia.
> Anhélame, retiéneme
> De pie te grito! Quiéreme. [...]
> Yo sólo te deseo, yo sólo te deseo!
> No es amor, es deseo que se agosta y se extingue,
> es precipitación de furias,
> acercamiento de lo imposible,
> pero estás tú,
> estás para dármelo todo,
> y a darme lo que tienes a la tierra viniste
> como yo para contenerte,

---

4 Pablo Neruda, *Obras completas* [Complete Works], IV, 1999, p. 1201.

y desearte, / y recibirte! [...]
Llénate de mí.
Ansíame, agótame, viérteme, sacrifícame [...],
Porque tú eres mi ruta. Te forjé en lucha viva.
De mi pelea contra mí mismo, fuiste [...]
Seré la ruta tuya. Pasa. Déjame irme.
Ansíame, agótame, viérteme, sacrifícame.
Haz tambalear los cercos de mis últimos límites.
Y que yo pueda, al fin, correr en fuga loca, [...]
correr fuera de mí mismo, perdidamente,
libre de mí, furiosamente libre.
Irme,
Dios mío, irme!

[Submerge me in your nest of vertigo and tenderness. / Yearn for me, retain me / Standing I cry out! Want me. [...] / I only desire you, I only desire you! / It is not love, it is desire that debilitates and extinguishes itself, / it is a precipitation of furies, / nearing the impossible, / but you are there, / there to give me everything, / and you came to give me what earthly self you have / and I to try to contain you, / and desire you, / and welcome you! [...] / Fill yourself with me. / Long for me, exhaust me, pour me out, sacrifice me [...] / Because you are my road. I forged you in a live struggle. / From my struggle with myself, / you were [...] / I will be your road. Come in. Let me leave. / Long for me, exhaust me, pour me out, sacrifice me. / Make the fencing around my last limits tumble, / And let me, finally, run, escape madly, [...] / run outside of myself, hopelessly, / free of myself, furiously free. / Leave, / oh God, I need to leave!]

Via the demanding and mad vehemence in this writing, Pablo thought he had found his most original language, the route to his definitive poetic affirmation and the achievement of fame. Upon hearing *The Ardent Slingsman*, his friend Aliro Oyarzún, who enjoyed a certain prestige as a keen reader, confessed to Pablo that he sensed the echoes of the Uruguayan poet Carlos Sabat Ercasty, whom they had read carefully. Neruda categorically denied that influence; after all he had written that very poem—which gave the collection its title—at night in Temuco under the stars he gazed upon through the window in his room, in a state of delirious inspiration, of creative euphoria. But, consumed by doubt, he anxiously wrote to his Uruguayan mentor, giving him an enormous responsibility in the case of a negative response. Fortunately for Pablo, Sabat Ercasty was not impressed by the young man and responded that he could see some of his work in the lines he received. Spiteful and furious, Pablo brusquely abandoned the project and let the many poems (almost one hundred) he had written for that book in 1923 go astray. Consequently, *The Ardent Slingman*—a book in which he had put so much faith—would never have been published had Luis Enrique Délano (thanks to the help of Albertina and other friends) not rescued a dozen lost texts ten years later.

Giving up on this project in early 1924 forced Pablo to recuperate his most sincere and authentic erotic language in *Twenty Love Poems* midway through that year. This was against the grain and without meaning to, because the language associated with his sincerity seemed poetically inferior in his eyes due to the pressure brought to bear on him by the idealized and false image of himself—the image of the slingman. Pablo proclaimed the triumph of that sincerity in Poem 1, written after Sabat Ercasty's reply, where he noted clearly the rise and fall of the slingman, and the return of authentic love:[5]

> Fui solo como un túnel. De mí huían los pájaros
> y en mí la noche entraba su invasión poderosa.
> Para sobrevivirme te forjé como un arma,
> como una flecha en mi arco, como una piedra en mi honda.
>
> Pero cae la hora de la venganza, y te amo.
> Cuerpo de piel, de musgo, de leche ávida y firme.
> Ah los vasos del pecho! Ah los ojos de ausencia!
> Ah las rosas del pubis! Ah tu voz lenta y triste!
>
> Cuerpo de mujer mía, persistiré en tu gracia...
>
> [I was alone like tunnel. Birds fled from me / and night inhabited me with its powerful invasion. / To survive myself I forged you like a weapon, / like an arrow in my bow, like a stone in my sling. // But now revenge's hour has come, and I love you. / Body of skin, of moss, of avid and firm milk. / Ah your breasts' cups! Ah your absent eyes! / Ah the roses round your pubis! Ah your slow and sad voice! // Body of my lover, I will remain in your grace...]

---

[5] For more details, see Hernán Loyola, *El joven Neruda* [The Young Neruda], 2014, pp. 97–100.

3

On October 5th, 1929 the Consul[6]—still under name Neftalí Ricardo Reyes—began writing a long letter that he wrote over different and sporadic stages until he completed it on November 21st in his bungalow next to the sea in Wellawatta, a suburb of Colombo, Ceylon (today Sri Lanka). The letter was bound for Buenos Aires where his faithful Argentine friend—whom he never met in person—lived. Eandi had the cheerful and priceless resolve to nudge Pablo with his own letters to write a marvelous collection of letters which is crucial to understanding his life in Asia and to interpreting his *Residencia en la tierra* 1 [Residence on Earth 1].

After thanking Eandi for his obstinate and unbelievable support, at the beginning of his letter, Pablo declared for the first time what he had hidden out of dignity: the ongoing humiliation of having an unbearable economic situation: "I make 166 American dollars a month, around here that is the salary of a low-level shop assistant." To which he added a confession that is extremely interesting for our purposes:

> If my salary were stable and unchanging—that is, if I could count on receiving it at the end of every month—then I would not mind living in any corner [of the world], cold or warm. Yes, I who made of irresponsibility and movement a doctrine for my own life and those of others, now feel an anguishing desire to settle down, to dedicate myself to something, to live or die peacefully. *I also want to marry, but soon, tomorrow, and live in a big city.* (My emphasis)[7]

Coincidentally, just as Pablo was writing these lines to Eandi, Albertina Rosa Azócar was disembarking in the La Rochelle-Pallice port on October 16th, and, not yet settled in serenely, she sent Pablo a postcard from Brussels with some news. A researcher and instructor at the University of Concepción in pedagogy, Albertina was sent to Europe to study teaching methods with Ovide Decroly in the renowned École de l'Ermitage, near the Soignes Forest.

It is not difficult to imagine the commotion this caused Pablo upon receiving the news, in November, and the anxiety it produced. Forgetting about Albertina's snubs of his desires from 1924 to 1927, he immediately begged

---

6 Translator's note: Neruda was the lowest ranking consul.
7 Pablo Neruda, *Obras completas* [Complete Works], V, 2002, p. 940.

her to travel to Colombo to wed him, suggesting in letters sent on December 17th and 18th the way to change her return ticket to Chile for one to Colombo from Marseille. Between his reborn attraction and his disastrous economic situation, his anguish got to the point that he asked his ex-lover to postpone the hypothetical trip to Colombo until the end of February to be able to welcome her with some decorum. One could only imagine the terrible humiliation our miserable Consul faced given his inability to even provide a decent place for the girlfriend he had dreamed of and desired.

She had other worries in the meantime. In mid-December she traveled to London with several classmates without leaving a forwarding address. One of Pablo's urgent letters was returned to Colombo with the note *Parti sans laisser adresse* [Left without leaving an address], while a postcard arrived from London with only four words written on it: "Your silence troubles me" along with her new address in Brussels. Pablo responded on January 12th, 1930, with a letter as pathetic as some from years before:

> My Albertina, I can barely contain my fury and write to you calmly... I have been madly thinking about you all this time... and awaiting word from you with anguish, and when I thought it had arrived, my letter was returned because you have not deigned to respond with your ideas.
> Yesterday I thought I would go mad with rage, disillusionment, sadness. I imagine my other six or seven letters sent to that same address will end up lost too... And, of course, a small postcard in one month! After five years of complete silence, what you have to tell me fits on a postcard!
> Tell me, Albertina, should I doubt you?

Knowing that Albertina's embarkation was set for the first day of February, Pablo's stubbornness became more pronounced and turned even more pathetic. He wrote to her summing up the plan and asking for forgiveness for his demands in his last letter ("All of this should happen now or never"), adding a postscript confessing how lonely he felt. Little did he know that that would be even less convincing to the undaunted Albertina, who, without getting upset, set out on the sea for Chile.

Ironically, her commitment to the university (which she brandished as the reason for not traveling to Colombo) was left as unattended as Pablo's desperate desires. Upon returning to Concepción, she appeared before the director of the program who had sent her to Brussels and who reprimanded her for the content in her last letter to Pablo, which he had just opened. Furious due to this breach of her privacy, Albertina abandoned her post at the university and with it her project to apply the Decroly Method for which she had traveled to Brussels, and for which—according to her last letter to Pablo—she refused the idea of reuniting with him in Ceylon.

4

On June 13th, 1930, traveling from Colombo, Pablo disembarked in Batavia, an island of Java, and on December 6th that same year married a Javanese woman (of Dutch descent) somewhat his senior, and whose name he immediately Chileanized as Maruca. The obvious rush was the result of his attempt to fulfill his dream with Albertina—in Ceylon—to, as he declared in his letter to Eandi, "*marry, but soon, tomorrow.*"

He had arrived in Batavia as the Consul of Singapore, which meant that he doubled his salary and seemed to reassure him that he would have a married life free from economic distress. As unfortunate as his honeymoon was, nobody notified the Consul in Batavia of the catastrophic effects of the Great Depression and Wall Street Crash that ensued in 1929, which unleashed its delayed fury on the Chilean economy at the end of 1930 and not before, due to the trade agreements between the government of the United States and General Ibañez del Campo,[8] which held up until the end of that year. In early 1931 shipments from Chile were almost cut in half, and nominally, because they did not always arrive. Moreover, Pablo began to understand that marrying had been an enormous mistake. "Why did I get married in Batavia?" he would ask himself decades later, in 1958, in *Extravagaria*.

5

Pablo Neruda and his wife Maruca Hagenaar arrived in Temuco on the train from Puerto Montt on April 19th, 1932 in the afternoon. They had disembarked from the freight ship *Forafric* they boarded in Colombo. In addition to the Batavia-Colombo connection, their trip included two terrible months of

---

8 Translator's note: Carlos Ibañez del Campo (1877–1960) was a general and the president of Chile twice—from 1927 to 1931 and then again from 1952 to 1958. He assumed dictatorial powers in his first term, whereas in the second his center-right positions were more tempered (even counting on some support from the Popular Socialist Party).

travel on the Indian Ocean and the Atlantic Ocean, passing through Cape Town and through Magellan's Strait. Those two interminable and lugubrious months were projected onto his poem "El fantasma del buque de carga" [The Phantom of the Cargo Ship].

Returning to the family home was not a bundle of joy nor painless for Pablo. His father, José del Carmen Reyes, did not hold back on his reproaches and sarcasm toward the restless son who had abandoned his university studies in order to continue writing his 'worthless' poems. Five years before, he had traveled overseas without going to Temuco to bid farewell and had not sought his father's permission when he got married on a remote Asian island. And now he had returned in even worse shape than the brusque rail worker had predicted: without money, without employment, without any signs of having gained at least some fame...and besides, with a wife in tow. But his *mamadre*, doña Trinidad, and his sister Laura balanced out the rough reception his father had given him with their affection and delight, and they welcomed Maruca warmly and kindly.

At the end of a week, April 26th, Pablo and his wife took the night train to Santiago, where they settled finally in a boarding house on Santo Domingo Street and later in a small apartment on the third floor of a building on the promenade Huneeus, behind the congressional building. Thanks to friends and his relative Rudecindo Ortega Masson, the poet managed to secure a provisional post at the Ministry of Foreign Affairs. Yet he returned to his country with a new vigor to promote and distribute his work. On May 11th he recited his poems and gave a talk at the Chief Magistrate's Lodge [Posada del Corregidor], and was introduced by Alfonso Bulnes, the Undersecretary of Foreign Affairs, with great acclaim and articles in the press.

His old and new friends helped him keep his mood up and his energy in swing. His homecoming to the modest bohemian Santiago life furnished him with enthusiasm and optimism, which allowed him to overcome the sadness he felt over his married life, with which he nonetheless carried on responsibly.

6

Only marital unhappiness which he brought upon himself could explain why Pablo, renouncing his most basic sense of pride, wrote a letter to Albertina on May 15th, 1932, a month after his return to Chile, asking if they could meet "as friends." Around that time, she was teaching French in some school or high school in Concepción after having abandoned her position at the university. Although he feigned a distant tone in his letter, his homecoming and his falling out of love with Maruca reignited his never extinguished desire to reunite with Albertina.

Nearly two months later, another letter dated July 11th, 1932 detailed the expected failure and incredible blindness Albertina was able to stir up in him:

> I answered your letter about a month ago, and you do not address anything I asked you. You are always that way, how can I have any confidence in you? ... When are you coming? Will you be coming in September? For the first time in your life, why do you not write a long letter telling me about things?

For the umpteenth time—though this would be the last—these letters written in 1932 repeated the same stubborn pattern of complaints, reproaches and requests which, with a wealth of variations, he had proposed in dozens of letters over the course of ten years. No other woman would beat Albertina's record.

Some years later she married Ángel Cruchaga Santa María,[9] a prominent poet and a very dear friend of Pablo's. Their own love story had (finally) concluded for Pablo, but not for Albertina who later—with a not very well disguised nostalgia—joined the court of the bard's ex-lovers and friends who, now harmless, continued to visit him during the reign of Delia del Carril. Out of loyalty to Delia, they rejected Matilde when the revelation of Pablo's new love became apparent, and naturally Albertina and the rest were expelled from Matilde's kingdom.

"La estudiante" [The (female) student], 1923, reappeared in the autobiographical Canto XV, titled "Yo soy" [I am], which concludes *Canto general* (1950). From the beginning of the poem, it confirmed the experience of love founded on sex and sensuality:

> Oh, tú, más dulce, más interminable
> que la dulzura, carnal enamorada

---

9 Translator's note: Ángel Cruchaga Santa María (1893–1964) was a Chilean poet and communist who was influenced by French Symbolism and was considered part of the aesthetic movement right after the turn of the 19th century, termed "postmodernism." He was awarded the National Prize for Literature in 1948 for *Paso de sombra* [A Shadow's Steps, 1939], which dealt with the Spanish civil war.

entre las sombras: de otros días
surges llenando de pesado polen
tu copa, en la delicia. Desde la noche llena
de ultrajes, noche como el vino
desbocado, noche de oxidada púrpura,
a ti caí como una torre herida,
y entre las pobres sábanas tu estrella
palpitó contra mí quemando el cielo.

[Oh, you, sweeter, more never-ending / than sweetness, fleshy lover / among the shadows: you arise from / other days filling your goblet / with heavy pollen, in the delightfulness. From the night / full of offenses, night like an uncontrollable / wine, rusty, purple night, / I fell before you like a wounded tower, / and among the poor sheets your star / beat on me burning the sky.]

In 1964, *Isla Negra* naturally included Albertina in the intervening series "Loves": evocations of the women the poet had loved—each in a different poetic register. The two texts Pablo dedicated to the young woman of the incandescent rendezvous in Santiago were entitled "Amores: Rosaura (I) [Loves: Rosaura (I)"] and "Amores: Rosaura (II)" [Loves: Rosaura (II)], a name he had invented to cover up the allusion to Albertina *Rosa*, who was still alive. They are two long poems that follow the course of their love "de la hora / diurna, erguida / en la hora resbalante / del crepúsculo pobre, en la ciudad" [from the morning hour on, / standing still in the slippery hour / of the poor dusk, in the city] (because her oldest sister made sure that she did not spend the night out away from the boarding house that they shared with their brother Rubén); and the dates "en la esquina / de la calle Sazié, o en la Plazuela de Padura" [on the corner of Sazié Street, or the small square on Padura]. These poems were Neruda's last farewell to that love.

7

Albertina died in November of 1989. A few years before, she confessed bitterly to the journalist Inés María Cardone: "Once a fortune teller told me that I had cheated fate."

The Second Sin

Fable-Spinner

"Oh Maligna, ya habrás hallado la carta."
[Oh Maligna, you must have already found the letter]
Tango del viudo [The Widower's Tango]

"Hablo de cosas que existen, Dios me libre
de inventar cosas cuando estoy cantando!"
[I talk about things that exist, God forbid
I invent things when I am singing!]
Estatuto del vino [Statute of Wine]

I

NOT LONG AGO I had the opportunity to read the research of some academics on Southeast Asia, who at various moments improvised as Neruda scholars by putting together a series of pieces in which they denounced Pablo Neruda's behavior with regards to his passionate and turbulent love affair with Josie Bliss in Rangoon.

Among these Asian scholars, the most battle-hardened is Roanne Kantor (University of Texas—Austin).[1] Without showing any particular interest or sensibility regarding the scarce number of poems in *Residencia en la tierra* [Residence on Earth] about the Orient she was familiar with, she submits them to an instrumentalized reading in order to launch a virulent attack on this area of Neruda's poetic production, particularly "Tango del viudo" [The Widower's Tango].

The principal point of the attack is to negate the existence of Josie Bliss: in his writing the poet allegedly invented "the Josie myth...calculated to massage

---

[1] Roanne Kantor, "Chasing Your (Josie) Bliss: The Troubling Critical Afterlife of Pablo Neruda's Burmese Lover", *Transmodernity*, 3, no. 2 (spring 2014).

Neruda's ego."[2] This delicate judgment comes at the end of a convoluted labyrinth of accusations whose grave and magisterial tone, nonetheless, does not manage to cover up the very modest knowledge she has about *Operation Josie Bliss*. Kantor opens fire at the very beginning of her article:

> Neruda and generations of critics analyzing his life and work have filled reams of paper with descriptions of Josie as exotic, passionate, animalistic and homicidally jealous. Behind all these descriptions, however, is an absolute void: we lack not just the archival evidence to corroborate this particular version of Josie, but the evidence to suggest that there was ever any Josie at all.[3]

And her article concludes that "generations of Neruda scholars have been writing about Josie Bliss in the wrong way." Except her, of course.

But the true guilty party must have obviously been Neruda, whose vanity conjured up the myth of Josie Bliss. I have to admit that this denunciation is a novelty. We already know that while our poet was alive and even today he was and has been the subject—48 years after his death—of hostilities and attacks that, looking to destroy him, end up confirming his vitality. There is more or less an established and even canonical repertoire. But once in a while there are unique assaults, like this one by Professor Kantor (there are no Josie Bliss archives) which merit some clarifications.

Let us start with Neruda's *ego massage*. Like anybody, the versemaker was not at all immune to those types of massages. From the time he was a young man the collision with José del Carmen forced him—so as to hold up his poetic vocation—to develop a high regard for himself and a corresponding strong ambition. He had to show his father that writing poetry was a respectable profession, and not an activity for idle (or effeminate) intellectuals, and, in the process reach the highest level among poets—which he accomplished.

The first major massage his ego benefited from was the whole unexpected and incredible reception that his *Veinte poemas de amor y una canción desesperada* [Twenty Love Poems and a Song of Despair] (1924) acquired in Chile, and later in Latin America and the rest of the world. Penned between 1923 and 1924 by a nineteen-year-old writer who did not want to become famous due to those poems, which he considered minor among his works,

---

2 Kantor, p. 73.
3 Kantor, p. 60.

that chapbook was an absolute best seller for Western lyrical poetry in the 20th century, with at least ten million copies sold and read.

That being said, at 20 the poet rejected other possible ego massages, refusing to ride the wave of fame by writing another twenty or forty love poems, thus frustrating the expectations of hundreds of young women with his new book: *Tentativa del hombre infinito* [Attempt of the Infinite Man] (1926), an avant-gardist work, which was a difficult read and little given to sentimentality. Later the Nerudian ego was also sweetly massaged by the success and the admiration *España en el corazón* [Spain in my Heart] (1937) and *Canto general* (1950) elicited.

And so, we now return to the "myth" of Josie Bliss, considering the topic in relation to those generations of scholars and critics that according to Kantor wrote "reams of paper" with descriptions of Neruda's mythical lover. As far as I know, these "generations of Neruda scholars" who were so prolific in writing about Josie in the 20th century, only existed in Kantor's imagination, and I think they are even more scarce in this first stretch of the current century. Unless Kantor considers "Neruda scholars" to be chroniclers or casual commentators (I am not referring to the professional ones) in the press and on television, or simple scribblers who in these first couple of decades in the 21st century—especially after the publication of *Los amores de Neruda* [Neruda's Love Affairs], by Inés María Cardone, who have transformed the love "fable" of Pablo and this 'Burmese panther' into a commonplace story which is more or less spicy.

2

We have at our disposal the original version of "Tango del viudo" [The Widower's Tango], which is dated "Calcutta 1928" (November-December) and was sent to Héctor Eandi. Neruda first published the poem in the journal *Atenea* 58,[4] later included in *Residencia en la tierra* 1 [Residencia on Earth 1].[5] Kantor affirms that "The Widower's Tango" is the first poem "explicitly and unequivocally linked to Josie Bliss."[6] Wrong. Although it might seem incredible today, the connection between "Tango del viudo" and the woman Josie

---

4 (Concepción 1929).
5 Pablo Neruda, *Residencia en la tierra* [Residence on Earth] 1 (Santiago: Nascimento, 1933).
6 Kantor, p. 63.

Bliss was explicitly revealed—for the first time—by Neruda in some succinct paragraphs in one of the ten autobiographical chronicles which he agreed to write for ten issues in the journal *O Cruzeiro Internacional* (Rio de Janeiro), in 1962.

That means that for 33 years Neruda wanted the poem to be read without anyone, except a few friends (undoubtedly Tomás Lago and Rubén Azócar), connecting "The Widower's Tango" to Josie Bliss—not named in the entire text of *Residence 1*—and without anyone being able to remotely identify the poem titled "Josie Bliss"—written during the first half of 1935, or six years after he had composed "The Widower's Tango"—with her. As if that were not enough, the poem "Josie Bliss" (whose anecdotal background was completely unknown until 1962, like the character in the title) was placed at the end of the second volume of *Residence on Earth*. In publishing the two poems together for the first time in September 1935 in Madrid Neruda was deliberately (and not by chance) providing "Josie Bliss" with the privileged role of rounding out the entire work.

Meaning that there are two temporal gaps at work: the major one of 33 years (1929 to 1962) and the smaller one of six years (1929 to 1935). The large gap buries Kantor's elucubrations about the ostensible *Operation Josie Bliss* calculated to "massage the poet's ego," as well as her musings about the infinite reams of paper wasted by generations of "Neruda scholars" who read and analyzed the myth of the Burmese panther "in the wrong way." The shorter gap is a story in and of itself. For now, let us turn to the big gap.

Between 1935 and 1962 Neruda did not mention Josie Bliss in public, not even in his lengthiest and beautiful autobiographical speech "Viaje por las costas del mundo" [A trip around the Coasts of the World], 1942-1943. Besides the final poem in *Residence*, where he did not identify to whom he was referring, the name Josie Bliss did not appear in Neruda's writing until those aforementioned paragraphs in *O Cruzeiro Internacional* which would later be included—with certain changes—in his posthumous memoirs. They did so without explicitly providing a link between the poems "The Widower's Tango" (1928) and "Josie Bliss" (1935), without, that is, explaining the big gap. Only a few perceptive readers of *Residence on Earth*, who also had the good fortune of reading the chronicles in the journal *O Cruzeiro Internacional*, were able to find the nexus in 1962, but they were left without an explanation for the temporal distance between the two poems. New information and hints appeared in "Amores: Josie Bliss" (I and II), two poems included in *Isla Negra*, but they were still enigmatic.[7]

Is it not strange that Neruda would have created the myth of Josie Bliss with the "calculated" purpose of "massaging his own ego," as Kantor contends, and nonetheless have let thirty years go by before revealing the source, in other words, the unleashed and indispensable secret or mystery which would have served his vain purpose? Because the story of love and fear, which are at the center of the alleged myth, was created not only in "Tango del viudo" but also in seven other poems in 1928 that the poet was careful to distribute—in the 1933 edition—in a *deliberate, anti-chronological way*, so as to *hide* rather than reveal the secret nexus between them. I demonstrated this in my 1987 book for the first time.[8]

Why hide the nexus? Because Neruda was interested in the way those poems might be read precisely as poems and not as episodes in *an erotic story which he had no interest in telling*, although he was surely aware that that tale would have had a wide readership (as this 21st century has confirmed) and it would have furnished him with a substantial "ego massage." It turns out that in 1933 Neruda already agreed with the future Asian scholar Kantor that that would imply reading his poems "in the wrong way," which she attributes to "generations of Neruda scholars."

There is another question that comes to mind: on what archives or bibliographic information (of which I am unaware and would want to know) does she base her reiterated supposition that "generations and generations of critics analyzing [Neruda's] life and work" have filled reams of paper with

---

7 It might surprise Kantor to find out that the voluminous and exhaustive *Pablo Neruda: An Annotated Bibliography of Biographical and Critical Studies*, by Hensley C. Woodbridge and David S. Zubatsky (1988), includes only one article, *only one*, up until 1988, about "The Widower's Tango". And it is humorous that that only lengthy article analyzes the poem from the perspective of the Argentine tango. For example, one section is titled "La cumparsita y el viudo" [The Cumparsita {a famous tango} and the Widower]; another is titled "*La mujer fatal* en el tango y en el poema de Neruda" [Femme Fatale in the Tango and in Neruda's Poem]. It is not from the Orientalist perspective about the lack of archives, detritus and other possible evidence that the Chilean fabricator actually fled the house from a certain Josie Bliss, a resident of Rangoon.

8 Translator's note: The author is referring to his seminal critical edition of *Residencia en la tierra* [Residence on Earth] (Madrid: Ediciones Cátedra, 1987), long considered by scholars to be an indispensable source.

descriptions of an animalesque, passionate, sexy, etc. Josie? Among the 1500 pages in David Schidlowsky's well documented two volume *Pablo Neruda y su tiempo* [Pablo Neruda and his Time], the biographer dedicates six lines—on page 139—to the topic of Josie Bliss (in Rangoon). Volodia Teitelboim's *Neruda* dedicates five or six pages all told. And René de Costa (*The Poetry of Pablo Neruda*) a little more than a page. So where are these countless "reams of paper" that Kantor ostensibly examined?

3

Kantor writes that Neruda, based on his experiences with Burmese women, could have projected onto Josie the tendencies that she purportedly puts on display in "The Widower's Tango". With regards to that, Kantor says it "is important to remember that living in Burma for a year did not make Neruda an expert in Burmese culture.[9] The truth is that Neruda never pretended to be an expert on Burmese culture (it was enough for him to be an expert on seashells). In his memoirs he simply remembered that in Rangoon he was more interested in the people in that country than the boring English, and since those two worlds were incompatible, he had to choose:

> My British friends saw me in a vehicle called a gharry, a little horse drawn cab used mainly for ephemeral trysts in transit and offered me the kindly advice that a Consul should never use those vehicles for any purpose. They also suggested that I should not frequent a lively Persian restaurant, where I drank the best tea in the world in little translucent cups. Those were their final warnings. After that, they stopped greeting me.
>
> This boycott [...] and, after all, I had not come to the Orient to spend my life with transient colonizers, but with the ancient spirit of that world, with that large hapless [unfortunate] human family. I went so deep into the soul and life of the people, that [I fell in love with] a native girl.[10]

That native woman was Josie Bliss. Why is it so difficult for Kantor to understand that the poet was elaborating in his own language (always so precise and rigorous) the experience he was living? Besides being more

---

9 Kantor, p. 64.
10 Pablo Neruda, *Memoirs*, pp. 86–87.

interesting, the local area of the city was likely less expensive that the British area for a consul with financial difficulties, and that had an impact on his initial decision. Nevertheless, Kantor goes so far as to assume that, despite his precarious financial situation, Pablo appeared—in the eyes of a hypothetical Josie—aligned with the English colonial powers.

Unaware of her lack of information about Neruda and *Residence on Earth*, Kantor supposes that her "relationship with him, therefore, might have been motivated less by sexual passion than the pursuit of financial security or prestige; her performance of jealousy a calculation, rather than a compulsion... The perpetuation of the Josie myth...is one transparently flattering to the vanity of its creator."[11] In other words: not sexual passion but rather *the search for economic security and prestige motivated* Josie perhaps, whose jealous performances were not born out of erotic compulsion but rather *by calculation*, gratifying the creator's vanity of a mythic "panther" in his bed. Poor Neruda: even if Josie really existed, it would have gone awry for him, because the panther only feigned her wild eroticism, which was, rather, designed to hide her prosaic economic schemes.

Here the blind anti-Neruda fervor plays an ugly—or ridiculous—trick on Kantor, because she did not read well the oft cited David Schidlowsky, who on page 140 of his major study reproduces Neruda's cable to the Foreign Affairs Office in Chile, dated June 6th, 1928: "Two months without a salary. I beg you to cable me the 669 dollars for first trimester remit New York or authorized a wire transfer [autorización girar tesorería]." And Schidlowsky adds: "This situation continues for another two months. All told for almost five months without a salary." Was it this indigent individual who Josie Bliss was to deceptively seduce in search of financial security and prestige?

Schidlowsky's information about the cablegram is eloquent, and reliable, and consequently could acquire—even for Kantor, perhaps—the almost sacrosanct status of an "archive" that would indirectly tend to validate the existence of the real Josie Bliss. For five months, not moved by calculation, money or prestige, she lived with and nourished the no less real and poor poet, a fifth-rate consul without prestige, money (five months or more without a salary) or friends in the colonial bureaucracy in her two-story house on the shores of the Irrawaddy. Could it not be because of love?

---

11 Kantor, p. 64.

What is clear is that someone helped him survive and *grow as a poet*. That someone, who was not English, must have loved him madly (we should quote here: "la loca que me quería" [the madwoman who loved me] from *Extravagaria*, 1958). Thanks to Schidlowsky, we know for sure, that in Rangoon Neruda went through a desperate stretch in economic terms. How did he survive, then, without five months of salary, in which he even organized—allowing it to acquire a set form and a title—the project *Residence on Earth* (a title which emerged and was communicated to González Vera for the first time in August 1928, that is, in the midst of the consul's worst economic crisis)? As I understand it, all of this information constitutes an important archive which confirms the true existence of Josie Bliss, who, for Kantor is only a hypothetical figure, a figure conjured up by a vain poet.

4

Let us turn now to Mark Eisner, whose biography, *Neruda: The Poet's Calling* (2018), reiterates and amplifies—in chapters eight and nine—Roanne Kantor's thesis about the Great Fable-Spinner. On pages 153-154 Eisner refers to an episode in the *Memoirs* in which Pablo and Álvaro, during their stay in Paris in 1927, were miraculously invited by the Chilean millionaire Alfredo Condon to join the night pleasures of the city in a Russian nightclub—The Caucassian Club—accompanied by young women dressed like peasants from the Russian Steppes. Condon drank champagne and danced like a crazy man until he fell under the table. Frightened because they could not wake him and could not pay the bill, the two travelers managed at last to drag him to a taxi a young woman from the cabaret had called. She accompanied them to the luxurious hotel where the host was staying. Considering that the young woman was neither pretty nor ugly, "but was attractive because of the pointed nose Parisian women have," they invited her to share an onion soup with them at dawn in Les Halles.

> We then invited her to our miserable hotel. She had no problem with going with us.
> She went to Álvaro's room. I fell on my bed exhausted, but soon I felt that they were shaking me. It was Álvaro. I thought his crazy but placid face looked strange.
> "Something has happened" he said "This woman is exceptional, unique, I cannot explain it. You have to try your luck with her now."

Shortly thereafter this unknown woman got in bed with me looking drowsy yet indulging. Upon making love with her I confirmed her mysterious gift. What arose from her depths was indescribable, it harked back to the origin of pleasure itself, the birth of waves, the secret genes of Venus. Álvaro was right.

The next day, over breakfast, Álvaro warned me in Spanish:

"If we do not leave this woman right now, our travel plans will be frustrated. We would not drown in the sea, but in the bottomless sacrament of sex."

We decided to shower her with gifts: flowers, chocolates and half the Francs we had left. She admitted that she did not work in the Caucasian Cabaret, that she had visited it the night before for the first and only time. Later we took a taxi with her. The driver was cutting through an unknown neighborhood when we asked him to stop. We said goodbye to her with big kisses and we left her there, disoriented but with a smile on her face.

We never saw her again[12]

Eisner translates most all of this passage, summing up the last paragraph. I quoted the entire original passage because the biographer added the following footnote:

> The violent objectification of the woman described in this scene establishes a pattern of disturbing misogynistic behavior that would continue during Neruda's time abroad. Perhaps even more disturbing to today's reader is the fact that this description comes from what Neruda wrote in his memoirs, fifty years later. There are no archival records for this event. Therefore, it is impossible to verify this description, to fully assess whether these events took place and, if they did, whether the young woman consented to sex with Neruda or was raped by him.[13]

Frankly, I cannot understand the reason for this footnote, but it is evident that Eisner inserts it in his book under the influence of Roanne Kantor (whose 2014 article the biographer quotes from explicitly more than once). The proof is the demand for "archival records," even for recollections of two young Chileans' improvised night out in Paris, who had little money and were

---

12 Pablo Neruda, *Memoirs*, pp. 70–71.
13 Mark Eisner, *Neruda: The Poet's Calling*, p. 154.

on their way to Asia. Which seems to me *un po' troppo*. Why blame the young Pablo, who as yet did not have readers or fame in Paris, or paparazzi to pursue and photograph him that night, to produce the indispensable "archival records"? Can Neruda not even be believed when he tells this adventurous story as a young man in his memoirs? What about this story is particularly scandalous for a male or female adult reader? And, above all, what "violent objectification of the woman described in this scene" is he referring to?

According to Neruda's story (since we have no other "archival record"), the unknown young woman decided on her own to stop a taxi and accompany the Chileans to Condon's hotel, and later to Les Halles, and finally to the miserable, rundown hotel where, clearly—it cannot be clearer—she *willingly* went to bed with the two young men, who were nice with her and showed her respect and admiration (for her gift). So, where is the violence? What sense does it make, in the case of this story, to want to "fully assess whether these events took place and, if they did, whether the young woman consented to sex with Neruda or was raped by him"? I wonder why Eisner brandishes here this gratuitous offense against the poet of whom he is writing a biography? Why search by hook or by crook for a way to read between the lines when there is nothing there? Why prosecute the young Neruda for a night out in Paris that he described transparently? And this constitutes an "honest reading" of Neruda—a formula Eisner attributed to his own biography in an interview with a Santiago newspaper? This type of reading would not be possible if there were not a real or presumed *sin*, or one without any basis, as is the case here, of racism or misogyny or sexual violence or abandonment.

5

The reference to the "disturbing misogynistic behavior" which Neruda supposedly showed in Paris, anticipates and paves the way for Eisner to focus on the unforeseen sexual encounters the poet had during his residence in Asia, especially his shared life with Josie Bliss. His perspective is colored by the main assumption that Roanne Kantor developed about the inexistence of the "Burmese panther" in her article in 2014, and by how Neruda's representations of Josie fit with the "problematic narration" concerning race, gender, and the view that Neruda had of himself and the prototypical "Asian woman," according to the Western canons studied in Edward Said's postcolonial theory. Following on the heels of Kantor's argument, Eisner affirms that

Josie incarnated the fantasy of a sexually acceptable Burmese woman onto which Neruda projected "all his racialized—and racist—fetishes."[14]

I do not consider Neruda to be untouchable, nor walled off from serious criticism, as long as it is well founded. But I believe in the true greatness of his work, which I know very well, and I am dismayed that a certain type of Orientalism has provided a new gold mine for anti-Neruda scholars, especially for a group of Chileans who, as I am sure Eisner knows, are attracted to these kinds of topics for political and ideological—not literary—reasons. As the *questions* they asked him clearly demonstrated in his interview with the newspaper *La Tercera*, on May 26th, 2018, in Santiago, to which he responded by laying it on thick, even more than the interviewer might have expected, by resorting to vulgar insults (in Chilean slang) hurled at the poet.

As far as Josie Bliss is concerned, the biographer and casual Orientalist oscillates between "it is not impossible that there was a woman as extremely tempestuous and emotionally unstable whom he charmed" and "nevertheless, Neruda exaggerated and invented a lot in his writings, throughout his life."[15] Eisner carefully avoids providing proof or *archives* to document those exaggerations and inventions. There is, nonetheless, an interesting moment when he affirms that "the approximately two months [in truth, it was five or six] of the ostensible *Josie Bliss affair* were filled with furious, crude and uninhibited sexual activity for Neruda, with at least one woman, opening up a new level of eroticism in himself"[16], which was projected onto his writing and elevated the explicit content and images.

---

14 Eisner, p. 165.
15 Eisner, pp. 164–165.
16 Eisner, p. 166.

The Third Sin

Rapist

I

In Calcutta, on January 8th, 1929, Neruda embarked on the ship *Merkara* bound for Colombo, the capital of Ceylon, an island of 65,000 kilometers that is 50 kilometers southeast of India. At that moment a part of the British empire, it is an island that looks like an earring or a tear, "a pendant off the ear of India...the shape of a tear" according to the Canadian writer Michael Ondaatje, author of *The English Patient*, who was born and raised in Ceylon.

Neruda disembarked in Colombo on January 16th. He had not yet turned 25. Who knows how he was able to find a small, recently built bungalow on 42nd Lane in the Wellawatta suburb, far from the English with their tedious protocols...and next to the sea? It was a remote and modest tropical precursor to his house in Isla Negra. Shortly after having rented it, an episode occurred there that Neruda did not tell in his chronicles for the journal *O Cruzeiro Internacional*, but confessed to, on his own, some years later while he was writing his unfinished memoirs. This is Neruda's story:

> My lonely and isolated bungalow was far from any urban development. When I rented it, I tried to find out where the bathroom was because I could not see it anywhere. Actually, it was nowhere near the shower, toward the back of the house.
>
> I examined it curiously. It was a wooden box with a hole in the middle, very similar to an artifact I had known from my childhood in the countryside, in my country. But ours were set over a deep hole in the ground or above a running water. Here the receptacle was a simple metal pail beneath the round hole.
>
> The pail always appeared clean at dawn every day without my noticing how its contents disappeared. One morning I had gotten up earlier than normal. I was astonished at what I saw.

Coming through the rear of the house, like a dark statue that walked, was the most beautiful woman I had ever seen at that point in Ceylon, an ethnic Tamil, from a caste of pariahs. She was dressed in a red and golden sari, with rough cloth. She wore heavy rings on her naked feet. On each side of her nose there were two very small, shiny red dots. I suppose they were made of glass, but on her they looked like rubies.

She solemnly went toward the toilet, without even looking at me, without even noticing my existence, and disappeared with a sordid receptacle on her head, walking away like a goddess.

She was so beautiful that despite her humble profession it had me worried. As if she were a shy animal just arrived from the jungle, she had another life, a world apart. I called her, to no avail. Later on, I left a gift—fruit or satin—in her way. She passed by me without hearing or looking at me. That miserable trail she took had been transformed by her dark beauty into an obligatory ceremony of an indifferent queen.

One morning, with my mind made up, I took her by the wrist forcefully and looked at her face to face. There was no language I could use to talk with her. She let herself be guided by me without a smile and soon was laying nude on my bed. Her thin waist, her full hips, the overflowing cups of her breasts, made her a replica of the millennial sculptures in southern India. The encounter was between a man and a statue. She stayed there the whole time impassively, with her eyes wide open. She was right to despise me. I did not do that again.[1]

The episode just turned 90 years old—it happened when Neruda was not famous nor a communist—but I believe this story was written after 1966. That year, in London, Neruda acquired a copy of *Growing*, a reprint of the brilliant autobiography that Leonard Woolf, Virginia's husband, dedicated to telling of his years as a young civil servant in Ceylon between 1904 and 1911. No doubt this reading activated Neruda's memories and had an influence on the last part of his memoirs on the people of Ceylon. Among them was the episode of the beautiful Tamil woman, first published in *Confieso que he vivido* [Memoirs] and read for over 40 years without any important

---

1 Pablo Neruda, "Confieso que he vivido" in *Obras completas* [Complete Works], V, 2002, pp. 504–505.

commentaries that I know of,[2] until 2013, when a Spanish journalist threw it out there to the anti-Nerudian international crowd—which provoked scandalous rumors.

2

Since then, this Neruda text has been the privileged object of an avalanche of attacks from different ideological trenches, which the social media have disseminated with much fanfare.

Among the attacks, I think the most particularly representative one was the one published by the columnist Joaquín García-Huidobro in the newspaper *El Mercurio*, under the title "El toro y la diosa" [The Bull and the Godess].[3] To head off the Parliamentary proposal to name the international airport in Santiago *Pablo Neruda*, García-Huidobro—who, besides being a journalist, is a professor at the University of the Andes, connected to the Opus Dei— glosses over that fragment from *Memoirs* in his special way. The first paragraphs set the tone for what follows:

> He, our poet, was a pioneer in terms of Chilean sexual activity in Asia. As though it were the most common of things, in his memoirs he tells us of brown and golden women who slept with him "sportingly and disinterestedly", those "[women] friends of different colors" who went to bed with the Chilean diplomat "without leaving anything behind except their flashing physical presence." However, there was one in particular who was different, the most beautiful women he had ever seen in Ceylon, a Tamil, from the pariah class… [but who] did not deign to look at him. She did not receive his gifts nor respond to his greetings. She walked like a goddess, carrying a receptacle full of excrement on her head, because no human filth could stain her divine purity. Such a spectacle was too much for *the bull with Latin blood*.

> The episode with the goddess occurred when the Consul Neruda (a.k.a. *the bull*) was examining (or moving into) the bungalow: *"When I rented it* I tried to find out where the toilet was because I could not find it anywhere."

---

2 For more details, see Hernán Loyola, *Neruda. La biografía literaria* [Neruda: The Literary Biography], pp. 394–396.
3 *El Mercurio*, 11/11/2018.

In other words, having just arrived in Ceylon. Consequently, he could hardly have been able to carry on with his patriotic mission as a sexual pioneer, now in Wellwatta, with "brown and golden women" whom he had not met yet. There cannot possibly be a connection, then, between the free-spirited friendship with these women and the episode of the goddess, as García-Huidobro distractedly notes. And he does so with partiality, for he also denounces in a reproving way that Neruda mentions, as "the most common things" in the world, having slept with these spontaneous women when he was 24–25 years old. I wonder why the professor thinks this is such an *abnormal* thing.

3

With this point García-Huidobro begins his devious gloss of Neruda's story, to whom he assigns the role of the "embravecido toro latino" [enraged Latin bull], driven crazy by his desire to possess the Tamil goddess. I wrote a letter to the Editor of *El Mercurio*—published on Tuesday, November 20th, 2018— that sums up my point of view:

REGARDING THE BULL AND THE GODDESS

Dear Editor:

I was late in reading—in Italy—the article "The Bull and the Goddess" by Joaquín García-Huidobro (Sunday November 11th) who, based on a short story Neruda tells in his *Memoirs*, concludes with this invitation: "Please keep this in mind, parliamentarians, and read these dark pages." I would like to be added to this invitation asking the parliamentarians and all Chileans in general, to read those "dark pages" without blinders on (118–119 in the recent Seix Barral edition, 2017). You will read a serious and honest *unsolicited* confession. A Chilean who was about 65 years old confesses spontaneously, and without mitigating circumstances, to having obliged a woman of humble extraction and, in his eyes, very beautiful, to have sex with him when he was 25 years old in Ceylon (1929). It is a succinct story of his failed seduction of that woman, in which the exaltation, wonder and praise for that Tamil woman (who rejected Neruda's arousal with statuesque passivity and immobility) does not tend to lessen the abuse, but rather, on the contrary, reinforces his sincere remorse which is summed in one phrase: "[She] was right to despise me." For all who know Neruda's proud personality and work, this phrase has to strike them as a very rare and strong act of self-criticism, one which indicates that he despised himself—heightened by the high worth he attributes to the victim—which is followed by an explicit corrective: "I did not do that again." That layman's confession is so unusual that it acquires an ethical value that Joaquín García-Huidobro [whom I presume is Catholic] should have recognized instead of instrumentally using it against Neruda. I do not believe there are many authors of sexual abuse in the history of our country [*especially in recent history*] who have confessed spontaneously, and who have shown remorse. Joaquín García-Huidobro's political blindness (or whatever it is) does not allow him to admit that without this confession nobody would have known about what he calls this "dark episode," almost 40 years ago now (illuminated by the author himself). But, above all, nobody would have known of that beautiful Tamil woman in Wellwatta in 1929 who Neruda heaps praise on, making it obvious that there is an intention to rescue her humble figure from the abyss of nothingness, without the need of any #MeToo protests. As the facts show, Neruda's words were more than capable of rescuing her [paying a high price in the process]. Consequently, I not only invite anybody and everybody to read these "dark pages," but also ask the readers to compare them to Joaquín García-Huidobro's article, which transmutes Neruda's sober and honest story into a *steamy erotic encounter*. In the end, this article says more about García-Huidobro than it does about Neruda. Under the pretext of attacking the poet and managing to disqualify him from the honor of having the airport named after him, Joaquín García-Huidobro delights himself by inventing a caricature of the "bull with Latin blood," of a "enraged Latin bull" who "burned with desire to possess the goddess," until "he was able to delight in his own pleasure and devour with his eyes that pure and fleeting face." Where Neruda writes that "there was no language with which I could talk with her," a riled up Joaquín García-Huidobro imagines that "there were no words exchanged between them, because the goddess' language was incomprehensible to that bull who only knew how to roar" and she had no recourse but to follow the "stallion [who] took off her clothes," the "bull [who] threw himself on her," etc. She was impotent standing before the "rich, powerful, influential, communist, strong bull" (Neruda was none of that in 1929); "while the bull's blood rushed, she possessed the calmness of the gods," etc. So much insistence and delight over the unchained bull, which Neruda does not confirm, would seem to invite us instead to a psychoanalytic session.

Let us return to Neruda and his confession that he disregarded the lustful abbot Boccaccio's opposite reflection: *peccato celato è mezzo perdonato* [a hidden sin is half forgiven]. The version, which makes its way around in Italy today, *peccato confessato, mezzo perdonato* [a confessed sin is half forgiven], has not stopped the great majority of the opinion pieces I have read in the Chilean press from condemning Neruda as a low-class rapist—without extenuating circumstances—and often expressing it in vulgar language. I sense in the younger writers a type of generational reaction against a sacred monster of whom, in general, they know little and by way of rumors. However, not too many decades ago that was a militant flag which other young people raised against the military dictatorship. When the dictatorship fell, coinciding with the collapse of the wall in Berlin and socialism in the Soviet Union and Europe, it set off a growing wave of indifference to—if not hostility against—the memory of the bard, although he is holding on in the not so young poor and educated sectors of society. Within this domain it is infrequent to read an opinion piece like the one the writer and visual artist Claudia Donoso wrote for a "top survey" that *The Clinic*[4] did over the episode in Ceylon:

> I consider Neruda to be a man of his time and nothing more. What I see in his text is that he was aroused by exotic attraction, in a similar way that Rimbaud was. I do not think there was a rape because the guy courted the Ceylonese woman, in other words, he did not throw himself on her like a dog. And when he sees that *she is not the least bit interested*, that she obeys like the pariah she is and that she responds like a statue, Neftalí feels despicable and out of place. Therefore, I do not see it as a rape but rather a huge mistake in terms of affect, an anthropological blunder.[5]

---

4 Translator's note: *The Clinic* is a satiric publication that is similar to *The Onion*, in the United States.
5 *The Clinic*, 10/1/2012.

4

The history of the reception of Neruda's life and works in Chile is so complex and pulled along by ups and downs that it would merit an in-depth study of its decisive factors. His communist militancy has not been the least of them and is generally tied—favorably or unfavorably—to the world-renowned appreciation of his poetic work. The persistence and latest attacks hurled at him—explicitly or implicitly—from the national conservative trenches, are not due so much to the poet's communist militancy per se, but rather to his unpardonable tenacity, having persisted in that commitment well beyond his own death (with the famous 1973 funeral which twisted the dictator's arm). There is no way to rescue Neruda for the sake of "democracy," so he has to be diminished, belittled, cut down to size.

The American CIA made an all-out effort to prevent Neruda from receiving the Nobel Prize for literature in 1963,[6] but there are signs that our poet will continue to be the *bête noire* for the Agency. Among the signs, as I understand it, there are the modulations, sudden dissemination and international resonance which the recent scholarly "rediscoveries" of episodes like the one with the beautiful Tamil woman, and others that we examine below. Paradoxically, that is the reason why Neruda does not lose his vitality nor relevance despite it all: the enemy takes care of that.

5

Neruda was 22 when he left Chile en route to Asia. Although accompanied by his friend Álvaro Hinojosa, during the trip Pablo began to understand that he had embarked on a much more complicated adventure than he had imagined. On the day of his 23rd birthday (July 12th, 1927), he wrote to his sister Laura from the *Baden*, two hours before arriving in Lisbon:

> Up to this point the trip has been excellent, comfortable and without any mishaps. I hope to be in Paris in six days and embark for Asia at the end of the month. I am a bit afraid of arriving because here on the boat I have found out that life there is very expensive, that the cheapest

---

6 For more details, see Francis Stonor Saunders, *La CIA y la guerra fría cultural* [The CIA and the Cultural Cold War (London: Granta Books, 1999)].

boarding house costs $1600 per month, and I am traveling under precarious conditions. Besides, there are epidemics, tertian fevers, and fevers of all types. What can I do? One has to give in to life and struggle with it especially knowing that no one is taking care of you.

The little fear he felt was actually enormous. Let us try to imagine the state of mind of this young provincial man, inexperienced and ultimately timid, always looking for symbolic feminine support which as a child and an adolescent he found in his *mamadre* Trinidad, along with the unconditional solidarity of his sister. That is clearly evident in the final phrase in the cited passage: "One has to give in to life and struggle with it especially *knowing that no one is taking care of you.*" But the first part of the phrase, on the other hand, set up a counterpoint to his anxiety: proud determination, action and struggle. That mixture was always characteristic of Neruda.

In every one of the experiences of anguish and helplessness he encountered when arriving at his different destinations in Southeast Asia, we find a first sign of disquiet in his immediate search to find sexual solace in the strong bond with a woman. However, his instinctual desire unmasked the need and anxiety-ridden search for the ideal partner, possibly a young and beautiful woman, but above all an expert in local culture. In sum, a woman capable of helping him and supporting him in carrying out his diplomatic and poetic missions, which he was only able to find in Josie Bliss.

Hence Consul Neruda's (officially Reyes') destinations and professional changed during his exile in the Orient left their mark every time in the form of the anxiety or anguish which he variously recorded in his literary work and in his correspondence. His arrival at three destinations—Rangoon, Colombo and Batavia—had in common an episode linked to the sexual dimension in his life. And it was engraved in his memory in an intense, unique and lasting manner as it made their way into his writing, as we just verified in the case of the story about that violent impulse which he was not able to control when faced with the beautiful Tamil woman, shortly after disembarking in Colombo. It was an anomalous behavior, but something he did not try to justify.

There is something *enigmatic* about the importance which Neruda gave to that episode in Wellawatta, compared to the relative lack of interest with regard to other, similar (like the "the brown and golden young women" incident) episodes. Why the difference?

6

A year and half before, in October 1927, an episode Neruda lived just before his exile in Asia engendered two texts that are even more enigmatic. And they have yet to be clarified. The problems the new Consul faced in settling down in the Burmese capital did not appear in his memoirs, as they did in Wellawatta. Whereas the poem "Rangoon 1927", in *Memorial de Isla Negra* [Isla Negra], in evoking Pablo's arrival to his new destination, does dedicate more than half of its lines to an erotic experience the consul had—as the lines suggest—the very day he disembarked, in the afternoon. Or it might have taken place a few days later.

While Álvaro stayed in their living accommodations sleeping or writing, Pablo—after having showered and eaten something—went out for a walk around the surroundings. The walk took him to the port area, abandoned at that time of the afternoon. There, also alone and seated on a bench, was a young woman. What happened next between a lonely man and a lonely woman in Rangoon, some afternoon in October 1927, was buried by the poet in a deep cave for decades. It finally emerged with all its repressed energy in the poem "Rangoon 1927": an evocation with an unusual intensity, a sexual encounter between two strangers, unable to understand each other, but whose loneliness crossed paths to such a degree that it left Pablo with an indelible memory. So much so that he had already insinuated it in a part of the 1934 poem "Las furias y las penas" [Furies and Sorrows]. Why so? Why did both poems evoke this episode with a dramatic and intense tone? What was so special and unforgettable about that encounter?

7

The third destination. Upon arriving in June 1930 in Batavia (the capital of Java in the Dutch Indies), the initial anxiety or anguish had been announced and confronted "theoretically" months ahead of time in Wellawatta. In a long letter to his friend Héctor Eandi, mailed November 21st, 1929, he showed a need to apologize—or come clean—with his faithful pen pal about his economic situation and about what he called the "sexual matter." Here I transcribe some of the most important passages:

> I should explain to you [the meaning] of my first cable. Consuls of my rank—honorary or chosen consuls—have a miserable salary, the lowest

among all the personnel. The lack of money has made me suffer immensely up until this point, and even today I live consumed by ignoble conflicts. I make 166 American dollars a month, around here that is the salary of a low-ranking shop assistant. And it is even worse: my salary depends on the number of [shipping] entries at the Consulate, in other words, if there are no exports to Chile on a given month then I do not get paid. It is really awful and humiliating: I was in Burma five months without a salary, that is, without anything. [...]

Thanks a million, Eandi, and pardon my terrible details which are the reality I live and that torments me every day. (...). *I also want to marry, but soon, as soon as tomorrow,* and live in a big city. Those are my only persistent desires, maybe I will not be able to achieve them ever.[7]

The night before he disembarked in Batavia (today Jakarta), during the final farewell party on board, Neruda met Kruzi, a Jewish woman with whom he had drinks, danced and later shared secrets and his cabin bed. Neruda told the story of Kruzi in an unforgettable way—very Somerset Maugham-like—in one of the best parts of his memoirs.[8] The young woman was "blond, Rubenesque, brimming, with orange-colored eyes and fun loving... That last night we made love in my cabin, in a friendly way, conscious that our destinies were meeting by chance and only once. I told her about my misfortune. She empathized with me softly and her passing tenderness stirred my soul." But she also told him about the true motive for her trip. An international organization had chosen her as the European concubine of a rich Chinese businessman who was bored in Batavia. Upon disembarking, Pablo caught a glimpse of the magnate's Rolls Royce.

8

This casual episode involving sex completed the erotic triad that intertwined the stories Neruda wrote about his arrivals in Asian cities during his exile. Let us recapitulate in chronological order. *First episode*: the "story of ports," that was what Pablo called the silent and intense encounter between two strangers on the docks, perhaps the afternoon that he disembarked in Rangoon,

---

7 Neruda, *Obras completas* [Complete Works], V, pp. 945–946.
8 Neruda, *Obras completas* [Complete Works], V, pp. 507–510.

October 1927. *Second episode*: the forced copulation with the beautiful Tamil woman who cleaned bathrooms in Wellawatta, January 1929. *Third episode*: almost a repeat of the first, but with a lighter touch: it was the friendly, drink and dance filled solace, both verbal and sexual, shared by two anxiety driven, desperate, and wandering travelers, Pablo and Kruzi, at dawn on June 13th, 1930, a few hours before they disembarked in Batavia. In his memoirs the third episode almost reached the point of comedy. The tragedy would begin several weeks later.

The Fourth Sin

Bad Husband

"¿Para qué me casé en Batavia?"
[Why did I get married in Batavia?]
Estravagario [Extravagaria]

"...wooing, wedding, and repenting..."
Shakespeare, *Much Ado About Nothing*, II, 1

"j'eusse aimé vivre auprès d'une jeune géante,
comme aux pieds d'une reine un chat voluptueux."
[I should have liked to live near a young giantess,
/ Like a voluptuous cat at the feet of a queen]
Baudelaire, *La Géante [The Giantess]*

I

A MONTH BEFORE TURNING TWENTY-SIX, June 13th, 1930, Neruda disembarked in Batavia—capital of Java, the Dutch colony—and stayed in the Hotel der Nederlanden, located in Weltevreden, the prestigious neighborhood in the city. Determined to not repeat the experience of being lonely in Ceylon, he attempted to quickly establish social connections in the city. The Cuban consul, Gustavo Mustelier y Galán, helped him out: he opened the doors of his house and invited him to dinner often. He was the political representative of the dictador Machado, but after having a few glasses of top-notch rum, he had no problem talking in detail about the abominable situation in his country. Via meetings like these Pablo gained access to other things, and in particular to the tennis club, where he met Maria Antoinette Hagenaar Vogelzang, or simply Marietje, "a very discrete and beautiful young woman."[1] She belonged to a colonial dynasty of

---
1 Hagar Peeters, *Malva*, pp. 25, 29.

illustrious and affluent lineage in the past, but her father's bad business deals had ruined the family's favorable economic standing, and Marietje was forced to work as a secretary in the Bataviascha Afdeling Bank.[2] "She received a very good salary at the time: the equivalent of three hundred Swiss francs a month."[3]

Pablo was seeing Marietje (immediately "rebaptized" Maruca) no doubt when in August or September he left the hotel to rent a small chalet on Probolingo Street, in the Weltevreden neighborhood. In a very short period of time, he decided to get married. They were married on December 6th, barely five months after he arrived in Batavia. Why the hurry? In a letter to his father he pointed out, with some trepidation: "I had wanted to communicate with you to let you know of my decision to marry and wait for your approval, but due to numerous circumstances we tied the knot much earlier than we had hoped."[4]

What were those circumstances? Was Maruca pregnant with the child she would later lose in a miscarriage? It could be, according to the clues Pablo offered in a letter to his sister Laura, dated March 23rd, 1931, in which he told her of two recent calamities. First, that Maruca "has been very ill and I had to call a number of doctors and specialists in women's health, but, fortunately, she did not have an operation. Here a doctor can cost $100 per visit. Everything is very expensive."

2

The second calamity was of an economic nature. The giant wave of the Wall Street crash in 1929 fell on Chile with an indulgent delay due to the fact that North American loans kept coming in until the end of 1930 (as a sign of thanks for General Ibañez's government's support of American economic interests in the country, to the detriment of British interests, which, to that point, had been dominant). Pablo surely would not have married in December if he had been informed about the imminent danger (who knows why he did not suspect it himself?), and Maruca would not have given up her bank job. He wrote about this—in more detail—to Morla Lynch in March 1931: "my salary has been slashed in half, leaving me with starvation wages. I was

---

2 Adam Feinstein, *Pablo Neruda: A Passion for Life*, p. 77.
3 Peeters, p. 29.
4 Neruda, *Obras completas* [Complete Works], V, p. 817.

making $333.32 dollars and they have cut it to $166.66 and I write to you with a heavy heart since I got married only three months ago and I do not know what to do. With what I had, getting by was not easy, now it is impossible."⁵

He asked Morla Lynch for help several times in anxious letters from July 1st to September 8th, but with no tangible results. Whereas he wrote to Eandi on September 5th, 1931 in a very different tone, sparing him the details about his daily miseries with proud dignity and even referring to Batavia warmly, a place with an apparent serenity for literary endeavors. But the most significant paragraphs in this long letter refer to his married domestic life:

> My wife is Dutch, we are exceedingly close, exceedingly happy in this house, which is smaller than a thimble. I read; she sews. Consular life, the protocol, the meals, the dinner suits, the frock coats, the chaqué, the uniforms, the dances, the cocktails all the time: it is hell. Our house is a refuge, but pirates surround us. We burst out of the place and take off in our automobile for the mountains or the coast with thermoses and cognac and books. We lay down on the sand and look at the black island, Sumatra, and the subterranean volcano Karakatau. We eat sandwiches. We return. I am not writing. I am reading Proust for the fourth time. I like his work more than before. [...]. Even the strangest thing or the most endearing thing becomes routine. Every day is the same as the next on this earth. Books. Films.⁶

The sequence "we exceedingly close, exceedingly happy," is rare in Neruda's language, and it is rather ironic. Boredom. Sterility. Colonial time as the absence of history and personal time with the absence of stimuli. Along with the letter to Eandi he included a poem that "I wrote a few days ago" titled "Duelo decorativo" [Decorative Mourning], which he changed to "Lamento lento" [Slow Lament], which, along with "Madrigal escrito en invierno" [Madrigal Written in Winter] and "Fantasma" [Phantom] (1926) would constitute the madrigal triad published in the Nascimento edition of *Residence on Earth 1*. This 1931 addition testified to the reemergence of his nostalgia for Albertina (the addressee of the other two preceding madrigals) and opened up a gap in his relationship with Maruca. Rereading Proust meant rereading about Marcel's erotic obsession with a figure called *Albertine*. And in the

---

5 Pablo Neruda, *Epistolario viajero* [A Traveler's Diary], p. 63.
6 Neruda, *Obras completas* [Complete Works], V, p. 960.

title "Decorative Mourning", the term *mourning* (for having failed to reunite with Albertina in Ceylon toward the end of 1929) now seemed *decorative* because his current situation was useless mourning, a heartbreak that was purely ornamental:

> En la noche del corazón
> la gota de tu nombre lento
> en silencio circula y cae
> y rompe y desarrolla su agua.
> [In the heart's night / the drop of your slow name / circles and falls in silence / and breaks and swells its water.]

Time's homogeneous and lethal passage was the theme of the last two poems Neruda wrote on those Asian lands: "Cantares" [Songs] and "Trabajo frío" [Cold Work]. Using language laced with somber sadness, or dread, they revealed the secret process, hidden in the recesses of his soul, while on the surface Pablo declared that he was *exceedingly* happy. He could not admit that his marriage to Maruca was acquiring the terrible semblance of a grave mistake. In Batavia in 1931 he was discovering that his notion of marriage had not been anarchic at all. And towards the end of 1936, in other words over the course of six years, he carried on responsibly—at times in a heroic way—with his marital commitment to Maruca.

3

> "O Mort, vieux capitaine, il est temps! Levons l'ancre!
> Ce pays nous ennuie, o Mort! Appareillons!"
> [Oh Death, old captain, it is time! Lift the anchor! / This country bores us, oh Death! Let us set sail!]
> Baudelaire, *Le Voyage*
> [The Voyage]

Lacking any documentation of the last months the couple spent in Batavia, we are left to imagine them. Pablo's enthusiasm from the year before to get married had disappeared, since Maruca, besides not inspiring the passion he shared with Josie Bliss or Albertina (this he always knew), was not the day-to-day partner that the poet had hoped for. Margarita Aguirre judged her the following way: "very tall, slow, inexpressive, *lifeless.*" Despite what his letters affirmed (which were part sincere and part form), Pablo's *poetic* silence about his conjugal situation was more poignant. Perhaps alone he harbored doubts about his interest in returning to Chile with Maruca. But at the same time, he was unable to break off the ties he had accepted. Besides, as we now know, part of him had easily grown accustomed to domestic life, which he always lacked.

Did they consider the possibility of Pablo traveling alone and Maruca staying with her parents, or alone in the tiny house on Probolingo Street until he was able to firm up his economic situation in Chile? More than likely Maruca did not even entertain that idea. Although it might sound strange, given the financial misfortune she shared, and which she shared later in Chile, her attachment to Pablo was based in great measure—as we will see—on the importance she always placed on *being a consul's wife*, even if it meant being with a negligible consul with an almost invisible status. Consequently, Maruca the dreamer threw herself heart and soul into the preparations for the long trip. She began packing suitcases and trunks—at least a couple of trunks since Pablo's things were stored in one. Especially the masks he has been collecting since the year he spent in Rangoon and which, a few months later, would surprise his Santiago friends.

In a letter on November 25th, 1931 Neruda asked Morla Lynch to write to Alfonso Bulnes, recently named the Undersecretary of Foreign Affairs, "so that he can get me out of this bad situation," and he urged her, "Since I am writing to you directly at the same time, I beg you to do so right away, hoping that these dual efforts might help me."[7] Maybe he had not yet received the cable in which the Ministry informed him of the news that administrative measures were being implemented to cut the budget, and specifically of the inevitable restructuring of the consulates given the catastrophic situation Chile was facing in 1931. The final blow came with the arrival of that cable in the early days of December, coinciding with the couple's first anniversary (I know of no details regarding their melancholic celebration). From January of 1932 on, Neruda stopped receiving his miserable stipend for good.

It was an absolute tragedy. Without any resources, the poet could not stay in Batavia nor go back to Chile. But finally, *in extremis*, someone heard his complaints in the Ministry, and he sent Neruda two tickets and showed his friendship once the poet returned to Santiago. That was Alfonso Bulnes.

---

7 Neruda, *Espistolario viajero* [A Traveler's Diary], p. 73.

4

"A long, two-month trip on the sea allowed me to return to Chile in 1932": this brief line is all that appears in his memoirs about his return to his country. Incidentally, in distancing Maruca from her native Java, he saved her from Japanese concentration camps which were set up ten years later, during the Southeast Asian front of the war.

At the beginning of February, in Batavia Pablo and Maruca embarked on a Dutch ship bound for Colombo. It was the third time Pablo had disembarked in the Ceylonese capital, but on this occasion, he did not muster the enthusiasm to write a diary. Since they had to wait a couple of days before the ship (the *Forafric*, a cargo ship owned by Andrew Weir's company) departed for Chile, Pablo and Maruca probably went to the bungalow in Wellawatta where he had lived nearly a year and a half by the sea. And maybe he hunted down his friends Lionel Wendt and Andrew Boyd to talk over coffee.

In mid-February of 1932 the *Forafric* set sail from the docks in Colombo. Having twenty years of sea waring experience, this cargo ship would last almost another ten years on the vast oceans, visiting exotic ports. Christmas night in 1941—a few weeks after Pearl Harbor—Japanese bombers sunk it. Identifying itself as a peaceful cargo ship did not help at all. The commanders and the crew never knew the ship would be immortalized in "El fantasma del buque de carga" [The Phantom of the Cargo Ship], a poem Pablo Neruda wrote aboard it and was able to finish before disembarking in Puerto Montt on April 18th.

5

About midway through the voyage, the *Forafric* docked in Cape Town. Just prior to that it had made a layover in Mozambique. Pablo left no written trace of either of these two probable landings: he was not in the mood to write chronicles of his trip. Following on the heels of that, there was the interminable thirty-day navigation across the southern Atlantic Ocean on the way to Magellan's Strait. During those days, Pablo and Maruca's cohabitation must have been very sad because they had little to talk about, whether it was due to Maruca's lack of literary, artistic or other types of interests—that lack of a lively spirit Margarita Aguirre saw in her—or whether it was due to the poet's scarce or depressed life energy, documented in "The Phantom of the Cargo Ship".

The *Forafric* did not help. It was a cargo ship that had some passenger cabins, at affordable prices, but without the comforts and entertainment transatlantic cruises tend to have. On this type of ship, two months must have been hard to bear even for an enthusiastic adventurer returning to his home base, exhausted from his experiences, but satisfied and at ease. Imagine how a 27-year-old young man must have experienced that return trip which was defeat writ large: he had no money, no employment, he had not published his book…and he had no love. Although his pride would not let him write openly (though he did so cryptically), I am sure that for Pablo Maruca's company during that trip was, at least in part, a load added to his desolation.

I am not aware of any information about the captain, the officials or the crew, nor about the passengers Neruda must have met during dining hours or chatted in some living room or in the inevitable café-bar, or during the interminable hours walking on the deck or overlooking the sea by the railing and watching the waves being left behind. "The Phantom of the Cargo Ship" leaves us with the image of a ship that is truly ghostly, without a crew and with only one passenger: Pablo. Not even Maruca seems to exist. The poem refers to stairs, railings, cabins, storage rooms, kitchens, furniture, chairs, closets, corners and halls, the rumor of "fatigadas máquinas que aúllan y lloran / empujando la proa" [fatigued engines that howl and cry / pushing the bow] of an "desventurado comedor solitario" [unfortunate solitary dining room] and "las verdes carpetas de las mesas" [the green table covers]. But he does not allude to any of the human beings with whom Pablo shared the trip.

Written while he was crossing the sea, the first version of the poem was published in *Atenea* 87 shortly after his having returned to Santiago (May 1932). A second corrected version was sent to Eandi almost one year later, at the end of March 1933, when the book that included it, *Residencia en la tierra I* [Residence on Earth 1], had already gone to press with Editorial Nascimento in Santiago.

Significantly, "The Phantom of the Cargo Ship" (a poem which was not going to be included with the originals in *Residence 1*, already organized before the trip) was added to section III, which included "Caballero solo" [Gentleman Alone], "Ritual de mis piernas" [My Legs' Ritual] and "The Widower's Tango", notably the three-part work about sexual solitude or about conflicts and anxieties of a sexual type. That being said, by adding "The Phantom of the Cargo Ship" to the thematically common triad, Neruda revealed to us his most secret (and bitter) key to reading them: his sexual and affective solitude related to the (invisible) woman in the text who traveled with him for seventy-five days from Batavia to Puerto Montt.

6

"Instead of the cross, the Albatross
About my neck was hung."
Coleridge, *The Rime of the Ancient Mariner*

Besides the poem about the phantom and a few lines he wrote to Eandi about the Batavia-Colombo-Puerto Montt trip in 1932, Neruda's silence was almost complete. I say 'almost' because ten years later he penned some fleeting (and also cryptic) lines in his speech *Viaje por las costas del mundo* [Voyage along the Coasts around the World] whose first edition, organized in Mexico, he read in Havana in 1942, and, with a few tweaks, in Bogotá in 1943. Neruda read the third and definitive version in the National Library in Santiago, back in the country in December of 1943.

The second paragraph of that speech was a rapid flight over the entirety of Pablo's Asian experience, from the beginning until the return trip:

> For a long time, solitary names of unknown and distant regions accompanied me, where I had a house, some books, maybe a wife. Those names were never of interest to anybody [...]. What would a month, a thousand days, many of my weeks, many seasons, the Gulf in Martaban, wandering the shores of the Irrawaddy river, whose mouth is in Rangoon [...], or a cold morning by Magellan's Strait, freezing, sick and without work, looking at the snout of an imprecise manatee with his big, frosty moustache, mean to anybody?[8]

After describing this frigid image of desolation, the subsequent paragraphs tell us about seas and rivers, from the Gulf of California to "the fabulous Genil river," written by the Andalusian Pedro de Espinosa in true octaves. Pablo names three rivers, after which he includes these enigmatic lines:

> The division of the sea is always different. My long walks next to the cliffs, my navigations to frozen corners, *where I deserved to carry a dead albatross hanging from the neck of the ancient mariner,* made me look

---

8 Neruda, *Obras completas* [Complete Works], IV, pp. 498–499.

beneath the waves, impregnate myself with its ghostly zoology, tremble at the very site of the shipwreck. And after many years had transpired, I turned my life toward the solitary sea of my childhood [...], and toward the deserted sea which always rocks my dreams and opens up for me night's doors of time, so I once wrote in "El sur del Océano" [The South of the Ocean] (my emphasis).[9]

With what other glacial navigations—before "The South of the Ocean" (1933)—could Neruda have been associating Coleridge's paraphrase, save his journey through Magellan's Strait in 1932? Thus, the ancient mariner's dead albatross, and now about his neck, was a metaphor for Maruca, encoded in such a way so as to have remained undeciphered until now. No need to explain the terrible meaning of that image. But it is important—very important—to underline the *I deserved* with which the bard honestly accepted responsibility for the ancient mariner's *crime* (in this instance, the hurried and loveless marriage), declaring unequivocally that he deserved the *punishment*. And thus refuting, many years ahead of time, a recent accusation that—without the least bit of proof—a certain Argentine writer whose name I prefer to not recall attempts to hang something else around his neck: "His *cynicism* allowed him to live life without feeling the 'miseries or sorrows' though he inflicted them on others."[10] In light of what is written in this book so far, let the reader judge how accurate it is to say that Neruda was a cynic.

As we know, over the course of six years Neruda somehow managed without complaints, and with verifiable responsibility, the weight of the albatross around his neck.

7

Having disembarked in Puerto Montt on April 18th, 1932, Pablo and Maruca continued their journey by train to Temuco, where they arrived the following day in the afternoon. Awaiting Pablo were his father's bitter reproaches and sarcasm. Would he ever return triumphantly to the wooden house? Maruca did not understand much of the conflict between her husband and don José del Carmen, but her European and colonial education pushed her to make

---

9 Neruda, *Obras completas* [Complete Works], IV, p. 501.
10 *La Tercera* (Santiago), 1/19/2019.

a good impression with her new Chilean relatives. With doña Trinidad, and especially with Laura, she did so fully.

After a week, Pablo and Maruca took the night train to Santiago. In her scant Spanish Maruca wrote to Laura on May 2nd: "We are now in the boarding house, 736 Santo Domingo, which is very good and cheap, we pay 400 pesos for two people." That is exactly what the Ministry of Foreign Affairs paid Pablo for the temporary position he was assigned. Who knows how they were able to eat? I wonder why they did not think, for example, that Maruca could teach private English classes. Maybe she was too inert to propose that type of initiative.

In renewing his ties with his friends, Neruda felt as though he was being reborn in Santiago. "He was no longer the somber, melancholic and absent young man. Now he talked a lot and laughed no matter what the pretext."[11] His metamorphosis was also a surprise for Maruca, but in the opposite sense. She did not understand nor was she pleased with the change since Batavia, although Pablo did all he could to better their financial situation. Maruca never understood—in Santiago, in Buenos Aires or in Madrid—that the way to stay with Pablo was to accompany him (and share in) the socializing and fun with his friends. She insisted on remaining by herself, not even bothering to learn Spanish, unable as she was to be a part of the husband's *real* life. She would make a scene whenever he arrived late, which only gained her the opposite of what she wanted.

8

And yet she had a good opportunity, since Pablo was isolated as regards his affective life. In December 1932 he wrote "Barcarola" [Barcarolle], a poem which, together with "The Phantom of the Cargo Ship", he sent to Héctor Eandi on February 17th, 1933, and was later included in *Residence on Earth 2*. "Barcarolle" was a like a summons for a woman with braids. It was a vehement and desperate summons for help to recuperate the lost territory of his dreams and prophetic impulse.

---

11 Diego Muñoz, *Memorias. Recuerdos de la bohemia nerudiana* [Memoirs: Recollections of Bohemian Life with Neruda], p. 180.

Considering Pablo's intimate life towards the end of 1932, a close reading of the poem has led me to this hypothesis: extratextually, that unnamed addressee was Maruca—she was the key to this enigmatic composition. I have not seen any photos of Maruca with braids, but the Dutch tradition (or Germanic tradition) allows me to presume that she used them when Pablo met her in Batavia, or in old photos of her. At any rate, the reference to the braids harks back to the couple's past, to the blissful phase of falling in love, in contrast to the unfortunate present. The summons petitioned the return of the Edenic disposition of that woman with braids. It pleaded with her to show a sign of the restoration of that moment, to which the poet would respond with a symmetrical offer of availability which the following lines, as I understand it, allude to:

Si solamente me tocaras el corazón,
si solamente pusieras tu boca en mi corazón,
tu fina boca, tus dientes,
si pusieras tu lengua como una flecha roja
allí donde mi corazón polvoriento golpea,
si soplaras en mi corazón, cerca del mar, llorando,
sonaría con un ruido oscuro, con sonido de ruedas de
    tren con sueño,
[...]
si tú soplaras en mi corazón, cerca del mar,
como un fantasma blanco,
al borde de la espuma,
en mitad del viento,
como un fantasma desencadenado, a la orilla del mar,
    llorando.
[...]
Quieres ser el fantasma que sople, solitario,
cerca del mar, su estéril instrumento?
Si solamente llamaras,
su prolongado son, su maléfico pito,
su orden de olas heridas,
alguien vendría acaso,
alguien vendría,

desde las cimas de las islas, desde el fondo rojo del mar,
alguién vendría, alguien vendría.

[If you only touched my heart, / if you only put your mouth on my heart, / your delicate mouth, your teeth, / if you put your tongue like a red arrow / where my dusty heart beats, / if you blew into my heart, near the sea, crying, / a dark noise would sound, a sound of a train / wheels with dreams, [...] if you blew into my heart, near the sea, / like a white Phantom, / next to the foam, / amid the wind, / like an unchained Phantom, at the seashore, / crying. / [...] Do you want to be the Phantom who, lonely, plays, / her sterile instrument near the sea? / If you would only call, its prolonged son, its harmful whistle, / its order of wounded waves, / maybe someone would come, / someone would come, / from the heights of the islands, from the red depths of the sea, / someone would come, someone would come.]

There is a group photo, taken at María Luisa Bombal's house during the New Year's disguise party in 1933, which supports my reading of "Barcarolle". In that photo[12] Tomás Lago, Joaquín Edwards Bello, Pablo Garrido, Gabriela Rivadeneira, Álvaro Yáñez (Juan Emar), Alberto Rojas Giménez, and Regina Falcón appear. And in the background, the Nerudas, pressed against each other and smiling, happy and in harmony. He is shown embracing her. It is an image that is not at all common, but rather extremely rare. It is the only Chilean photo is which Maruca is smiling and seems to be happy. In a letter to Laura on January 4th, 1933 Neruda confirmed that "Maruca and I were very happy that night [New Year's] and we remembered you."

9

In the winter of 1933 Neruda was finally able to receive an assignment as selected consul in Buenos Aires. Although his salary was still barely enough, he was at least able to leave behind the disastrous economic situation he lived in Chile. He took on his role on September 2nd and found his boss, Sócrates Aguirre Bernal, to be understanding and even a friend: "I could not demand anything other than his creative vocation and his literary ties," Aguirre Bernal

---

12 For more details, see Lizama and Zaldívar eds., p. 699.

wrote years later to his daughter Margarita, friend and biographer of the poet, who was then a child.

Pablo and Maruca settled into a spacious apartment on the 20th floor of the modern Edificio Safico on Corrientes Street, with a splendid, panoramic view of the city. However, the attempt to resurrect the couple's life, seen in "Barcarolle", spilled out everywhere. Argentine friends and intellectuals received Neruda warmly and invited him to be a part of the Café Signo group and other locales in Buenos Aires, a city which at that time boasted a high economic and cultural life far above Santiago's. But Maruca seemed unable to understand that her lack of interest in artistic and intellectual matters did not allow her to get the most out of the most interesting people surrounding her husband. She was impervious to any type of engagement in life and socializing in Buenos Aires that, to a greater degree than in Santiago, was her best opportunity to be in sync with Pablo. Instead, she made hateful scenes of jealousy and concocted conventional forms of violence. Neruda was certainly not a saint by any means, but he was more available to her than Maruca was able to notice.

Invited by her friend Pablo, María Luisa Bombal arrived at Edificio Safico in September fleeing from her own problems in Chile. She was the only woman who understood Maruca and became her friend: "[Pablo] never went anywhere without me and his wife, *but she got bored so often*, imagine, that in the social gatherings she would ask permission to go lay down. Pablo would run over and cover her..." (emphasis mine).[13] What would [Maruca] do without the daily company of María Luisa, so intelligent yet fun, who never pretends to know more than what she knows?"[14] Very little, and Neruda probably invited María Luisa to Buenos Aires not only for her own sake but also for Maruca's. He was aware that the two women were on the same wavelength.

---

13 María Luisa Bombal, "Testimonio autobiográfico" [Autobiographical Witnessing], in *Obras completas* [Complete Works], pp. 278–279.
   Translator's note: María Luisa Bombal (1910–1980) was a well-known Chilean novelist and short story writer influenced by feminism and the avant-garde. Her novels include *La última niebla* [The Last Fog, 1934] and *La amortajada* [The Shrouded Woman, 1938]. She lived in the United States for twenty-nine years, where she met the Nobel Prize winning poet Gabriela Mistral.
14 Ágata Gligo, *María Luisa*, p. 68.

10

Federico García Lorca[15] had yet to disembark in Buenos Aires when María Flora Yáñez, Álvaro's sister (Álvaro=Pilo Yáñez=Juan Emar),[16] arrived with the idea of spending a few weeks in the city. When the Andalusian arrived, María Flora would have the opportunity to attend a tribute and dinner for Federico and Pablo, put on by the PEN Club, and she witnessed the unique and brilliant "joint speech" the two poets dedicated to Rubén Darío.[17] But in her *Historia de mi vida* [History of my Life] María Flora remembered an earlier episode:

> Pablo Neruda, a friend of Pilo's, came to see me at the hotel. He asked me to join him for a cocktail which he would dedicate to me. [...] He lived in an ultramodern apartment on the 20th floor of a skyscraper, where he welcomed me with exquisite friendliness. With the low voice and slow manner of speaking of a preacher he introduced me to Norah Lange[18], Alfonsina Storni[19], Maruca, his Javanese wife who looked like

---

15 Translator's note: Federico García Lorca (1898–1936) was an internationally known Spanish poet and playwright. Along with Rafael Alberti, Miguel Hernández, Jorge Guillén, Pedro Salinas, Vicente Aleixandre, Luis Cernuda, Gerardo Diego, among others he was a member of Spain's Generation of '27, which also included such figures as Salvador Dalí and Luis Buñuel. His most famous books of poetry are *Romancero gitano* [Gypsy Ballads, 1928] and the posthumous *Poeta en Nueva York* [Poet in New York, written in 1929–1930 as Federico García Lorca claimed in the original edition, but a few poems were also written in Spain upon his return and others were edited and elaborated upon before he was assassinated in 1936 and then published in 1940]. García Lorca's best-known plays are *La zapatera prodigiosa* [The Shoemaker's Prodigious Wife, 1930 *Bodas de sangre* [Blood Wedding, 1932], *Yerma* [1934] and *La casa de Bernarda Alba* [The House of Bernarda Alba, 1936].

16 Translator's note: Álvaro Yáñez Bianchi (a.k.a, Juan Emar) [1893–1964] was a writer and one of the leaders of the Chilean avant-garde. A friend of Vicente Huidobro as well as Neruda, he was influenced by Dada and Surrealism. His works include *Ayer* [Yesterday, 1935], *Un año* [One Year, 1935], *Miltín 1934* (1935), and *Diez* [Ten, 1937]. His magnum opus, *Umbrales* [Thresholds], was published posthumously in 1996.

17 Translator's note: Rubén Darío (1867–1916) was a Nicaraguan poet and the leading figure of the modernista movement (a movement akin to French Symbolism) who revolutionized poetry in the Spanish language, in Spain and in Latin America. His classic books are *Azul* (1888), *Prosas profanas* (1906) and *Cantos de vida y esperanza* (1905).

18 Translator's note: Norah Lange (1905–1972) was an Argentine poet and novelist active during the avant-garde. She was a friend of Jorge Luis Borges and was the wife of the Argentine avant-gardist poet Oliverio Girondo (1891–1967). She was awarded the Gran Premio de Honor [The Grand Honorary Prize] by the Argentine Writers' Association in 1959.

19 Translator's note: Alfonsina Storni (1892–1938). Born in Switzerland, she is considered to be a popular Argentine poet known for her feminist stances—which were brought to light

a giant, blond police officer, and María Luisa Bombal, a young Chilean actress.

In that get together on October 3rd, 1933 Pablo also introduced her to others in the cultural world in Argentina, like Sara Tornú Rojas Paz (Blondie) and José González Carbalho.

> After the meal, Neruda suggested we spend the evening in Signo, a writers' hub. Maruca disappeared into their bedroom, getting Neruda's attention as she did so, and he followed her. Shortly thereafter we heard yelling from a heated discussion [until] Neruda and Maruca came out of the bedroom; he, sadder than ever, she, still full of anger. 'Let us go to Signo' Neruda ordered. And off we went. There, in that great underground café, there was no action, only sad dances. At two in the morning they dropped me off...[20]

This paragraph, written by María Flora Yáñez, and María Luisa Bombal's previous rendering of events, depict the sad domestic life Pablo and Maruca led in the Safico Building. It is clear that Neruda did not exclude his wife from the get togethers or other activities his status as poet and diplomat afforded him; quite the contrary he invited her to participate in them and surely tried to arouse in her an interest in this stimulating dimension of his life. It was all for not; she became bored, and nothing seemed to grab her attention. And it appears she hoped besides that Pablo would give up these types of experiences which he needed for his intellectual and emotional development. Or simply to have fun. It is no surprise, then, that the poem "Walking around" condensed the constancy of that desolation that suffused Neruda's life in Buenos Aires before García Lorca arrived to rescue him from that abyss.

II

And yet normal intimate moments were also present in the couple's life, as witness the fact that Maruca became pregnant in November. Pablo would say as much implicitly in his letter to don José del Carmen dated March 24th, 1934 in Buenos Aires. I quote here the pertinent passage:

---

by Latin American literary critics in the 1980s—and for her *postmodernista* and avant-gardist verse.
20 María Flora Yáñez, *Historia de mi vida* [A Story of my Life, 1980], p. 210.

Now let me share some great news, and it is—we assume—*that we will make you a grandfather in August this year*. Although Maruca has had some internal difficulties, I hope all will turn out well. We are still unable to save anything, but what can you do? Things will work out in time. I imagine Laura will be delighted with her new niece or nephew. And what do you think? / Maruca is doing very well, learning to sew...[21]

Pablo confirmed the news a few days later, on 28 March, in a letter to Laura: "You know, you are going to have a nephew in August."[22] But in that letter, he also wrote to his sister about his imminent transfer to Barcelona, asking her to let their father know of the news. Why did he not do it in the letter he wrote a few days earlier? He probably focused on the news of a future grandchild because he thought it would have more of a touching effect on the hardened rail worker. To understand Pablo's behavior before and after Maruca's giving birth, one has to consider how exceedingly important it was for him to get don José del Carmen to accept him. His father's disdain continued to be the most bitter price his son had to pay for his loyalty to the act of writing poetry. Hence, the possibility of making him a grandfather took precedence over his progress in the diplomatic field; it seemed to Pablo that he had finally found a masterful way to regain the long-yearned affection of his father.

At the same time that he wrote these letters, Neruda penned the long poem "Maternidad" [Maternity], which makes for difficult reading. On the one hand, it signals the favorable developments in his personal life (having reached a level of renown, having made friends and having reengaged in eroticism in Buenos Aires), and, on the other hand, there exists the interpellation with the principal addressee in the throes of maternity. That second dimension establishes an affinity between the poems "Maternity" and "Barcarolle" insofar as it appears to vehemently push him toward a complete renewal, a new beginning in a frank and open way. The affinity with "Barcarolle" is visible especially in the conclusive apostrophe:

Oh madre oscura, hiéreme
con diez cuchillos en el corazón,
hacia ese lado, hacia ese tiempo claro,
hacia esa primavera sin cenizas.
Hasta que rompas sus negras maderas

---

21 Neruda, *Obras completas* [Complete Works], V, p. 833.
22 Neruda, *Obras completas* [Complete Works], V, p. 834.

llama en mi corazón, hasta que un mapa
de sangre y de cabellos desbordados
manche los agujeros y la sangre,
hasta que lloren sus vidrios golpea,
hasta que se derramen sus agujas.

La sangre tiene dedos y abre túneles
debajo de la tierra.

[Oh, dark mother, wound me / with ten knives in the breast, / toward that side, toward that clear time, / toward that spring without ashes. / Until you break its black wood / call in my heart, until a map / of blood and overflowing hair / stains the holes and the blood, / beat until its glass cries out, / until its needles spill. // Blood has fingers, and it opens tunnels / beneath the earth.]

The poet urges the mother to shake and assault him emotionally until his determination is able to penetrate the walls of discord and dissolve the rancor and rejections, aiming to reconstitute them together. It is quite likely that García Lorca recommended the Gypsy-like formula "wound me / with ten knives in the breast," where the number 10 is rooted in the Arabian-Andalusian traditions and connotes totality, a return to unity. *Blood has fingers*: the pregnancy possesses a potent active force (*fingers* stands in for *hands*, a Nerudian symbol for *action*) capable of opening a subterranean passageway that will reconnect the couple.

12

"It was a good trip"—wrote Neruda to Eandi from the ship headed to Barcelona—"were it not for the death of the little monkey we bought in Brazil and who died and left Maruca weeping... I am a jerk for running and running around the world."[23] The trip had begun on May 5th. It was difficult to leave a city where he felt accepted and appreciated, where he had friendships and love affairs, where he met Federico, and return to his state of melancholy and emotional emptiness, to the weight of "the albatross around his neck." Besides, he was not interested in Barcelona; his dream was to live in Madrid. I believe it is likely that this new oceanic trek inspired the poem "El reloj caído

---

23 Neruda, *Obras completas* [Complete Works], V, p. 971.

en el mar" [The Fallen Clock in the Sea], an image reflecting the lethal passing of empty time: "Es un día domingo detenido en el mar, / un día como un buque sumergido, / una gota del tiempo que asaltan las escamas / ferozmente vestidas de humedad transparente" [It is a Sunday pausing over the sea, / a day like a submerged vessel, / a drop of time which assaults the [fish] scales / ferociously dressed in transparent humidity].

Scarcely had he disembarked in Barcelona when telegrams from Laura and other friends informed him of the miserable death of his great friend, Alberto Rojas Giménez[24], a victim of alcohol and of a heartless bartender who, seeing that Rojas did not have a penny on him to pay the bottle he had downed, made him leave his jacket as a tender. So, he left in shirt sleeves, in the middle of a cold night, and a week later he died of bronchopneumonia."[25] This terrible blow plunged Pablo into the worst type of grieving, and he found no other outlet in Barcelona than to enter

> the great cathedral of the seafarers, the Basilica of Santa María del Mar, immense, dark, full of stone and small votive boats and baroque hurricanes. But since I did not know how to pray, I went looking for a Catholic friend [the painter Isaías Cabezón] who prayed at every one of the altars. In the darkness only the three-foot-long candles I had bought my friend burned. I knelt before the main altar with my friend and was content. I then wrote a poem titled "Alberto Rojas Giménez viene volando" [Alberto Rojas Giménez Comes Flying], which I am sending to you separately in the magazine in which it was published. It is a solemn, funereal hymn, because it could not have been otherwise.[26]

There is precious little information about Pablo's brief stay in Barcelona, except that he was even more fortunate with his new boss—Tulio Maquieira, Chilean General Consul in Spain—than he had been with Sócrates Aguirre in Buenos Aires. "A very stern [he said of Maquieira] man, known for being a hermit, who was extraordinarily generous, understanding and warm with me."[27] Specifically, he approved Pablo's transfer to Madrid. We have no idea

---

24 Translator's note: Alberto Rojas Giménez (1900–1934) was a Chilean journalist, painter and poet influenced by the avant-garde and associated with anarchism. He published the book, *Chilenos en París y otras crónicas* [Chileans in Paris and Other Chronicles, 1930].
25 For more details, see Luis Enrique Délano, *Memorias. Aprendiz de escritor/Sobre todo Madrid* [Memoirs: An Apprentice Writer, Madrid Above All], pp. 86–87.
26 Neruda, *Obras completas* [Complete Works], V, pp. 1030–1031.
27 Neruda, *Obras completas* [Complete Works], p. 522.

where the Nerudas stayed in Barcelona and we have no particular news about Maruca.

13

On May 31st, Neruda took a train to Madrid, where Federico García Lorca was waiting for him, accompanied by Rafael Rodríguez Rapún and Luis Sáenz de la Calzada, who were both members of the theater group La Barraca, directed by García Lorca. Apparently, Maruca stayed in Barcelona this time. Pablo finally met the diplomat Carlos Morla Lynch in person. He had exchanged letters with him, and as noted in Morla Lynch's diary, dated June 2nd, he held a reception party at his house: "all the guests came to meet Pablo Neruda," the host wrote, without revealing the names of the guests, yet naming the protagonists of the event. It started with Acario Cotapos acting out his hilarious parodies, which Pablo would always remember. Federico improvised an Oriental dance covered in a rug, Bebé Vicuña sang her husband Carlos' compositions, and at the end, the main course, which all had been expecting: Neruda read some of his poems, among them "The Phantom of the Cargo Ship", "Sólo la muerte" [Only Death] and, ending with "The Widower's Tango" in that crescendo effect, which the bard always knew how to dramatize in his readings, as Morla Lynch's diary affirmed this time.

Among the guests who was not named in the diary, no doubt, was Delia del Carril. Although Rafael Alberti claimed more than one time that he was the one who introduced Delia to Pablo, the comparison of signs Morla Lynch's diary offers makes it difficult to imagine that the Argentine friend was not there that night of June 2nd. Many years later, Lola Falcón remembered Delia's intense curiosity prior to the poet's imminent arrival: "So, do you know this Neruda?"

14

On the next trip from Barcelona, Pablo arrived with Maruca and, together, they visited Rafael Alberti[28] and María Teresa León's house on Marqués de

---

28 Translator's note: Rafael Alberti (1902–1999) was Spanish poet and painter who belonged to the Generation of '27 and was a communist. Some of his best-known books of poetry published while Neruda was alive were *Marinero en tierra* [Sailor on Earth, 1924, winner of the National Literary Prize], *Cal y canto* [Lime and Song, 1927], *Sobre los ángeles* [About

Urquijo Street. María Teresa wrote the following detailing her impression of Maruca:

> In that house, among the plants which had made our terrace a garden, the doors would never close.
> Pablo Neruda knocked on that door. He put a finger over his lips: Shhh. I ask you please. My wife is below. Do not let her see the surprise on your faces when you set eyes on her. She is very tall!
> Yes, Pablo's wife was tall, very tall, capping off her body with a beautiful, clear head, which, though we were forewarned, surprised us. She sat in front of us showing her long legs—magnificent columns—as she faced us.

Alberti helped the Nerudas find a place to live in Madrid, nearby. Rather quickly—and still in June—Pablo was able to move into an apartment high up in a red brick building with Maruca. His poetic lines later made this place famous: la Casa de las Flores [the House of the Flowers], on the corner of Rodríguez San Pedro and Hilarión Eslava, in the Argüelles neighborhood. Recently built along with other apartments on the block, they all had balconies with geraniums and other plants. Neruda had a partition wall knocked down between two rooms and thus created a large living room where he began to place his books, swords, Asian masks and other objects.

Very soon that living room became the place for literary gatherings and parties with his friends, which were known for their large number and for including intellectuals, writers and artists who often made it up to Neruda's apartment in Madrid. Among them, Delia del Carril (known as "La Hormiga;" [The Ant]), who after living in Paris for three years—an intense period of introduction to Marxism and affiliation with the French Communist Party—had arrived in Madrid at the beginning of 1934, during the first dark months of the "Dark Biennium."[29] That situation intensified Delia's authentic political activism. The Albertis introduced her to the Alianza de Intelectuales [The Alliance of Intellectuals] and shepherded her transfer to the Spanish

---

the Angels, 1928], *El poeta en la calle* [The Poet on the Streets, 1938], *El hombre deshabitado* [The Uninhabited Man, 1931] and *De un momento a otro* [From One Moment to Another, 1938]. He won the Cervantes Prize in 1983.

29 Translator's note: This term refers to the two-year period following the elections in 1933, in which the Right made great gains in the Spanish Parliamentary elections.

Communist Party. Given her fluency in English and French, she was assured of countless activities, since Hitler's recent power grab in Germany made the Spanish Republic a focus of attraction and reference point for liberal-progressive Europe, which was on alert and was mobilizing.

Pablo and Delia needed each other without knowing it. It all happened as if Delia had dedicated her time in Paris preparing for the arrival of Pablo, offering him what he was looking for, and to receive from him what she, in turn, needed: especially on the emotional side. Neruda's *orthodox* communism, singular and tenacious until his death, cannot be explained without Delia.[30] Alberti's role as a communist intellectual was of no interest to him and he did not follow him. Besides, it was typical of Neruda's own style (so to speak) to await the intervention of a woman in his life to carry out decisive changes. So it was in the case of Albertina and the delirium of the Slingman (Hondero), so too in the case of Josie Bliss and the vicissitudes of the first volume of *Residence on Earth*. Delia inserted herself in a natural and opportune way into the intimate, clarifying process that Neruda's conscience had combated since well before their first encounter. This led to "Explico algunas cosas" [I Explain Some Things], the love cantos for Stalingrad, and *Canto general*.

The romance between Pablo and Delia developed night after a night in the Cervecería Correos. Delia would never forget that one of those nights the wordsmith entered, sat by her side, and "put his arm around me and we stayed there just like that."[31]

On August 12th, Neruda wrote to Morla Lynch—who was in Ibiza to avoid the terrible summer in Madrid—one of his vivacious letters, in which imagined her visiting him "in the midst of your pastoral life, singing a seamen's song with a hoarse voice. *But Maruca has yet to have her child*, so I must stay in Madrid."[32]

She did not have to wait long. Six days later Malva Marina Reyes was born.

---

30 Translator's note: By *orthodox* Loyola means the pro-Soviet line that Neruda adhered to until the end of his life. (Consultation with author, 11/5/2021.)
31 For more details, see Fernando Sáez, *La Hormiga. Biografía de Delia del Carril, la mujer de Pablo Neruda* [The Ant. Biography of Delia del Carril, Pablo Neruda's Wife], p. 89.
32 Translator's note: It should be noted that Neruda wrote this letter just before his daughter's birth and it shows that he was very excited about it.

The Fifth Sin

Bad Father

"Por unos dedos que el rosal quisiera..."
[For fingers the rosebush would like...]
Enfermedades en mi casa
[Illnesses at home]

I

PABLO AND MARUCA ARRIVED in Spain at the end of May 1934. As he had predicted in the letter Neruda wrote to his father from Buenos Aires in March, Malva Marina was born in August: August 18th, 1934. According to research Dr. Galo Corral—the Chilean obstetrician—did in Madrid, Maruca had a normal birth, at two in the morning that day in the maternity ward located at 66 Mesón de Paredes Street, in the Lavapiés neighborhood.

The girl only weighed 2.4 kilograms and was 47 centimeters tall, a weight and height that are completely insufficient for a newborn [who] was in grave condition the first few days due to complications from the labor [and] congenital hydrocephalus... The hydrocephalus in itself, with or without the cerebral hemorrhage, in those times was an incurable condition which included progressive mental damage, which left the human subject living oblivious to sensorial experience.[1]

The photos and data left of the child during her childhood in Gouda, Holland, always show her in a small wooden cart, in the arms of somebody, or seated on the edge of a table, thus confirming that she was never able to walk, nor grab anything with her hands, but they also show that she was able to see and maybe recognize the children of the family who took care of her. She

---

[1] For more details, see Galo Corral, "Dónde y cómo nació Malva Marina", *Nerudiana*, 21–22 (2017): pp. 46–47.

was also able to smile sweetly. In a letter in 1938 Maruca mentioned to Neruda that their child was making progress cognitively and "sang a lot," which was probably not accurate. Yet it suggested that in some way she was able to hear or at least perceive the vibrations of the melodies Maruca always sang for her since the time she was born, and Malva attempted to reproduce with murmurings.

For some years now, Neruda's behavior toward his daughter has been the object of judgmental summaries, condemnations and anathema which, in general, start off offering a scarce amount of information and—motivated ideologically and politically—seem interested in discrediting or demolishing the poet. By contrast, I intend to impartially review the objective facts and evidence that the available documentation offers (poems, letters, photos, chronicles, stories, confessions, criticism, etc.) to see what comes of this type of analysis. Based on those materials, I will reflect on and formulate possible hypotheses which, incidentally, will not attempt to be a defense of the accused, his own is more than enough ("I respond with my work").

2

Maruca was released from the hospital on August 24th, six days after her delivery.[2] During those days the little girl was oscillating between life and death while Pablo was going to pharmacies to get medicine, syringes and other necessary instruments. Before that date, he began writing the poem "Enfermedades en mi casa" [Illnesses at home]. When the mother returned with their daughter, Pablo wrote a letter to his father. Additionally, he had a small, folded card printed, designed by his friend the painter Miguel Prieto, announcing the birth of Malva Marina. At the bottom of the announcement Pablo placed the fish figure, in the same position that, fifteen years later, Miguel Prieto[3] would place the fish figure of the *ex libris* (which would later be Neruda's logo) on the cover of the monumental Mexican edition of *Canto general*. Let us read a fragment from his letter to his father, dated August 25th, 1934 and written in Madrid:

---

2 Corral, p. 46.
3 For more details, see Sara Vial, *Neruda vuelve a Valparaíso* [Neruda returns to Valparaíso], p. 253.

The 18th of this month our daughter, whom we called Malva Marina Trinidad (as a tribute to my dear mom), was born. I have not hurried to communicate the news because things have not gone well. It seems as though our daughter was born premature, and it has been difficult to keep her alive, we have had to have doctors with her all the time, and she has to be fed through a tube, an IV, and spoonfuls of milk because she does not want to nurse. There were many dangerous moments in which the little one was dying, and we did not know what to do. We have had to spend many nights and even sleepless days watching over her, to feed her every two hours. The doctor recently told us that there is no danger, but the little one will need a lot of care. I think that since I was such a pain [as a child], we will be able to raise her. In twenty more days, they will begin giving her cod liver oil, as they gave me, which is the only salvation for emaciated children.

Our daughter is very little—when she was born, she weighed only two kilos and 400 grams—but she is very pretty, a doll, with blue eyes like her grandfather's, Maruca's nose (fortunately) and my mouth. Everybody thinks she is very pretty and soon I will send a photo of her. Naturally her struggle has not ended yet, but I believe she has won most of the battle and will put on weight and will be chubby soon.

Maruca has been doing really well. She had no major soreness and her labor only lasted an hour and a half. She is in good shape and tomorrow will get up and get around. She has fond memories of you, mom and Laura, and feels bad that you are so far away and cannot come to see your granddaughter.

These lines from the letter Neruda wrote constitute one of the more painful documents in his entire life. Rather than the light and triumphant tone with which he wanted to communicate his pride as a father to don José del Carmen, he had to make an effort to paint the delivery in a relatively normal light. This only made his silence all the more glaring regarding the true tragedy: Malva Marina's hydrocephalus. A week after her birth, the baby's head must have grown a great deal, with the inevitable decline in her mental faculties due to the pressure the cerebral-spinal fluid exerted on her still weak brain.

The sudden collapse of his expectations connected to Maruca's delivery was, for Neruda, an intense blow that is terrifying to imagine. These were the normal expectations of being a father; Pablo had wanted to have a child despite the difficulties he and Maruca had had (years later, having a child with his lover Matilde Urrutia would become an obsessive dream). But above all there were the enormous expectations of giving the irascible railroad worker a grandchild, a new and solid basis on which to reestablish the father-son nexus.

3

In examining the documents Neruda wrote about Malva Marina, I invite the reader to pay attention to the details dealing with the tone, the lexicon and the syntax, especially the affective side and communicative intentionality (it was not always direct, sometimes ludic or ironic or cautious due to modesty or pride. In sum, it was not always transparent, but it was never designed to deceive or lie). The reason for the caution is that many attacks on Neruda are based on misreadings or misinterpretations of his writings—and not necessarily in bad faith—or literal explanations without any contextualization or lack of attentiveness to the semantic disguises that the poet tended to use in his messages to addressees in whom he had confidence, interlocutors whom he knew were able to grasp and understand what was not said or the word play.

So, for instance, in a letter to Morla Lynch on August 12th (days before the delivery) Neruda wrote that "Maruca does not yet have her child," whereas the letter he sent to his father on the 25th alluded to "our daughter." The difference between these formulations had nothing to do with the delivery but rather with the messages' tones according to the addressee and the circumstance, and also the time period.

The formula "Maruca does not yet have her child" was inserted into a message with a jovial tone, full of humorous details regarding friends in common (Delia del Carril, Rafael Alberti, Arcario Catapos, Federico García Lorca), sent to another Chilean with whom he was able to talk jokingly, and in this case it might even have been to strengthen his implicit request for help contained in the final paragraph: "I live with the perpetual fear that I will be sent to another place." The aforementioned statement *Maruca does not yet have her child*, devoid of solemnity and machismo, depended then on the factors implicated in the communcative situation.

Likewise, but determined by factors that were of a very different nature, the other formula, *our daughter was born*, was necessarily solemn, serious and objective, which requires no further explanation. Further down, the omission of hydrocephalus *with which our daughter was born* in the letter to his father does not require further explanation either, beyond what I wrote in the preceding section. For any reader with good will, it is not difficult to understand why he remained quiet; s/he could not imagine Neruda resorting to deceit or hypocrisy. The reason was called pain, infinite anguish.

4

Neruda probably wrote "Enfermedades en mi casa" [Illnesses at home] alone, when Maruca was still in the maternity ward on Mesón de Paredes Street. The poem was a private way of relieving the strain without explicitly revealing the ultimate cause of the pain, the terrible bitterness. However, it did reveal—with a faithfulness to Neruda's expressive code—the details, the objects, the material of the decisive circumstances of that personal suffering with which he pieced together the poem. From the beginning the synecdoche in a plural and not singular form and the abstract nature of the title (*illnesses* for "illness" or "ill child") established a pattern of emotional modesty.

Tragedy arrived when a certain stage of happiness and fulfillment were dissipating into a long period of sadness (*los azufres caídos durante muchos meses* [the fallen sulphur during long months]) and the dryness or depression in his domestic life (*mis habitaciones extinguidas* [my extinguished bedrooms]). The first section or stanza in the poem appears dominated by images which etch the contours of the invasion of extreme suffering in a neoromantic way: "la rosa de alambre maldito" [the rose with cursed wire], "arañas" [spiders], "el vidrio roto hostiliza la sangre" [the broken glass antagonizes the blood], "las uñas del cielo" [the sky's nails], "es tanto el humo convertido en vinagre" [the smoke converted into vinegar is too much], "el agrio aire que horada las escalas" [the bitter air that perforates the scales], until it dissolves in an obstinate lament:

> en ese instante en que el día se cae con las plumas deshechas,
> no hay sino llanto, nada más que llanto,
> porque solo sufrir, solamente sufrir,
> y nada más que llanto.

[at the moment in which the day falls with its damaged feathers / there is only sobbing, nothing more than sobbing, / due to lonely suffering, only suffering, / and nothing more than sobbing.]

Following this descent to the bottom of his personal anguish, so that the poem would then resume its ascent to a collective, universal level, Neruda abruptly changes the register by playing with his own imaginary notion of *the sacred* [lo sagrado], its *deities* [deidades], that is, the maximum nodal figures in his very unique symbolic and axiological system: *the sea—the night—the tree—the hand—the moon—blood—water—death*. These images occupy the center of the poem: "El mar se ha puesto a golpear por años una pata de pájaro" [For years the sea has begun to beat a bird's foot], "las raíces de un árbol sujetan una mano de niña" [the tree roots grasp a child's hand], "cada día de luna / sube sangre de niña hacia las hojas manchadas por la luna, / y hay un planeta de terribles dientes / envenenando el agua en que caen los niños, / cuando es de noche y no hay sino la muerte" [every moonlit day / a child's blood rises toward the leaves stained by the moon, / and there is a planet with terrible teeth / poisoning the water in which children fall, / when it is night time and death is all there is].

Under pressure from the pain, the symbolic code's values are inverted, and the poet's secular divinities suddenly acquire negative connotations. Such is the case of the sea, an image of paternal support, which unleashes its cosmic force on a miniscule being, only a *bird's foot*, only a *pajarito*[4] in popular Chilean Spanish. Such is the case of the tree, connected to the forest, which rather than symbolizing life devolves into a gigantic and ferocious vampire. Such is the case of the night, his ally, yet here it is the accomplice of the ill-fated moon, which functions as part of the complacent crime scene. All the poet's blasphemies conjure up a livid, bitter and especially authentic condemnation of this *betrayal*.

The poem introduces at this point indirect and persuasive speech: how can he capture the benevolence of cosmic powers toward a minimal being, irrelevant in the scheme of tragedies which affect society and humanity at large? "a quién pedir piedad por un grano de trigo? [...] a quién pedir por unos ojos del color de un mes frío / y por un corazón del tamaño de un trigo que vacila?"

---

4 Translator's note: In Chilean Spanish *pajarito* can mean "baby bird" as in other Spanish dialects, but it can also mean "a defenseless being," which is its meaning here.

[who should one ask for pity for a grain of wheat? [...] who should one ask for eyes the color of a cold month / and for a heart the size of bending wheat?]. This discourse flows into a personal conclusion, unprecedented until then in Neruda's writing:

> Ayudadme, hojas que mi corazón ha adorado en silencio,
> ásperas travesías, inviernos del sur, cabelleras
> de mujeres mojadas en mi sudor terrestre,
> luna del sur del cielo deshojado,
> venid a mí con un día sin dolor,
> con un minuto en que pueda reconocer mis venas.
>
> [Help me, leaves that my heart has adored in silence, / rough journeys, the south's winters, women's / wet locks in my earthly sweat, / southern moon of the defoliated sky, / come to me with a day without sorrow, / with a minute in which I am able to recognize my veins.]

In these lines Neruda returned to the province where he spent his entire childhood, as in a brief note written in 1924 and titled that way, but now from an opposite and unprecedented perspective.[5] No longer from the superior purview of the poet who controlled and conferred life onto this world ("desde el balcón romántico *te extiendo* como un abanico," "*te propongo* a mi destino como refugio de regreso" [from the romantic balcony *I extend* you like a fan; *I propose* you for my destiny for returning home]), but rather from a subordinate, afflicted and helpless position. The atrocious pain because of Malva Marina's condition led Pablo to reimagine the South of his childhood with this new *pleading*.

Yet we should point out that the ocean to the south is missing. With this pleading and via a secular gesture Neruda took on the sacred and feminine nature of the forests on the Chilean frontier, including doña Trinidad in it as well as the love affairs he had when he was twenty (all associated symbolically with the forests surrounding Temuco and the poppy garden—along with the lifesaver's boat—in Puerto Saavedra). Only by saying *no* to the ocean, but *yes* to the forests; *no* to the severe father, but *yes* to the kind-hearted mother, could the afflicted bard plead for help for his dying daughter. And plead for solace for his own pain.

---

5 Pablo Neruda, "Provincia de la infancia" [The Province of Childhood], in *Anillos* [Rings, 1926].

Estoy cansado de una gota,
estoy herido en solamente un pétalo,
y por un agujero de alfiler sube un río de sangre sin consuelo,
y me ahogo en las aguas del rocío que se pudre en la sombra,
y por una sonrisa que no crece, por una boca dulce,
por unos dedos que el rosal quisiera
escribo este poema que solo es un lamento,
solamente un lamento.

[I am tired of one drop, / I am wounded in only one petal, / and through a needle's hole a river of blood rises without respite, / and I drown in the dews' waters that rot in the shade, / and for a smile that will not grow, for a sweet mouth, / for fingers that the rosebush would yearn / I write this poem which is only a lament, / nothing but a lament.]

5

On September 15th, 1934, a few weeks after Malva Marina's birth, Morla Lynch's diary recorded a visit to Neruda's house in the company of Jorge Guillén: "He welcomed us with open arms. In his bright and joyful living room, which has a wonderful view of the hills, we drank barley water. We talked about the new *Antología de poetas españoles* [Anthology of Spanish Poets] and we read aloud various poems by different authors. I was near the window and the view furled out before me contributes to the enchantment I feel."[6]

Life in the House of the Flowers was returning to a sense of normalcy having overcome the danger the initial days posed for Malva Marina. During Maruca's pregnancy, Delia del Carril, Lola Falcón and other women in the group of friends Pablo had, would come to help her and offer their feminine solidarity. This critical situation led to Delia living with the Nerudas in the House of the Flowers. Delia would go more frequently to help Maruca out after she gave birth and also, of course, to be closer to her lover. She was sincere in both cases. In the end, she practically lived with the Nerudas, and she even subleted a room. And there were no signs that Maruca, who was silently

---

6 For more details, see Carlos Morla Lynch, *España sufre. Diarios de guerra en el Madrid republicano, 1936–1939* [Spain Suffers: War Diaries from Republican Madrid, 1936–1939], p. 421.

present, felt in the least bit bothered by it. The several letters she wrote to the family in Temuco, which Laura kept, do not refer to any bitterness or conflicts with Pablo, but rather to her admirable and serene dedication to their daughter.

On September 18th, the Chilean embassy celebrated the 124th anniversary of Chile's political independence. Morla Lynch's diary noted that the party continued at Neruda's house, "which had an impossible soireé, full of strange people. Among them was the Cuban painter, son of a Chinese father [he is alluding to Wifredo Lam]... Everybody was so inebriated, and they wore disguises..."[7] He made no mention of Maruca and their daughter among the racket, which would seem to eliminate the possibility of a conflict between the Nerudas on this occasion: the diplomat would not have let that detail escape him.

6

The following day after this lively party, Neruda wrote a long letter to his friend Sara Tornú *la rubia* [Blondie] in Buenos Aires, confirming that they were there to stay in Madrid and that the complicated city swap (Pablo to Madrid, Gabriela Mistral to Barcelona) had taken place. That brought an allusion to the party the night before to the attention of Tornú, and in it, as though in passing, he made special mention of Delia del Carril among many general references to the Peruvians, Cubans and Mexicans who went to the House of the Flowers. But for our purposes what interests us is what follows in the letter, which concerns Malva Marina:

> There are no writers [in Madrid], even though it is winter. Federico [García Lorca], in Granada, has sent some nice lines of poetry for our daughter. My daughter, or so I have called her, is a perfectly ridiculous being, a type of semicolon, a vampiress weighing three kilos. All is well, oh dear Blondie, [but] all was not well before. Our little girl was dying, she did not cry, nor sleep. We had to give her food through a tube, give

---

7 Morla Lynch, p. 421. Translator's note: Wifredo Lam (1902–1982) was a Afro-Cuban avant-gardist painter. In the 1920s he studied art in Madrid, where he worked with Salvador Dalí. In 1938 he moved to Paris, where Picasso introduced him to Fernand Léger, Henri Matisse, Georges Braque, João Miró, among others. His work shows the impact of Cubism and Surrealism. His most famous painting is "The Jungle" (1942).

her spoonfuls of food, injections, and we would spend all night, and all day, all week, sleepless, calling the doctor, running to abominable orthopedic stores, where they sell horrible baby's bottles, scales, medicinal cups, funnels with degrees and rules. You can imagine how much I have suffered. The little girl, the doctors told me, is going to die, and that tiny thing suffered horribly from a hemorrhage which she had when she was born. But cheer up, Blondie Sara, because everything will work out, the little girl began to breastfeed and the doctors come around less, and she smiles and is consistently gaining weight every day.

This paragraph contains one of the most damning things for biased readers or those who are not willing to place themselves in the context in which it was written, and naturally for anti-Nerudians of every stripe. Among them we should point out the Dutch writer Hagar Peeters, who in her novel *Malva* proclaims herself the mouthpiece or transcriber of the story of Neruda's daughter, chosen by Malva Marina from her life in the afterlife: a narrator for hire who relies on that fiction to dish out her personal ideas and opinions about the world (and about Neruda). Once and a while she appears in her own story (a whole chapter is dedicated to that purpose) to tell us about her own relationship with her father and other unexpected events, or to opine in first person about "mistaken ideologies" like the poet's, for example. Enough about that for the moment. The novel ambiguously collects the majority of the attacks on Neruda with regards to Malva Marina, which will make it useful incriminating evidence for some chapters dealing with the interminable trial against the poet. With regards to the scandal, then, nobody is better than Malva herself, the omniscient Malva (here mystifying) cast in the role by Hagar Peeters:

> In his letters, not scheduled for publication, he referred to me this way: "My daughter, or so I call her, is perfectly ridiculous, a type of semicolon, a vampiress weighing three kilos." He saw me as a bloodsucker, a monster, due to my homely little body and my enormous head. And, as the great poet he was, he could not think of anything else to call me other than a semicolon!
>
> Yes, I know he did not mean it, that he did not feel that way, that that laconic description of me was aimed at the beautiful blond before which he feigned an ironic distance, which is something beautiful women at a certain age appreciate from certain great men... [...]

There is a lot of ambivalence in my father's description of me as a "being who is perfectly ridiculous," because perfectly ridiculous is a paradox: the ridiculous is by its very nature imperfect. However, I was such a ridiculous child that my ridiculousness made me perfect.[8]

The letter to Blondie was dated September 19th, 1934, when Malva Marina was only a month old. Above I quoted one pertinent paragraph from that long letter. Hagar-Malva isolated the 24 words in that paragraph (*My daughter, or whom I call...vampiress weighing three kilos...*) and used them as projectiles against Neruda. The rest of the words in the paragraph—as the reader can readily confirm—reveal aspects associated with the drama of being a father, yet they were not worthy of commentary in the eyes of the omniscient narrator in the hereafter.

I cannot imagine any love affair with Blondie, who was the wife of the Argentine writer and friend of Neruda, Pablo Rojas Paz, during the poet's stay in Buenos Aires. She was a tireless cultural planner who put Neruda in touch with other writers and artists in her circle in the Río de la Plata region, and especially with García Lorca, who had just arrived by ship. She was, in other words, a very good and loyal friend to whom Pablo owed a letter since he left the Argentine capital, as he noted in the first lines. But I think, besides, that the undeclared nucleus of this long message was the paragraph about Malva Marina, whose illness Neruda was inwardly determined to nourish with the hopes of a cure, from the time she showed signs of improving, towards the end of August, until the final months of 1935, as we will see.

When he wrote the letter to Blondie on September 19th, 1934, Neruda was living a period of pure optimism with regards to his daughter's illness (and of feelings of love for Delia del Carril). That is what the 24 isolated words truly mean with regards to Hagar-Malva, and it is what explains their content. The clumsy or cruel aplomb with language that the Dutch writer (and along with her other accusers) wants to read in those words are inconceivable given his state of mind. When he lost hope, when his wishful thinking about a radical change in Malva Marina's health dried up, Pablo's reaction was very different: it was complete verbal silence. I say "verbal" because he found another language, as we will see later on, another way of remembering his daughter and perpetuating her memory.

---

8 Peeters, *Malva*, pp. 17–18.

Those 24 words, written to a dear friend, were intended to be a way of communicating in a ludic, humoristic, extravagant, and, consequently, in an open way, about a serious matter, soon to be resolved. Above all, they were meant to be a Chilean mode of communication devoid of solemnity. That was typical of Neruda when his state of mind was very good, such as when journalists asked him what impressions he had of Machu Picchu: "Well I thought it was great place to have a good goat cookout."

If Hagar Peeters had bothered to study Neruda's language more carefully, she would know that for a Chilean the term *vampiress* means a seductive, sexy, irresistible woman, or a type of *femme fatale* like Marlene Dietrich in *The Blue Angel*, and therefore, "a vampiress weighing three kilos" was a tender compliment to Malva Marina, and was nothing like a "bloodsucker, monster." Likewise, the formula "a perfectly ridiculous being," whose emphasis suggests (to any well-meaning reader) that it means the exact opposite of what it says, or better said, he was attempting to twist an expression in an endearing way (the way it is used in Chile, such as when Neruda called Matilde *Patoja* or *Chascona*[9]). Besides, a review of Spanish grammar would have reminded the omniscient Hagar-Malva that, in this case, *perfectly* is an adverb connoting praise with respect to the adjective *ridiculous* (a substitute would be "absolutely or totally ridiculous"), which has a very different syntactical role than the noun *perfection*, which is not germane. All this makes Hagar-Malva's paragraph about the "ambivalence in my father's description" *perfectly* inadequate or impertinent.

7

January 1935: Neruda wrote a letter to Eandi notifying him that they had finally officially transferred him to Madrid. At the beginning of February Maruca put her semi-fluent Spanish to work and wrote don José del Carmen a letter confirming Neruda's joining the embassy in Madrid—and retaining his

---

9 Translator's note: In Chile terms of endearment tend to be used with nouns or adjectives that could be initially perceived as negative. For example, in Sonnet XX in *Cien sonetos de amor* [One Hundred Love Sonnets] the speaker refers to his loved one (undoubtedly Matilde Urrutia) alternately as "mi fea" [my ugly one] and "mi bella" [my beautiful one]. So, when Neruda says *Patoja* he could mean that she walked like a duck; *chascona* means someone with disheveled hair. These were terms of endearment.

position as Consul—and also confirming the optimistic view she and Pablo still had regarding Malva Marina's development:

> Malva is now five and a half months old, and she is very cute. She has grown and gained quite a bit of weight: she is 71 centimeters tall, whereas she was 47 when she was born, which is something that frightens me a lot because I would feel so bad if she grew to be as tall as I am. She is always a happy girl, she never cries, she smiles all the time. Everybody loves her very much and thinks she is pretty and intelligent. Some days ago, she was eating a small potato like an adult not having to struggle at all. She drinks orange juice, tomato juice and grape juice with sugar and a few drops of an extract from cod liver oil. She has an ultraviolet treatment to fortify her bones, which is good for her health in general.

This letter, unquestionably written by Maruca at Pablo's urging, reveals that the optimism they both felt regarding their daughter persisted until February 1935. But as the months passed the optimism turned to anguish, uncertainty, and in the poet's inner self there grew a subjective will to impose his own wishes on the negative signs that persisted in his daughter's illness. In this battle against the harshness of reality, Neruda was definitely stimulated by the satisfaction he felt during 1935 in the literary world (the publication of his opuscule with the *Tres cantos materiales* [Three Material Songs], the tribute Spanish poets gave him, the publication of the complete edition of *Residence on Earth* in two volumes, and the inauguration of the journal *Caballo Verde para la Poesía* [Green Stallion for Poetry]. In the political realm (his trip to Paris, in June, to participate in the international conference For the Defense of Culture) and in the amorous realm, the company of Delia del Carril. That year of grace could not have been so without the triumphant recuperation of Malva Marina. His good friend and, at the same time, the mentor who introduced him to poetry of the Spanish Golden Age, Vicente Aleixandre,[10] left us with moving evidence of Neruda's blind, desolate and pathetic battle:

---

10 Translator's note: Vicente Aleixandre (1898–1984) was a renowned Spanish poet who belonged to the Generation of '27. Some of his most well-known books of poetry are *Espadas como labios* [Swords like Lips, 1932], *La destrucción o el amor* [Destruction or Love, 1935; winner of the National Literary Prize], *Pasión en la tierra* [Passion on Earth, 1935], *Sombras del paraíso* [Shadows of Paradise, 1944], *Mundo a solas* [The World on its Own, 1950] and *Historia del corazón* [History of the Heart, 1954]. He won the Nobel Prize for literature in 1977.

Pablo had a daughter, no older than two years old, whom I did not know. The poet came up with her name, which, pronounced by him, sounded like a light or shone like music...

Weeks and months went by. These were the days in which Neruda was preparing the inaugural issue of the journal *Caballo Verde para la Poesía* [Green Stallion for Poetry], which acquired a generous editor in his good friend Manuel Altolaguirre, the poet and magical printer besides, who gave birth to poetry books and journals and circulated his graphic art around the world...

Pablo lived in a building—the House of the Flowers—made famous by his presence there. He always urged me to go and visit his daughter. Finally, one day we agreed to go that afternoon to his home...

We arrived at his house, here a rose, flowers in the windows, green shades. The sun rays were softer, but the sun was persistent. It made you turn your head. Between buildings and right next to the apartment there were fields, which allowed the blue air to freshen the environment. It enveloped us and bid us farewell at the door of the house.

We went up some stairs. *Come in, Vicente.* A living room, and Pablo disappeared. In front of me, a wide balcony, and in back, an enormous piece of sky. I went out onto the narrow and adjacent terrace, like a dead-end road. On the way Pablo was hovering over what looked like a cradle. I could hear his voice, but he seemed far away. *Malva Marina, can you hear me? Come, Vicente, come! Look at this marvelous girl. She is the prettiest in the world.* Words blossomed as I approached. He called me over with his hand and stared full of joy at the bottom of that cradle. He was all smiles, full of blind sweetness in his gruff voice, a being absorbed by another being. I arrived. He stood up radiantly while he looked at me. *Look, look!* I came closer and then the bottom of the lace revealed what the cradle contained. A large head, an implacable head which would have devoured her factions, a ferocious and aimless head, overgrown without mercy, with any interruption. A child (was she a child?) whom one could not look at without feeling deep sorrow. A heap of matter in disarray. White, I raised my head, murmured some sounds for whomever awaited them, and I managed to simulate a smile. Pablo was full of light, radiating a fiction, a dream, and his dreaminess was as firm as a stone, his happy pride, thankfulness for this celestial being.

I understood, but I could not explain it.[11]

There are no other outside accounts about Malva Marina or about the intimate drama her father faced when confronted with the reality that are as explicit and heartrending as this one, written by Aleixandre. During the parties in the House of the Flowers, his friends, especially García Lorca, were playful and kind with the child, who had fun with them as Maruca wrote (and that allowed her to reconcile herself with her husband's social gatherings). But the written accounts elude any reference to suffering. So, for instance, when Luis Enrique Délano remembered Malva Marina

> as a pale little girl, with dark hair and eyes, like Neruda's. Did the Nordic features leave any trace in her? Come to think of it, maybe the contour of her face was similar to Maruca's. I remember her in her cradle and in the stroller in which her mother took her to the park, Parque del Oeste [West Park], which is the one which was closest to the House of the Flowers. [...] She did not talk, she just watched everything with her large, sweet and almost frightened eyes. And she sang! Her mother, who carried a nice tune, had taught her to sing and the little girl followed the melody of the songs with her good ears.[12]

Several months after Aleixandre's visit, in Maruca's letter to doña Trinidad (because he did not have courage to write it himself) Pablo revealed the terrible truth to his mother and father:

> My dear Mother: We received your letter some time ago and we hope that you will forgive our long silence [...], but we were unable to muster the energy because we had to write to you about the bad news regarding our Malvita[13]. When she was a few months old we discovered that due to her difficult birth (although I did not suffer at all) her little head started to grow excessively: an illness that the best doctors in Madrid and Paris were unable to cure, which was despairing for us.[14]

In accepting the truth about Malva Marina, life with Maruca lost all meaning for Pablo. However, there is no indication that he decided to formally

---

11 Vicente Aleixandre, *Los encuentros* [Gatherings], pp. 147–149.
12 For more details, see Volodia Teitelboim, *Neruda*, p. 183.
13 Translator's note: 'Malvita' is an affectionate way of saying 'little Malva' in Spanish.
14 Letter dated 5/2/1936 and written in Madrid.

break off the marriage. And he might have continued living with Maruca more, if, two months after sending that letter, the Spanish Civil War had not broken out.

8

In another moment of Peeters' novel, she "transcribes" how an omniscient and cultivated Malva Marina remembers a episode from her life on earth:

In the Gouda Museum there was an exhibition held for *Man with a Tall Cap* by Ferdinand Bol, and my mother (inspired perhaps by the man in the portrait) knitted me a small cap which would cover part of the enormous bulge that my head had become so that when I was in the street the other children would not make fun of me or stare at me.

Every time I recall that scene—my mother knitting the little white cap on her lap—I am overwhelmed with sadness. A detail like that, an action that is so vain, so superfluous, so dispensable, so unnecessary, is what transmits love. The historian who in reading Dante came upon the word *Bice*, the endearing nickname the poet used with his lover and who had hidden away in one of his poems must have felt a similar emotion. Moved, the historian understood at that moment that Beatriz really existed. *I wish my father would have done the same with me, he would have hidden my name away in a couple of his poems or, at least, some diminutive of my name.* It is true that he did mention me once in a poem [she is alluding to "Oda a Federico García Lorca" (Ode to Federico García Lorca)], but among a long list of names, which is next to worthless. A detail like this, I think, is what really matters and not the perfect proportions, the precious section, the grand gesture, the purity of race, the eternal truth or the Nobel Prize for Literature. Though, who am I to talk like that? In the end I have been dead for so long.[15]

Bice is in fact the Italian hypocoristic name for *Beatrice* but is also used as a name. After writing a letter to Eandi, dated September 1935, Neruda stopped mentioning and naming Malva Marina: "I do not want to talk about my little girl, because the poor thing has been ill."[16] But his silences were

---

15 Peeters, p. 134.
16 Pablo Neruda, *Obras completas* [Complete Works], V, p. 973.

always revealing, as Jorge Edwards writes. Neruda never disguised his daughter's *name* in his poems, to my knowledge, but did reveal it to her, "hiding it away" in another document that was very typical of him, "naming her" in a non-verbal way.

The key is the *little fish* that Miguel Prieto, following Pablo's request, designed on a card which announced Malva Marina's birth. It is well known that the overriding symbolic value of fish in Neruda's poetry "is the unflagging and profuse life that germinates in the sea's breasts [...] a symbol of the essential, of life and of the *original* [...] which converge symbolically with roses, doves, bells and grapes... The fish image as ebullient life also includes the representation of things that are changeable and slippery."[17]

Fourteen years later, in 1949, Neruda met up with Miguel Prieto again, now exiled in Mexico, and picked him to organize and typeset the monumental edition of *Canto general*, which he published there in 1950, with illustrations by Diego Rivera and David Alfaro Siqueiros. Now, Neruda asked his friend Miguel Prieto for a very special favor: an *ex libris* for Neruda on the cover and the book jacket, which later became the poet's logo: a fish encircled by armillary rings, inscribed in a circle surrounded by six letters of the name NERUDA.

I am certain the link between the two fish designed by Miguel Prieto—one in 1934 and the other in 1950—was deliberate, and that in the fish design in the Mexican edition of *Canto general* Neruda found a way to connect the memory of his daughter to his life and works. Via that sign he was able *to name and give a secret life and permanence* to little Malva Marina. The lyricist did not know how to do it in his writing, much as he was unable to respond to Amado Alonso's questions regarding some of his lines in *Residence on Earth*. Knowing Neruda, that fish was the reverse of the silence that he could not imagine empty. Rather, that fish incarnated the most revealing of his silences, which is why he never mentioned his daughter's name again, other than in this way. It would always be visible from this moment on in the editions of his books and on the flag which flies from the tower of his house in Isla Negra.

Likewise, he unconsciously forgot the name of the logo's creator, or I cannot remember him revealing it (no interviewer, myself included, thought to ask him about the origin and author of that famous logo). The truth is it was

---

17 Amado Alonso, *Poesía y estilo de Pablo Neruda* [Pablo Neruda's Poetry and Style], pp. 220–221.

not necessary, because the colophon of *Canto general* named Miguel Prieto as the creator of the design for the edition, including, implicitly, the design of the cover and the jacket. But I really believe Pablo forgot his name, much as he forgot when and how he baptized himself *Pablo Neruda*. There were no mysterious secrets or lack of gratitude, but rather—in both cases—something that was profoundly personal, about something (her name and the fish) to which the poet wished to give life and permanence, regardless of the origin.

The Sixth Sin

Plagiarist

"En mi cielo al crepúsculo eres como una nube"
[In my sky to dusk you are like a cloud]
Poema 16
[Poem 16]

I

At the end of April 1932—having just disembarked in Puerto Montt after an interminable trip on the cargo ship *Forafric*, and after a bitter week in Temuco—Neruda took up his life again in Santiago caught between the warm welcome his friends gave him and acute economic and domestic difficulties. The Wall Street crash of 1929 prompted in Chile the worst crisis in the West in 1931–1932, but Pablo managed to convince the Ministry of Foreign Affairs to give him a post paying him a provisional salary of 400 pesos a month, barely enough to pay for a boarding room. Despite these financial constraints, he felt as though he was renewed; he happily returned to the custom of going out at night, drinking cheap wine, and talking with his friends. On May 11th, he had a successful reading of poems written in Asia at the Posada del Corregidor [the Magistrate's Retreat].

A "group of writers of all tendencies" gathered to celebrate Neruda's return on May 29th in the restaurant *Giovinezza*. His usual friends went (Tomás Lago, Rubén Azócar, Ángel Cruchaga Santa María, Diego Muñoz, Rosamel del Valle) and acquaintances like Ricardo Latcham, Joaquín Edwards Bello, Mariano Latorre, Astolfo Tapia, Mariano Picón Salas, Juan Uribe Echevarría. Even Pablo de Rokha was present. "I want to thank you...and I hope that your fraternal support will continue protecting the expression of my secret," Neruda said at the end of the tribute.

During the month of June, the press Nascimento published his second and definitive edition of *Veinte poemas de amor y una canción desesperada* [Twenty Love Poems and a Song of Despair] with a re-elaboration of poems 2 and 4, and the substitution of Poem 9 of 1924 for a more recent version of Poem 9 (with poetic language that was similar to the *Residencia en la tierra* [Residence on Earth] poems). In a preliminary note, the editor declared that he had spared no effort in giving this now classic work the type of appearance it deserved, with the highest quality material which, given the economic situation, was almost impossible to obtain. "Nascimento Press wants to put this book by Neruda on display...the most important poetic success achieved by any Chilean author, in or outside the country."

Joaquín Edwards Bello announced a reading in the November 10th edition of *La Nación* for that afternoon in the Miraflores Theater: "Neruda is the top poet. Everyone yields to him, even the merciless sparrow hawk of *La Opinión*, the bristly De Rokha.[1] Everyone." That was too much for the poet from Licantén. He had silently put up with the reading in May, but Edwards Bello's allusion was the incentive he needed to inaugurate the next day his life-long mission with the article "Pablo Neruda, a Poet in Vogue."[2] Let us not forget this date. It was the beginning of an endless and pitiful litany of disqualifications regarding Neruda and his work, which Pablo de Rokha repeated with few variations, and in vain, the rest of his life.

> In *Crepusculario* [The Book of Twilights] Darío's little verse from *Prosas profanas* [Profane Prose] holds sway. The minimal rhyme follows the accent of a school rhyme, a used and tired monotonous rhetoric, an atrocious internal intonation... *Veinte poemas de amor*... It seems as though the sorrowful and cruel monotony would balance out the internal and superfluous laziness, a type of leftover of the soul, a sinister and dark residue of ruminant animality...the silly line, the simple insane line with its bad and assonate noise...that is how we understand the bovine delight, sheep, bovine and gallop of this mediocre book, without any height, without any tradition, a swing based on external rhythm, a twisted old bicycle.[3]

---

1 Translator's note: Pablo de Rokha [pseudonym for Carlos Ignacio Díaz Loyola] (1898–1968) was a renowned Chilean avant-gardist poet and an anarchist turned communist whose major work was *Los gemidos* [Howls, 1922].
2 Pablo de Rokha, *La Opinión*, 11/11/1932.
3 Quoted in Leonardo Sanhueza, *El Bacalao. Diatribas antinerudianas y otros textos* [Cod: Anti-Nerudian Diatribes and other Texts], 2004.

Neruda ignored the attack and, instead, wrote a letter of protest[4] to Raúl Silva Castro for the "unjust and confused judgment" in the newspaper reviews regarding Juvencio Valle's book, *Tratado del bosque* [Treatise on the Woods], published by Nascimento. Faced with the maliciousness of the individual who attacked him only due to the success of his reading at the Miraflores Theater, Neruda responded with a gesture of solidarity toward another poet. There is only an allusion to the enemy at the beginning, without naming him explicitly: "I do not like to write literary letters, nor articles, nor will I answer the merchant of paintings who insults me because he is envious."

Yet this jab was enough to unleash the enemy's fury and verbiage, who just two days later renewed his attack: "Neruda and Company."[5] From this moment on Neruda did not even resort to a jab: his most effective counter-attack was silence. The "merchant of paintings" took on the task of keeping Neruda's name alive—as if it needed a promotion—with his tenacious and pathetic battle.

2

At the beginning of 1933 Luis Enrique Délano, editor of the memorable Empresa Letras, with the help of Laura Reyes and Albertina Azócar, managed to salvage and publish twelve poems from *El hondero entusiasta* [The Ardent Slingsman] written ten years before, between 1923 and 1924, overcoming the resistance of Neruda who objected to the resurrection of that forgotten project. Short on money, the poet gave in, and the chapbook of thirty-four pages was published January 24th with a portrait of the author signed *Honorio* and a cautionary note to readers that these old poems "I handed over to the press as a valid document for those who are interested in my poetry." The edition was a big success and was sold out in a few weeks. Consequently, Délano arranged for a second edition, which appeared on May 5th with a change in the design: the portrait in ink, signed *Honorio*, was substituted for a sketch of Neruda signed by GEO (Georges Sauré).

In a letter to Eandi on February 16th, Neruda referred to the good literary beginning for 1933—although this happened in the midst of the poor conditions in which he was living—and it was followed by great news: "*Residence on Earth* is being published by Nascimento in a deluxe edition of only one

---

4 Pablo Neruda, *El Mercurio*, 11/20/1932.
5 Pablo de Rokha, *La Opinión*, 11/23/1932.

hundred copies. It will be a stupendous edition. You can count on receiving a copy, the only one I will be able to send to Argentina. It will cost $50 Chilean pesos and I do not think it will be available in Buenos Aires."[6]

Nascimento finished printing *Residence on Earth* on April 10th: one hundred enumerated copies from one to one hundred and signed by Neruda, in addition to ten author copies marked A to J, all on Dutch Alfa Loeber paper and in a 34 x 26 cm. format. The book Neruda had so bitterly fought for since his stay in Asia, was not published in Madrid, as he would have liked, nor in Buenos Aires, but rather in rundown Santiago in 1933. Yet in Madrid and Buenos Aires he could not have counted on the conviction and resolve of a publishing house like Nascimento, which believed in the young—almost unknown—poet, and which took the plunge and brought out an exceptionally beautiful and impeccable edition. And not only according to Chilean standards.

Pablo de Rokha was the first to proclaim—without meaning it obviously—the renown of the publication of *Residence on Earth* via the pathetic note "Epitaph for Neruda".[7] The grotesque sequence of insults and disparaging remarks confirmed deliriously a drama that would only heighten pathologically and out of control in direct proportion to Neruda's recognition and success: "more crafty and more sick...prankster...mystifier...swamp of silly and discontinuous forms...the cemented grimace of a grimace...that ferocious rattle...such a horrendous and sinister thing..." In the end, and against the grain, this arbitrary attack only rendered a tribute to *Residence on Earth*.

3

Like Neruda, Vicente Huidobro[8] also returned to Chile in 1932, but at the end of the year. Many artists who had gone to Paris to work on their artistic

---

6 Pablo Neruda, *Obras completas* [Complete Works], V, p. 966.
7 Pablo de Rokha, *La Opinión*, 5/22/1933.
8 Vicente Huidobro (1893–1948) was one of Chile's most prominent poets. From an aristocratic family, he became the voice of the avant-garde and Creationism (his own aesthetic theory) in Chile and Latin America. He spent nine years (1916–1925) in France and Spain, where he befriended most of the major figures of the avant-garde, including the luminary writers and painters of the day. *Altazor o el viaje en paracaídas* [Altazor or Traveling by Parachute], begun in 1919 and published in 1931, is considered to be one of the classic works of the Latin American avant-garde. Politically he was a fellow traveler of the communists, then a Trotskyist and then finally became disillusioned with left-wing praxis.

skills with the support of Pablo Ramírez, the Minister of Finance during the Ibañez government and the unusual sponsor [*mecenas*] for artists and writers at that time, had their monthly checks cut due to the collapse of the financial budget. And they had to return to Chile; among them were Camilo Mori and Marcos Bontá. According to Volodia Teitelboim:

> Huidobro also faced difficulties with payments, which in his case were not budgetary but rather connected to his family situation. Although it might seem incredible, his influential mother could not continue providing him with financial help during his stay in Paris. The crisis had reached that extreme. Go back to Chile! Rot in that hole in the ground! He would rather wrench his heart. He did not have a choice. [...]
>
> I always thought that there must have been another motive that made him return: the feeling that in Paris an era had come to a close. And not only for him. The amazing Aesthetic Revolution had in fact ended. The spring of innovations and cultural eruptions in the arts had come to an end. The creative euphoria in the first post-war era—the twenties—was fading and yielding to a new, grayer period, in which the preoccupations were different. From a state of (cultural) rebellion, from the challenging gesture and the intent to disassemble forms, from the rebellion of poetics, Europe moved, and the world tormented by the crisis also, to a phase in which social matters became more prominent. Most of the great artists felt that they were revolutionaries and many of them proclaimed themselves communists. They rejected bourgeois society, which some did not hesitate to call inhumane or rotten. Fascism has arisen in Europe. Mussolini had been in power for years. And Hitler was preparing to come to power.[9]

Now back in Chile with Ximena Amunátegui, Huidobro established ties with young poets who would go to the General Fund of the National Library and the semi-clandestine bookstore run by his friend Julio Walton. Volodia Teitelboim and Eduardo Anguita were among the members of that group, anxious to learn, practice and publicize avant-gardist poetry: "we were his first catechumens."[10]

---

9 Volodia Teitelboim, *Huidobro. La marcha infinita* [Huidobro: The Infinite March], pp. 179–180.
10 Teitelboim, *Neruda*, p. 205.

The Sixth Sin: Plagiarist 91

Volodia, who was 16 years old when he went to Neruda's November 1932 reading in the Miraflores Theater, surely told Huidobro of Neruda's strange performance and of the event's success:

I arrived ahead of time and I found a seat in the upper deck to be able to see the poet's face from afar. The curtain opened. The stage was decorated with painted Oriental masks. There were some strange room dividers or curtains. It gave the impression that we were at a Chinese opera and there was an air of faraway and enigmatic places. Suddenly, from behind the enormous masks, and taller and wider than a man's body, a nasal, slow voice, like a lament, began to say: "Qué pura eres de sol o de noche caída, / qué triunfal desmedida tu órbita de blanco, / y tu pecho de pan, alto de clima, / tu corona de árboles negros, bienamada..." [How pure you are of sun or nightfall, / how triumphant your boundless white orbit, / and your breast like fresh bread, warm weather, / and your crown of black trees, beloved...].

He continued, most of all, with [forthcoming] poems from the first *Residence on Earth*. He muttered almost without inflections, in a monotone, moaning voice, as though he were handing out dream-inducing pills. That was the feeling I had after a few minutes. The recital lasted about an hour. The melodic arc of his voice did not change a bit. But after a while it was like the sound of slow-moving water, like a breath of fresh air, not because the message that came out of that throat was cristaline and refreshing, but rather because what those words meant was like giving a thirsty soul an inebriating liquid, it created an enveloping atmosphere... At the end of the recital, would Neruda appear to the applause of or indifference to the crowd? At least half of them fluctuated between admiration, astonishment and bewilderment. Neruda never appeared. And we were left with the desire to meet him.[11]

Thanks to the young man's story, Huidobro knew immediately that Neruda had matured in Asia and had returned with the impetus and experience which put him heads and shoulders above most Chilean poets. And, consequently, he was a potential danger for Huidobro's ambition of being the dominant poet. But he had many practical problems to deal with, some having to do with Manuela Portales, from whom he had separated in 1927, and other

---
11 Teitelboim, *Neruda*, pp. 168–169.

kinds of problems having to do with living with Ximena and his finances. That explains why he decided to move from his apartment on Cienfuegos Street to a more modest one near the Central Station. So, for a while he contented himself with inaugurating—on March 4th, 1933—a vaguely Parisian version of the Walton bookstore, from which he preached the new good literary word he had brought from Europe and promoted revolution:

> In his resolute communist period, he showed himself as a man for whom it was all red or nothing... and his declarations made no room for other options. Anyone who was not a communist was an 'idiot'... Politically speaking, that was the categorical communist we welcomed to Chile after his sojourn in Europe. He hoped his call to arms would be heard by all open souls, by all who were not 'idiots.' In the journal *Síntesis* [Synthesis], in April 1933, he spoke loudly and without circumlocutions... He looked the part of a passionate communist. Experience tells us that sometimes those who burn too much end up being consumed in their own fire.[12]

Huidobro kept silent publicly about Neruda, although in coffee and bar groups he attempted to diminish his importance. Not a single comment was issued when *Residence on Earth* was published in April. Around that time, he suffered a concussion. On May 1st, Ximena wrote to Juan Larrea about his recovery. At the end of August Neruda left with Maruca to Buenos Aires to assume his consular duties and disappeared from the local scene. But the news of the warm welcome Argentine writers gave him, his meeting with García Lorca and the tribute the PEN Club gave both poets (along with the amazement caused by the duo speech the poets gave), worried Huidobro.

In 1934, besides facing a lawsuit that Manuela Portales filed against him "for abandoning his children and depriving them of a father,"[13] Huidobro, by way of Juan Larrea and other friends, followed Neruda's successful tour in the literary world in Madrid with increasing unease. Although Vicente was more fortunate than Pablo on one score: on October 9th, Ximena uneventfully gave birth to Vladimir Huidobro Amunátegui.

---

12 Teitelboim, *Huidobro. La marcha infinita* [Huidobro: The Infinite March], pp. 187–188.
13 Cedomil Goic, "Cronología [Chronology] in Vicente Huidobro, *Obra poética* [Poetic Work], p. 1399.

4

1934 was a year of many activities for Huidobro, including family disputes and numerous publications. Vicente García-Huidobro Portales, a son from his first marriage, born in 1915, declared around that time, "He abandoned us. My mom, me, everybody. He abandoned us all without any sense of remorse."[14] During evening get togethers, his young disciples, Teitelboim and Eduardo Anguita, listened to Huidobro's reading of long passages from *Papá o el diario de Alicia Mir* [Dad or the Diary of Alicia Mir], a book with made up names he would later publish with Ediciones Walton (1934). Yet "what stood out was that he was telling a terrible part of his own autobiography through the voice of a daughter who, despite living surrounded by the dimwittedness of the tribe, understood her father. She was a reliable speaker [but], without a doubt, the real first person was the author of the book..."[15] Other publications in 1934 included *Cagliostro. Novela-film* [Cagliostro: Novel-Film] (Zig-Zag); and *La próxima. Historia que pasó en poco tiempo más* [Next: A story that Happened in a Little More Time (Ediciones Walton)], which had three editions.

One of his disciples, the young Volodia Teitelboim,[16] discovered something in the spring that, like all things (in the past or the present), set the stage for attacking Neruda and caused a big stir. And he placed in Huidobro's pen the weapon he was missing. Unlike Pablo de Rokha, who needed no pretext to use his artillery against Neruda without the slightest provocation, Huidobro—given his intelligence and his European education—had not found up to that point a culturally justifiable reason. Consequently, he received Volodia's gift with poorly veiled delight, initially feigning a sense of superiority and distance. But let us take this one step at a time. There is no one better than the protagonist who unleashed the tumult to bear witness to what happened in the first person and many years later:

> It was all rather complicated, but we had to be new poets in order to be total revolutionaries. That is what I thought. Anguita had other

---

14 Goic, p. 1399.
15 Teitelboim, *Huidobro*, p. 197.
16 Translator's note: Volodia Teitelboim (1916–2008) was a Chilean novelist, poet, biographer and politician of the Communist Party. In his youth he was a follower of Vicente Huidobro and then, years later, became one of Neruda's best friends. His biographies on Neruda, Huidobro and Borges are must reads for any scholar or lay reader.

ideas. He never abandoned his religious principles. In the afternoons I devoured books in the General Fund section of the National Library. I devoured everything that came from France...[and] I continued to read as much poetry as I could get my hands on. One day in El *jardinero* [The Gardener], by Rabindranath Tagore, I heard the echoes of number 16 from *Veinte poems* [Twenty Poems]. I compared the two texts. They were almost the same. [...] I shared my thoughts with a poet friend. With all the flair of a condemnation it was published [Issue number 2, November 1934] in the journal *Pro*, edited by Vicente Huidobro. A lot was made of the matter at that time. Friends from Neruda's generation clarified that it was not plagiarism, but rather paraphrasing. Several of them remembered suggesting to Neruda, before the first edition of *Twenty Poems* appeared in print, that he include a note in the book making it clear that number 16 was a paraphrase of *El jardinero* by Tagore. Neruda himself recalled that in one of those provocative all-nighters in those days, walking along at dawn along the streets of Santiago with Joaquín Cifuentes Sepúlveda, he asked him suddenly, "Help me remember something. I need to include a note in the book at the publishers about the paraphrase of Tagore." Joaquín said to him, "Don't be silly, Pablo. Don't do it. They will accuse you of plagiarism. It'll be sensationalist propaganda. The book will sell like hot cakes."[17]

I deleted a few lines from Volodia's text that include a quote by the Mexican poet Efraín Huerta, which I find more appropriate here: "I prefer the paraphrase a thousand times over. In order to paraphrase the Romans or the Italians one would have to be called Garcilaso de la Vega; to paraphrase Tagore, to be Pablo Neruda."

René de Costa, a Huidobro expert, recognized that "Neruda knew how to handle himself well. Rather than suffer from what a critic has called *the anxiety of influence*, he admitted publicly he paraphrased his source."[18] Since the third edition of *Twenty Poems* was published,[19] poem number 16 includes this note: *Paraphrase of R. Tagore*. Years later, Neruda would make it clear that that poem was written as a deliberate paraphrase of a poem in "The

---

17 Teitelboim, *Neruda*, p. 205.
18 René de Costa, "El Neruda de Huidobro" in Hernán Loyola, *Neruda en Sássari. Simposio internacional* [Neruda in Sassari: International Symposium], p. 108.
19 Editorial Ercilla [Ercilla Press], 1938.

Gardener", by Tagore, "dedicated especially to a young female reader of that poet."[20] Pablo never named that young woman—perhaps because he had subsequently married—but he was not lying. In 1971 I showed documentary proof that it was not a late justification he made up: the young woman was Teresa Vásquez, Terusa in *Memorial de Isla Negra* [Isla Negra]. In February of 1923 her beloved Pablo had copied for her poems 1 and 4 from *La cosecha* [The Harvest]—another book of Tagore's—in the first pages of *Album Terusa* [The Teresa Album].[21]

5

On December 6th, 1934, in Madrid, and with a generosity that is not all that common among literati, Federico García Lorca gave his renowned presentation prior to Neruda's poetry recital before a large crowd of students and academics at the university. That same day, in Santiago, Chile, the poet Pablo de Rokha published the article, "The Scheme of the Plagiarist" in *La Opinión* [The Opinion], in a fury and in step with Huidobro's accusation against their common enemy: "To be plagiarist, one needs to be won over by an unbridled opportunism, a dirty and tremendously objective vanity, like an idiot or failed buffoon... There is a megalomaniac and a beggar in every plagiarist."[22]

A few days later, Huidobro (or in his place some scribbler) published "Pablo Neruda, Plagiarist or Great Poet?"[23] but he penned it under the pseudonym *Justiciero* [The Righteous One], which allowed him to put on display his literary knowledge, pretend to some resonant equanimity in his critical observations, and, above all, allude to himself in the third person with dishonest and almost infantile praise, sprinkled with self-criticism, which was not that at all, but rather disguised compliments. Here are some passages from that long article:

[...] While the young poet Volodia Teitelboim discovers in Chile Neruda's plagiarism of Tagore, Huidobro, Díaz Casanueva, etcetera, in Spain,

---

20 Pablo Neruda, author's prologue commemorating the one millionth edition with Losada in 1961. *Obras completas* [Complete Works], IV, p. 1055.
21 For more details, see *Anales de la Universidad de Chile* [Annals from the University of Chile], 157–160, p. 45.
22 Faride Zerán, *La guerrilla literaria* [The Literary Guerilla], p. 179.
23 Vicente Huidobro, *La Opinión*, 12/15/1934.

Federico García Lorca proclaims him the best poet in the Americas after Rubén Darío.

García Lorca's proclamation would be valuable if he were worth something, but all of the major poets who write in Spanish deny the Andalusian that status, they consider him a mediocre poet, a simple song writer. Seen in that light, his opinion is of no importance. By contrast, Teitelboim's accusation is not an opinion, it is a fact. [...]

Shakespeare was accused of plagiarism and the truth is that almost all his themes were borrowed from prior legends or works [...]. Searching the roots of Goethe's poetry, one finds the sources of another poet's verse. Should we then reject the works of Shakespeare and Goethe? [...] This proves that what matters is not plagiarism, but rather the quality, the value of plagiarism. [...]

When analyzed according to true value, we believe Pablo Neruda is a second-or third-rate poet. Proof of this is that no poet has come to his defense after he was accused of plagiarism in *Las Últimas Noticias* [The Latest News]. [...]. By contrast, an authentic poet like Pablo de Rokha left his mark in just a few phrases in the Thursday issue of *La Opinión*.

We have been able to verify that the most talented young poets, here and in other Spanish speaking countries, consider Neruda to be a mediocre poet or a simple bluff overinflated by a group that is just as mediocre as he is.

One of these young men declared yesterday: "I have no interested in being the best poet since Rubén Darío, I am more interested in being the best poet after Huidobro."

Nevertheless, Huidobro's [work] lacks a major defect and that is that it is too difficult, it is akin to the music of Schoenberg, which is music for musicians. Huidobro's poetry is only for poets and it becomes more hermetic and complex every day. [...]. To lock oneself up in a chapel full of the initiated to my mind is a useless gesture especially now when poetry should have a grand social role and display itself in the sun.

They tell me that among the Chilean poets Huidobro only admires Díaz Casanueva and Pablo de Rokha. It is an opinion that is too harsh, and it proves that love for the enclosed chapel..."[24]

---

24 Quoted in Sanhueza, pp. 22–24.

This article had all the appearance of a serious and well-documented accusation, but it wasn't difficult to catch the trick, the dirty trick Huidobro (unlike Neruda) did not have qualms about resorting to, although he was always outed, as happened with the famous kidnapping he feigned in the twenties and that cost him his friendship with Juan Gris. Here he begins pointing out various cases of plagiarism committed by Neruda, which the ostensible accuser, Volodia, himself would then disprove:

> It was not the only time Huidobro would let things go to his head. In the book *Neruda* we told the story of the well-known *affaire* which in his time caused such a fuss...with regards to poem number 16 in *Twenty Love Poems*... But we never talked about Neruda's plagiarizing Huidobro and Díaz Casanueva because we still have not found a single case.[25]

The *Justiciero* (The Righteous One, that is, Huidobro or one of his scribes) could not be bothered with the ineffable task of proving his assertion that "we believe Pablo Neruda is a second- or third-rate poet." It was an arbitrary affirmation—like Pablo de Rokha's—which convinced no one, not even himself. What mattered to him was the next sequence, which began with the recognition that very soon he himself would refute: "Proof of this is that no poet has come to his defense after he was accused of plagiarism in *Las Últimas Noticias* [The Latest News]. [...]. By contrast, an authentic poet like Pablo de Rokha left his mark in just a few phrases in the Thursday issue of *La Opinión*."

After having established such unquestioned and condemnatory authority, he turned to the vague or ill-defined jury of "the most talented young poets, here and in other Spanish speaking countries" (?!) who considered Neruda a mediocre poet. This led finally to the Supreme Court incarnated in "One of these young men declared yesterday: 'I have no interested in being the best poet after Darío, I am more interested in being the best poet after Huidobro.'" This was the nucleus, the core, the heart of the article. Which is reminiscent of the *boutade* attributed to Nicanor Parra (I quote by heart), when a journalist asked him if he aspired to be the best poet in Chile he responded: "Look, I am modest, I have no interest in being the best poet in Chile: I would be happy being the best poet on Isla Negra." Both quotes refer to Neruda implicitly, but Nicanor does so humorously and tongue in cheek.

---

25 Teitelboim, *Huidobro*, p. 219.

The rest of the *Justiciero's* article included a series of ridiculous critiques of Huidobro brought to the fore to feign evenhandedness, yet from the point of view of the (undeclared) *Justiciero*, high praise was to be lavished on him. Who did he want to fool with that type of a transparent subterfuge? By affirming that Huidobro's poetry was too difficult or refined, that it was a poetry "only for poets," it was clear that the *Justiciero* did not at all intend to point out Huidobro's "major defect," but rather give him the highest praise, as when jazz critics refer to Bill Evans, author and performer of "Waltz for Debby," as a "pianist for pianists."

6

Not satisfied with the charge of presumed plagiarism in his little journal *Pro*, issue number 2,[26] nor with Pablo de Rokha's articles (as well as the *Justiciero's* piece), in January of 1935 Huidobro dedicated the second issue (was there a first issue?) of the journal *Vital*, entirely under his direction, to the "Neruda-Tagore Affaire." To eliminate any doubt about the animus behind the publication, the cover included several bellicose catchphrases. Under the title we read: "Against the cadavers, reptiles, gossipers, poisoned, microbes, etc. etc." In case there was any doubt about their content, the next line proclaimed "Journal of Social Hygiene" and at the bottom of the page we read the following: "You want a brawl, now you're going to see what a brawl is."

In reviewing the journal, we can confirm that it was solely dedicated, from beginning to end, to one specific recipient: Pablo Neruda, the plagiarist. Secondly, against two writers, chosen because they were friends of the poet: a letter overblown with insults for Tomás Lago, accusing him of vague and imprecise falsehoods, and a note which denounced Diego Muñoz for ostensibly being with the police.[27] Several questions come up based on this which, apparently, nobody has bothered to ask.

1. Why such an uproar and persistence with regards to the plagiarism? Once Volodia denounced the plagiarism charge with pertinent documentation and seriousness, the matter must not have been of any more than slight interest to Huidobro. Having followed through with what he considered to

---

26 Published in November 1934.
27 For more details, see Diego Muñoz, *Memorias. Recuerdos de la bohemia nerudiana* [Memoirs: Recollections of Bohemian Life with Neruda], pp. 199–205.

be his duty it was the accused's turn to respond. Why then did Huidobro carry on as though it was something personal and grant the ostensible "literary crime" the category of State importance? Why did he go to the extreme of wasting the time, effort and money publishing a *monographic* issue of the journal *Vital* dedicated solely to rehashing the well-known condemnation of Neruda's plagiarism? Why? What else did he purport to do? Huidobro's behavior was strange, to say the least.

2. Why did that monographic issue of *Vital* wave its bellicose and aggressive flags so, as if it were a matter of a life and death situation? Besides the plagiarism, which was publicly known, what had Neruda—the recipient of this special issue—done to deserve this type of verbal assault? To which of the plagiarist's attacks was the accuser reacting with that feisty piece?

These questions are rhetorical and useless because the answers are evident. I believe I have shown the motives that drove Huidobro's attack. The repressed violence, hidden for years, exploded aimlessly until fixating on some support. But elaborating these questions allows me to call the reader's attention to the title of Faride Zerán's book, *La guerrilla literaria. Huidobro-De Rokha-Neruda* [The Literary Guerrilla: Huidobro, De Rokha, Neruda, 1992]. In my view, the title refers to something that never existed. The term *guerrilla* involves skirmishes between different hostile or enemy forces (writers in this case). That was not the case when Huidobro published *Vital* 2. Between October of 1932 and January of 1935 only one faction (Huidobro and De Rokha) attacked the common enemy, who did not reciprocate and did not exist because he was not aware of the projectiles directed at him. If the reader thumbs through Zerán's book s/he will not find a single article or diatribe, nor a polemical piece by Neruda against Huidobro or against De Rokha during that time period. They do not exist. What guerrilla are we talking about then?

Unless we apply the definition guerrilla to the term *asymmetric warfare*. Two combatants, each on his own, fire on the common enemy who lets them fire away without responding. He simply ignores them.

The situation changed a few months later. On April 2nd, 1935 Neruda sent a potent missile from Madrid, as we will see. But even in that case it is not accurate to talk about *guerrillas*, because the projectile Neruda—not at all given to skirmishes—sent begins an all-out war, a real war, not simply a *guerrilla* war.

The Seventh Sin

Insolent

"Aquí estoy con mis labios de hierro"
[Here I am with my iron lips]
Aquí estoy [Here I am]

I

Teitelboim notes:

In April 1935 we showed a new sign of disrespect. *The New Anthology of Chilean Poetry* was published, and it rapidly became a source of scandal. Anguita and I were the editors. Abusing our positions, we included ourselves among the ten selected poets. Mistral was not included, but Neruda was. Among them were some of the recent unedited poems at this point,[1] which later appeared in the second *Residence on Earth*. De Rokha was also included, in our view—even in hindsight today—rightly so. He charged that Huidobro had colonized the collection, a charge that was unfounded.[2]

This sign of disrespect was really a game among young men (Volodia had just turned 19 years old and Anguita 20), especially compared to the sign of disrespect which arrived from Madrid in typed copies, without the name of the author, but with the unmistakable mark of Pablo Neruda.

Morla Lynch's diary noted the arrival of Huidobro's package with *Vital 2*, clearly to be assured that Neruda would read it and would finally become infuriated. This time it worked, and exceedingly so, but before doing so Huidobro would have to read about the welcoming *Tribute* Spain's major poets—invited by García Lorca and Aleixandre—gave to Neruda and in fact relieved

---

[1] "Sólo la muerte" [Only Death], "Ode with a Lament], "Alberto Rojas Giménez viene volando" [Alberto Rojas Giménez comes flying].
[2] Teitelboim, *Neruda*, p. 206.

him from the attacks coming from Chile and which included "local" poets like Juan Ramón Jiménez. *Tribute* initially was a *plaquette* titled, *Homenaje a Pablo Neruda de los poetas españoles / Tres cantos materiales* [Tribute to Pablo Neruda from the Spanish Poets / Three Material Songs] (Madrid: Plutarco, April 1935). It included an introduction which deserves a place of honor among Chilean cultural documents:

> Chile has sent the great poet Pablo Neruda to Spain, whose obvious creative powers, fully in possession of his poetic destiny, is producing very personal works, which honor the Spanish language.
>
> By publishing these unpublished poems—the latest demonstrations of his magnificent creations—we, the poets and admirers of this distinguished Latin American writer, underline his extraordinary personality and his indisputable literary status.
>
> In reiterating on this occasion our hearty welcome, this group of Spanish poets is glad to show once again and publicly its admiration for a work that unquestionably constitutes one of the most authentic realities in poetry in the Spanish language today.
>
> [*Signed:*]. Rafael Alberti, Vicente Aleixandre, Manuel Altolaguirre, Luis Cernuda, Gerardo Diego, León Felipe, Federico García Lorca, Jorge Guillén, Pedro Salinas, Miguel Hernández, José A. Muñoz Rojas, Leopoldo y Juan Panero, Luis Rosales, Arturo Serrano Plaja, Luis Felipe Vivanco.

Besides including an extraordinary list of signees, this booklet of sixteen pages published three poems included in the subtitle: "Entrada a la madera" [Opening to Wood], "Apogeo del apio" [Celery's Peak] and "Estatuto del vino" [Status of Wine], the *Three Material Songs* pertaining to *Residence on Earth* 2, set aside for this occasion. They were not sent to Teitelboim and Anguita, as Neruda and the editors of the anthology would have liked.

García Lorca and Aleixandre had some problems publishing the *Tribute* motivated by Pablo's insistence on including a condemnation of Huidobro's insults. That served as pretext which furnished Juan Larrea with a reason not to be among the signees and put Gerardo Diego's and Luis Cernuda's signatures in danger (the latter, a communist, refused to attack his comrade Vicente). Consequently, and fortunately for Neruda's sake, Huidobro's name was removed. His ire due to *Vital 2* had hindered his ability to understand how naming Huidobro had harmed the *Tribute* (even without it, it led to Larrea's belligerent account of the episode published in 1967).[3] And yet, although Juan Ramón did not sign either, the *Tribute* had the effect for which Neruda had hoped.

2

With this grandiose confirmation in place, Neruda decided it had come time to jump in the ring to challenge and respond in kind to his enemies. To carry it out he needed the legitimation which the *Tribute* provide him. It was not lost on him that he intended to attack his elder rivals by demoting them from the hierarchy by proclaiming, in fact, his own superiority. For once he abandoned the silence he had held as a weapon against De Rokha's and Huidobro's attacks since 1932 and charged at them with his missile-poem "Aquí estoy" [Here I am] on April 2nd, 1935. It took them completely by surprise and silenced them. Neither of them—neither Huidobro nor De Rokha—was able to muster a reply.

Neruda counterattacked with crushing efficiency. His strategic key was to reject the terrain which his enemies had chosen in order to assault him, ignoring completely the content of their articles and pamphlets. Since 1932, De Rokha and Huidobro had dedicated themselves to publishing attacks on Neruda, that is, not openly directed at him, but rather at a reader-recipient for whom they enumerated, unfurled, explained, argued why negating the place of the poet from Temuco access to the poetic Olympus in Chile was necessary. Both referred to this reader-recipient, a person called Pablo Neruda, in the third person: a novice who assumed he could succeed to the throne which both had considered theirs.

Both passed judgment and prosecuted the fruits of this modest aspiring poet from the perspective of the consecrated, superior and omniscient poet. Each of them attacked Neruda from the point of view of the poet who has already arrived, been confirmed and installed in the local (and international in Huidobro's case) Parnassus, established, deified and beyond discussion. Both judged the intruder from the height of their positions. Each went out of his way to waste time and energy in a disguised performance of criticism

---

3 Juan Larrea, *Del surrealismo a Machu Picchu* [From Surrealism to Machu Picchu], pp. 104-108.

or literary denunciation (or *social hygiene*), whose only real objective was to demolish the other.

In brief, in the case of Neruda, De Rokha and Huidobro behaved like nineteenth century *ritual* poets: they had already arrived, completed their development, saw themselves fulfilled and rewarded, and wrote their poems from that overarching and immobile point of view. From that vantage point they unleashed their furies against the novice who aspired to behave like them. Each had his own style. De Rokha, via a torrential and pathetic parody of a theoretical and critical discourse whose infinite variations he gave voice to from October 1932 on, unabated until his death. Huidobro made efforts to be more objective and distant, and even elegant, as his contact with French culture had taught him, but the publication of *Vital 2*, as we have seen, was proof that he had lost control of his own security.

3

The titles of the writings which marked this storytelling were, on the one hand, "Pablo Neruda, Poet in Vogue," "Neruda and Company," "The Neruda-Tagore Affair" (De Rokha and Huidobro), on the other hand, Neruda's "Here I am." De Rokha and Huidobro made Neruda the protagonist of their writings, as an indirect way of highlighting their own personas, of making an impression and shining with critical speeches which sought to demolish the protagonist. By contrast, from the title on, Neruda portrayed himself as the protagonist of his own text. It was a challenging and explicit self-exaltation based on the strength of his sincerity. Whereby he began his broadside with an introduction to who he was, with a self-representation, with an ongoing self-portrait:

> Estoy aquí con mis labios de hierro
> y un ojo en cada mano
> y con mi corazón completamente,
> y viene el alba, y viene
> el alba, y viene el alba,
> y estoy aquí a pesar
> de perros, a pesar
> de lobos, a pesar
> de pesadillas, a pesar

de ladillas, a pesar de pesares
estoy lleno de lágrimas y amapolas cortadas,
y pálidas palomas de energía,
y con todos los dientes y los dedos escribo,
y con todas las materias del mar,
con todas las materias del corazón escribo.

[Here I am with my iron lips / and an eye in each hand / and with my heart complete, / and dawn arrives, and dawn / arrives, and dawn arrives, / and I am here despite / the dogs, despite / the nightmares, despite / the crabs, despite it all / I am full of tears and cut poppies, / and pallid doves of energy, / and I write with all my teeth and my fingers, / and with all the matter of the sea, / and with all the matter of my heart, I write.]

I am here, during this phase of my journey, of my evolution. I still have not won the right to pen *Yo soy* [I am], but I am headed in that direction. The humility is of a person who openly recognized that he had not reached that status to which he aspired yet, but of particular import was the difference—the advantage—Neruda held over De Rokha and Huidobro, who, feeling that they were fulfilled and rewarded, had lost the agility of the poet who is still developing. At the beginning of his battle Neruda placed a passionate self-portrait brandished in a neo-Romantic and visceral way ("with my heart completely... and dawn arrives... I am here despite the dogs... despite the nightmares, despite the crabs... I am full of tears and poppies... and with all the sea has to offer, all the heart has to offer, I write") in opposition to the pseudo-literary and 'academic' façade which his aggressors showed for years.

4

In the next stanza, and unlike his enemies, who alluded to him and insulted him *in the third person*, Neruda met them at the pass swiftly and stood before them without any formalities or ambiguities, an uncovered face and—importantly—employing an apostrophe to refer to them in the second person:

Cabrones!
Hijos de puta!
Hoy ni mañana

ni jamás
acabaréis conmigo!
Tengo llenos de pétalos los testículos,
tengo lleno de pájaros el pelo,
tengo poesía y vapores,
cementerios y casas,
gente que se ahoga,
incendios,
en mis *Veinte poemas*,
en mis semanas, en mis caballerías,
y me cago en la puta que os malparió,
derrokas, patíbulos,
vidobras,
y aunque escribáis en francés con el retrato
de Picasso en las verijas,
y aunque muy a menudo robéis espejos y llevéis a la venta
el retrato de vuestras hermanas,
a mí no me alcanzáis ni con anónimos,
ni con saliva,
existo, entre los metales, la harina y las olas,
entre el mundo y el cielo, con un corazón lleno de sangre
y de rocío.

    [Bastards! / Sons of bitches! / Today, tomorrow / never / will you be able to finish me off! / I have testicles full of petals, / I have hair full of birds, / I have my poetry and steam, / cemeteries and houses, / people who drown, / fires, / in my *Twenty Poems*, / in my weeks, in my calvary, / and fuck you, motherfuckers, / *derrokas, patíbulos,* / *vidobras*,[4] / and though you write in French with a portrait / of Picasso between your legs, / and though you often steal mirrors and sell / your sisters' portraits, / you will not reach me with your anonymous attacks, / your saliva, / I exist, among the metals, the flour and the waves, / among the earth and the sky, with a heart full of blood / and dew.]

---

4 Translator's note: The three terms are altered allusions to Pablo de Rokha (*derrokas*) and to Huidobro (*vidobras*). There is no consensus regarding the name *patíbulos*. It could refer to a friend of de Rokha's or Huidobro's.

The challenger did not waste a single line in his counterattack against his enemies' 'academic' criticism and went directly to the point: to proclaim his existence and his place as a poet. "I exist" was his battle flag, and with it he unveiled the hypocrisy of their pseudo-criticism which, in various ways, De Rokha and Huidobro had put into play to annihilate Neruda, to deny him his status as a poet and hasten his literary disappearance. The assaulted one returned their violence and energy in kind, which they displayed in their attacks, but he did so in a sincere manner whereas they used theirs in the guise of 'artistic' criticism and pejorative irony.

Beyond the rudeness and lexical immoderation, Neruda's "Here I am" is not lacking in rhetorical knowledge nor in honest vehemence, Philippic denunciations of classical times. The invectives were the salt and pepper of his main self-affirmation, of his proclamation "I exist," which was the main response to De Rokha's and Huidobro's attacks. By facing the sacred monsters of Chilean poetry at that time with unprecedented insolence, the young Neruda desacralized them and forced them to deal with him carefully. And to fear him. In other words, he forced them to recognize his "I exist" in the same modality they had used in vain to annihilate him.

In passing let us say that the invectives "Here I am" generally used the facts and anecdotes of literary cliques, more or less known to the average reader at that time, like the abusive selling point De Rokha made with regards to Paschín Bustamante's paintings, or Picasso's ostentatious portrait of Huidobro, or Huidobro's invented episode about his kidnapping at the hands of "Finnish scouts" in 1924. The violence and coprolalia which suffused these invectives were only the staging for the fundamental and conclusive apostrophe:

Conocedme:
soy el que sabe y el que canta,
y no podréis matarme aunque os partáis las venas
y volváis a nacer otra vez entre orines!
Adiós a muerte,
adiós a vida, fracasados...!

[Know me: / I am he who knows and who sings, / and you will not kill me off even if you cut your veins / and even if you are born again among urine! / Goodbye for death, / goodbye for life, losers...!]

The Eighth Sin

Abandoner

"Qué bien estar sin Maruca: me sentía vivir de nuevo."
[How good it was to be without Maruca: I felt like I was living again.]

I

IN SEPTEMBER 1936, TWO months and some days after the beginning of the civil war, it was imperative that the Nerudas leave the House of the Flowers, situated in a neighborhood in Madrid which faces the Castilian mountains, and which was ever more in danger due to Franco's artillery, which had the whole city under siege. The danger was real and imminent. (When Neruda returned from Valencia a year later, all that was left of the beloved apartment were a few destroyed objects and some standing walls.). The bard managed to transfer Maruca and Malva Marina to Barcelona under the protection and care of the consul Tulio Maquieira. Pablo stayed in Madrid to carry out the difficult task of continuing with his consular duties at this time because the Chilean ambassador, Núñez Morgado, sympathized with the rebels.

On November 8th Morla Lynch jotted down in her diary: "There is a huge bombing around the Mediodía Station. The newspapers have yet to publish the exodus of the Government [to Valencia], but there is talk of a Defense Committee, *including, undoubtedly, communists. The communists have done their part, in high spirits.*"[1] That same day his diary included the following: "Pablo Neruda, *fearful, and thinking about no one but himself,* closes up the consulate. He is leaving early in the morning, via the Valencia highway, the only one open, with Alberti and Delia del Carril, naturally" (the emphasis is

---

[1] Morla Lynch, p. 103.

mine).² In fact, Pablo and Delia traveled with Délano-Falcón and not with Alberti-León on November 9th, according to Lola Falcón's account:

> Pablo came to our house and said, 'Let us go. We have to leave now. The car is waiting for us outside and we do not know if we will have another chance to get away. There is no room for anything, so take as little as possible...the minimum.' And we had to leave everything behind, having barely enough time to pack a couple of small suitcases... I do not know how I thought about putting one outfit over another...and on top of that, a coat. There were five of us when we were ready: my son Poli, Luis Enrique and I, Pablo Neruda and Delia del Carril. It didn't seem strange to us that Delia was going along on the trip...³

It was surely true that the poet left the capital fearing the bombing because the House of the Flowers was closer each day to the rebels' artillery fire (indeed, I repeat, when he returned to Madrid in 1937 it was in ruins). We know that Neruda did not have it in him to be a hero, and besides there was little he could do to help out with the defense of Madrid in a practical way. But it was not only his own safety or the fear of the bombs that led him to leave. He needed peace and quiet to finish his most important, irreplaceable, urgent and effective contribution: the *España en el corazón* [Spain in my Heart] poems. That is what he knew how to do. Besides not being at all congenial regarding the idea of providing refuge to the enemies of the Republic, a task that ambassador Núñez Morgado took on with such enthusiasm and irresponsibility that by the end of 1936 the Chilean diplomatic corps had taken in more than 2,000 "opposition members to the regime" without any prior approval of the ministry.

2

After an eight-hour car trip, Neruda and Delia—with Luis Enrique Délano, Lola Falcón and their son Poli—arrived in Valencia on November 9th, 1936. The group continued on its way to Barcelona the next day: in Pablo's case to reunite with Maruca and Malva Marina, given protection there by the

---

2 Morla Lynch, p. 103.
3 Edmundo Olivares, *Pablo Neruda. Tras las huellas del poeta itinerante* [Pablo Neruda: Following the Tracks of the Nomadic Poet], p. 371.

general consul since the end of September. Delia and Délano-Falcón stayed in another place. "They gave us safe passage"—Lola recalled—"and Delia came along with us. We rented an apartment in which we all lived crammed together. We would eat on the diplomat Tulio Maquieira's billiard table. We would cook for eight and fifteen would show up, among them Manuel Altolaguirre, Santiago del Campo, Raúl González Tuñón."[4]

That November 10th the general consulate in Barcelona received orders to move to Marseille. Neruda's situation became ever more complicated. The Ministry asked Maquieira for information regarding consul Reyes' "close concomitances" with communists and anarchists in Madrid—which appeared in the Chilean press—and his reasons for abandoning the consulate in the capital. Neruda was forced to ask Délano for a difficult favor: "Amid those horrors"—Lola continued—"Luis Enrique had to travel to Madrid to bring the seal and documents belonging to the Consulate and, in the process, he would be risking his life and leaving me with my heart in my mouth. We received orders later to leave Spain and return to Chile via Marseille. We traveled in an unsanitary boat almost like prisoners."[5] Lola's detailed description of that infernal trip can be found in Olivares. I cite the first few lines:

> ...we had to travel in the Immigrant Class of an Italian ship named *Virgilio* [which set sail from Marseille on December 5th, 1936]. The Immigrant Class section was not at all poetic; it was the equivalent of Fourth Class, which was something that wasn't even mentioned in the case of a ship as elegant as that one. I was traveling with our ten-month old son [the future writer Poli Délano] and I remember a decision Neruda made to protect me from what he saw coming. The "cabin" we were assigned was for one hundred passengers. There was a cabin for one hundred men and another for one hundred women. Neruda told me: "You cannot travel with Poli in a cabin like that. Let us talk with captain." We went to talk with the captain, and he was not receptive. There were so

---

4 Lola Falcón, "Testimonios sobre Delia del Carril." *Boletín Fundación Pablo Neruda*, pp. 33–34.
5 Lola Falcón, pp. 33–34. Translator's note: Raúl González Tuñón (1905–1974) was an Argentine poet, journalist and communist. He is best known for *La calle del agujero en la media* [The Street of the Hole in the Sock, 1930] and *La rosa blindada* [The Armored Rose, 1936].

many people in the same situation...so many people... Those were difficult times.⁶

One can infer from this paragraph that on November 5ᵗʰ Neruda was in Marseille—location of the Chilean General Consulate after the move from Barcelona—with Maruca and Malva Marina, undoubtedly helped by consul Maquieira since Pablo no longer had a consulate and was without any economic means.

3

The following days marked an important moment in the poet's life. Maruca had managed to contact a Dutch friend who was the witness at Neruda and Maruca's wedding in Batavia in 1930. Barend van Tricht, who lived with his wife in a small apartment in Montecarlo, agreed to take Maruca in along with Malva Marina. There was no other option at that moment. Pablo accompanied his wife and daughter on December 8ᵗʰ, left them with the van Tricht, and returned to Marseille. From there he wrote one of the most interesting letters in Neruda's collection of letters—for what it reveals about the bard—to Delia (who was in Barcelona at the time):

Marseille 10 December [1936]

My dearest Hormiguita [my little Ant],⁷ I just received your letter and telegram, you are not understanding what I mean, your letters have not been lost, I received them all, but naturally I do not why you would want to stay in Barcelona for months, you had plans, you have changed them, I have told you many times about my matters, I think I will only know by the end of next week if the Chilean government will allow me to stay in Marseille or not. If you were thinking of going to Valencia you could have gone there and been back in Barcelona by this time. I have told you what my situation is from the very beginning, I do not understand why you are waiting in Barcelona, or maybe you have decided to

---

6 Olivares, pp. 373–374.
7 Translator's note: Delia del Carril was known in Madrid as *Hormiga* (ant) and *Hormiguita* (little ant) because she was a busy body, always involved in some political activity. It is likely a nickname Acario Cotapos or Isaías Cabezón gave her. (Conversation with the author.)

stay there. I cannot give any advice in that regard: I can only tell you what is going on.

I took Maruca to Montecarlo the day before yesterday, I returned yesterday at five in the morning. Her situation is not set up yet, the van Trichts have a well-placed apartment but it is small, she will have to look for a boarding house for at least 26 Francs a day, and that's not counting the expenses for my girl: fortunately, my little girl has recovered, and I left her singing and laughing as before. The important matter is to manage so Maruca can have that monthly income, so she can be at ease.

I am in a very old hotel in front of the port, I watch the sailboats every morning, we would be so happy together; but I think it is best to bear with things for a while longer; Cádiz and other Chileans have arrived here, they get together in their very small circles. As I was saying, I do not understand what your plans are, I will know more about my fate within a week. What will you do? They might send me back to Chile although no one here believes it, you could come with me, but what if they leave me here? Do you plan on coming here or staying in Valencia? All I want is for you to come here, I feel alone, this morning I washed myself off using the hotel's portable bidet, I cut my nails by myself for the first time, and despite the difficulties, it is good to be without Maruca: I felt like I was living again. But here I cannot speak with anybody, almost all of them are disgusting fascists, it pains me, but I bite my tongue. Van Tricht gave an idea of what human beings can be like for the first time since my arrival: intelligent and refined. Did you know that Jef Last's wife is Van Tricht's cousin? The world is so small.

If you come here, if you decide on that, even if it is for a couple of days, send me a telegram at the *Hotel Nautique. Reyes*, not the Consulate, for other things it's the Consulate. I would like you to see Iduarte and tell him that I received the books for Rubén Romero, but I have not received the ones I asked him to buy me, have him send them to me as soon as possible. Mr. Antonio Pirretas, the father of the Chilean who worked in the Embassy, will give you a check for 500 pesetas from the account in Buenos Aires. Tell me right away if you received it, but not by telegram, do not get so used to sending telegrams every day, I note this because of your financial situation. I would be much more grateful if you wrote me every day, if the letters are delayed due to censorship go see the Miratvilles and they will help you. I would also like you to buy me the model ship we saw with Manolo Ángeles, it costs 35 pesetas, Manolo does not like it but do not pay attention to him, I need it urgently because I live in the Nautical Hotel. You can bring it with you or send it to me via the Consulate, here those little ships are very expensive.

Please do not forget the errands. Do not misundertand my growls: I am not suggesting that you should go to Valencia, but I do not like it when you are disoriented: I do not want any complaints, please say farewell to my friends, I think I will be with them again sometime, so far I have not found out anything about things in Chile, I suppose you will find that out. A big hug with all my heart and I love you every day more, seeing you is all I hope for. *Pablo*.[8]

4

The letter follows an erratic path of an informal conversation with a well-known interlocutor, moving on from one matter to the next without any apparent logic. The tone is calm, without dramatic flairs on the surface. Nevertheless, Neruda was facing a very difficult moment on several fronts. It was a "time for decisions"[9] in his private life. He informed Delia about his trip to Montecarlo with Maruca, which was equivalent to a separation which proved to be final: they would never live together again. At the same time, he invited Delia to decide affirmatively, as he had done, about a life together without Maruca which was now possible, although it was problematic due to his professional uncertainty.

Verbalizing his emotions emerged with an unintended poetic modulation, a simple fruit of his sincerity. So, from the window of the "very old hotel in front of the port, I watch the sailboats every morning, we would be so happy together": the brusque juxtaposition of two dimensions of his love (Delia and the sailboats) came to Pablo spontaneously, with no danger of any immediate return to reality: "it is best to bear with things for a while longer," let us see how things go. The same is true further down: "All I want is for you to come here, I feel alone," a not so original confession with Romantic overtones, which, however, took on an unexpected meaning—also with

---

8 Pablo Neruda, *Obras completas* [Complete Works], V, pp. 976–977.
9 Olivares.

the spontaneous naturalness of *Residence on Earth*—in joining the prosaic nature of the images: "I washed myself off using the hotel's portable bidet, I cut my nails by myself for the first time." Immediately after that, this confession: "despite the difficulties, it's good to be without Maruca: I felt like I was living again."

It was the first time Pablo had explicitly spoken about his lack of love for and weariness with regards to Maruca. Four days earlier (December 6th) marked six years of marriage, which Neruda upheld responsibly despite his unhappiness and Maruca's inertia. He did not do it only because of his ethical or ideological principles, but rather because of his lack of energy or courage to break things off with her or also due to inertia. He did not abandon Maruca and had made tireless efforts—in Santiago, Buenos Aires, Madrid— to meet the material challenges the couple faced over six long years (a fact Neruda's moral prosecutors tend to forget). This lasted until an external circumstance—the Spanish civil war—made the separation real, since Chilean law, and later Maruca, denied him the option of a normal divorce which would have authorized the breakup, which existed in fact, between these two adults. The question of Malva Marina was a different and very delicate aspect of this family situation. I will return to the significance of Neruda's alluding to "the child" and "the little one" in his letter below.

There is another passage in the letter that is noteworthy: "I would also like you to buy me the model ship we saw with Manolo Ángeles, it costs 35 pesetas…I need it urgently because I live in the Nautical Hotel…here those little ships are very expensive." What is of import in this fragment is his conviction and self-assuredness, even allowing himself a *boutade* regarding the urgent need for the sailboat: "because I live in the Nautical Hotel." There is not the least bit of an indication of excuses for such a "unique yearning for banal things"[10] amid a precarious situation. The recipient of this letter [Delia] would later respond to this harsh judgement several years later (quoted paradoxically by the severe Schidlowsky):

> I stayed in Catalonia… I had to buy a play sailboat that Pablo had seen and which he asked for persistently. You should have seen what a state León Felipe was in when he came along with me. He was furious. Naturally I bought him the sailboat. These were childish things. I used to call Pablo mentally handicapped and Louis Aragon would get angry with

---

10 David Schidlowsky, *Neruda y su tiempo: las furias y las penas* [Neruda and his Time: The furies and the Sorrows], p. 312.

me, but it did not amount to much, because I called him handicapped too. Pablo's love for certain objects, toys, is proof of his authentic innocence. I liked that side of him. Everybody likes a big, manly guy who is a child at heart. It is good for men to retain that side of themselves.[11]

Delia's memory of her love for Pablo led her to understand the "unique yearning" of this manly guy in 1936. Yet the absolute naturalness which made buying the ship an urgent matter, was more than a "proof of his authentic innocence" and the survival of that "child at heart," it was an indication of the strength of the intimate hierarchy of values and needs the poet had been developing since his childhood and based on his personal experience. It was a unique and nontransferable hierarchy to which he was faithful until his death and which (sometimes appearing to be a whim and, consequently, misunderstood) came to the fore when he was at peace and reflected the coherent undergirding of his most diverse types of behavior in love, friendship, literature, politics...and in his relationship with nature and objects, including his collections. As strange as it might seem, the need for that ship was a sign and a root—among many—of Neruda's singular greatness.

5

In that private and revealing letter, Neruda confirmed on December 10th, 1936 his commitment to keep on helping Maruca and Malva Marina: "*The important matter is to manage so Maruca can have that monthly income, so she can be at ease.*"

A few days later, on December 16th, Pablo sent a letter to Germán Vergara Donoso, the Subsecretary of Foreign Affairs in Chile, asking for an alternative to the assignment the general consul had communicated to him: "Is there a chance you could assign me to Europe, for example, to be at the orders of Tulio Maquieira, and retain the entrance permission to Marseille or any other place that would not force me to repatriate? I am bothered by the idea of arriving in a turbulent atmosphere full of passion and being thrown into a political battle which goes against my temperament."

---

11 Schidlowsky, p. 313.

Neruda was forced to resort to ingenious juggling to achieve his goal, but Vergara Donoso knew and shared the poet's hostility towards the Ministry, which is why his response on December 23rd sounds like a joke:

> As far as the fear you show of having yourself thrown into a political battle, I think you need not worry. In our country people are inconsistent, so political campaigns are abandoned shortly after having started. In your case I do not think it even amounts to a campaign, but rather a polemic between "Nerudians" and "anti-Nerudians." I count myself as belonging to the former...[12]

In December of 1936 Neruda was not able to respond to Vergara Donoso, but years later, in hiding, the poet-senator dedicated a ferocious satire included in *Antología Popular de la Resistencia* [A Popular Anthology of the Resistance, 1948], which began like this: "I became a fascist / and Francoist in Spain."[13]

Faced with that rejection, and without any clear alternatives in Chile, Neruda left Marseille at the beginning of 1937 and moved to Paris in the company of Delia, who had just arrived from Barcelona. Juan Larrea provides proof of this: "In January 1937 Neruda and I met in Paris...he was arriving from Marseille, where he had spent three months." Truth be told, it was a little more than two months. In Paris, Louis Aragon's lasting friendship offered Pablo a modest but interesting job with the group, which was preparing the conference of anti-fascist writers, slated for June in Madrid. Neruda remembered it in his memoirs:

> I had been left without a consulate and, consequently, without a cent. I started working, for four hundred old francs, in an association for the defense of culture, directed by Aragon. Delia del Carril, my wife at the time and for many years, was known as a well-to-do rancher's daughter, but the truth was that she was poorer than I was. We lived in a suspect, run down hotel where the first floor was reserved for couples who would have rendezvous [and] who came and went. For several months,

---

12 For more details, see Schidlowsky, p. 314. This is the same deceitfulness as in the case of Vergara Donoso's in Buenos Aires, when the poet was still fleeing from the Chilean authorities in 1949. See José Miguel Varas, *Tal vez nunca. Crónicas nerudianas* [Maybe Never: Nerudian Chronicles], pp. 206–207.
13 Neruda, *Obras completas* [Complete Works], IV, p. 754.

we ate little and poorly. But the conference of anti-fascist writers was a reality.[14]

Pablo's censors should take notice of this quote: he did not stop sending money to Maruca despite his economic dire straits. There is more. Thanks to a letter Delia wrote for her sister Adelina, Amparo Mom and Victoria Ocampo on January 19th, 1937, we know that she lived with Pablo at "7 rue Belloni chez Mr Vargas Paris XIV," which was the address of the suspect, run down hotel. "I am living as frugally as possible because I left Madrid with what I had on and in Paris everything is expensive... Write to me please. I am very sad."[15]

In that same letter Delia—whose mother had just died in Buenos Aires—mentioned incidentally that "Pablo is going to give a talk about Federico García Lorca on the 20th [of January]." To be courteous and exercise some caution, Neruda had written to his ex-boss and friend Tulio Maquieira notifying him that he was going to be giving that talk. In a diplomatic tone like Vergara Donoso's, but with authentic friendship and fondness, the general consul in Marseille showed his displeasure with the idea. Maquieira reasoned that Pablo still had options in the diplomatic service: "You know very well that your talk will explode in the Chilean cenacle like Franco's bombs in Madrid."

But Neruda had understood that the increasing polarization in the Alessandri government between conservatives and pro-clerical groups—in particular due to the ties established between the Spanish conflict and the upcoming presidential election of 1938—made their prospects uncertain and precarious in Chile. Whereas the "the conference of anti-fascist writers was a reality" for the poet, not only as an immediate type of work but also as a rite of initiation into the cultural battles promoted by the Comintern. For Neruda, the months in Paris in 1937 became an important training school and preparation for the political and cultural activism in which he engaged later with surprising skill, ability and efficiency in his country.

Let us return to the matter at hand. Despite his precarious financial situation in the first half of 1937 in Paris, which I just outlined, Neruda continued to send Maruca money which allowed her to remain in Montecarlo until July that year. During this period, he worked on his return to Chile, unquestionably helped by the Comintern and by political and cultural projects, but he

---

14 Neruda, *Obras completas* [Complete Works], V, p. 538.
15 Olivares, p. 381.

also managed to convince Maruca that she should move to The Hague with Malva Marina. Naturally, he was determined to find her a job. At the beginning of September Maruca wrote to doña Trinidad from The Hague. As we shall see later, it was a serene letter that indicated that she and Pablo had come to an agreement, which included a job in the Spanish Republic's Legate Affairs Office in Holland and a living situation for Malva Marina in the city of Gouda. A Christian couple with three children agreed to take care of her and gave Neruda's daughter genuine love and the highest degree of happiness possible for her.

6

"I returned to my country in third class again," Neruda recalled in his memoirs, without adding another word.[16] Thanks to González Tuñón we know that he, his wife Amparo Mom, Pablo and Delia, boarded the cargo ship *Arica* in Antwerp on August 28th which took them to Valparaíso via Azores, Martinique, the Panama Canal, Callao and Mollendo. There are no other details about the ship, though its name, which carried the name of the northern most city in Chile, must have meant it was from that country. Diego Muñoz seemed to confirm that detail in his memoirs at the beginning of 1936: "The next day I went to Valparaíso and I boarded the *Arica*, which was scheduled for a round trip to Rio de Janeiro via Magellan's Strait."[17]

More than a month went by between the closing ceremony of the Conference in Paris (17 July) and the boarding in Antwerp (28 August). I have no information about what Pablo did during this period, besides writing nine poems about Spain, the failed attempts to find a job in a consulate in Europe and an agreement with Moisés Vargas. What is clear is that by this stage he had already managed to have Maruca moved to The Hague and had secured her a post with the Spanish Legate. He dedicated the rest of the time to organizing his own trip with Delia, who accompanied him in his unavoidable trip back to Chile:

> Delia began her preparations then, which consisted of reading Chilean history books, novels and poetry. Their relationship has been growing

---

16 Neruda, *Obras completas* [Complete Works], V, p. 547.
17 Muñoz, p. 214.

and is fortified in love, but also in practical and common endeavors. In that new world that opened up, new relationships got Pablo thinking about his projects, seeing in those people the goodness, the warmth and the whiff of fame, world fame which was practically impossible in a small country like Chile. He had to find new strength, return to that small country, to the small daily affairs, but he was accompanied by Delia, who was now his partner, his correspondent, his secretary, a woman who had a magical social touch. While she had no flair for dealing with reality, and forgot everything, and lost everything, [on the other hand] he had a true skill with regards to knowing who to contact, whom Neruda should meet. She never forgot what was best for Pablo: that was her goal.[18]

Now, there are indications that during the preceding weeks before the trip Neruda contacted Maruca to let her know of his imminent departure and to discuss their conjugal life with her. Although I have no documentary proof of this, I presume that they must have met secretly so that he could bid farewell to Malva Marina, perhaps thinking that he would be seeing her for the last time (since her illness gave the young child only a few more years of life—but he would see her later, in 1939). Choosing Antwerp as the boarding port might have allowed for a meeting between them given its proximity to Dutch territory (a little more than 120 kilometers separates Antwerp and The Hague).

The main indications are found in two letters: one dated August 20th, 1937 in Paris, where Pablo wrote to his sister Laura: "Mom's illness fills me with anguish. Fortunately, I am about to leave for Chile: I board the 28th, that is, in another week. Maruca is staying in Holland with our little child and with the family until we know what my destination is going to be. [...] Many warm greetings from Maruca and all of my love to you and dad and others, *Neftalí Ricardo*."[19] Dated in The Hague, the second letter consists of Maruca writing to doña Trinidad:[20]

---

18 Sáez, pp. 121–122.
19 Neruda, *Obras completas* [Complete Works], V, pp. 837–838.
20 Facsimile in Bernardo Reyes, *Retrato de familia. Pablo Neruda 1904–1920* [Family Portrait: Pablo Neruda 1904–1920], p. 181.

> The Hague, 2 September 1937
>
> Dear Mother,
> Several months have gone by since I last wrote. We have lived through a horrible time, the war, travels and a lot of sadness due to the little one's illness. All of that makes it difficult to write, it is not for lack of love for you all. I remember you all the time and always with lots of love. I feel so badly that you are ill, my only hope is that you get better soon.
>
> Neftalí is traveling to Chile and will arrive in Valparaíso on October 8th more or less. He will tell you all about it. I hope he finds you all in good health.
>
> My love to all of you and a big hug for you, my dear mother, from your daughter,
>> Maruca

The two letters overlap in terms of their fictional account of a normal, conjugal life. Maruca's "gives the impression, as many of her actions in those years, that she did not consider the relationship with Neruda over."[21] For Pablo it was difficult to communicate the news of the end of his relationship with Maruca with his family, and particularly his father, because he knew he would interpret it as another failure. He knew also that Maruca did not accept that decision, but he managed to convince her to wait in Europe while he worked out the arrangements with the Ministry and his eventual return to the diplomatic corps (which is what interested her most), since there was no other way of guaranteeing his economic support in any other way. That explains the tone of Maruca's letter, which, written to doña Trinidad from the perspective a normal couple in the throes of resolving external and circumstantial problems, obviously wanted to win over her husband's family's support for her "cause." Maruca even let them know about Pablo's ship's scheduled arrival in Valparaíso. The fact that she had this information on hand indicates that there must have been some previous meeting between the distanced couple.

I tend to imagine that only by meeting her personally could Pablo have pushed back against Maruca's firm intentions to return with him to Chile. So determined and set was Maruca, that in March 1937, on her own initiative, she wrote a personal letter to Chile's president Arturo Alessandri Palma from Montecarlo asking for a consular post for her husband or support so

---

21 Schidlowsky, p. 345.

the entire family could return to Chile. Germán Vergara Donoso, the Undersecretary of Foreign Affairs, whom we have met before, responded to her:[22]

Santiago, 17 April 1937

Mrs
Maruca Neruda
Montecarlo

Esteemed Maddam,
It is a pleasure to answer the letter you sent on March 16th to the President of the Republic, who has asked me to reply.

Although the law stipulates that repatriations should be in third class, we have decided that we will furnish you with better conditions once you decide to travel.

I ask that you notify me of your decision with regards to this issue...

Nothing is known about Pablo's reaction when he heard about Maruca's reply (with regards to a letter he had not seen). Naturally, his commitment to Aragon—to joining the organizing committee of the Conference in Valencia—was a good reason to postpone the decision in April. Traveling to Chile before August was impossible. After the Conference and a failed attempt to find a new position with the Ministry, Pablo had no other choice but to face the burning issue in his relationship with Maruca, whose letter to president Alessandri had begun and loudly proclaimed her obsessive determination to latch onto her position as the legitimate wife of the Chilean consul. She had underestimated the failure of the marriage and had not taken into account Neruda's own feelings.

The letter to president Alessandri Palma was a red flag which helps to explain Neruda's behavior afterwards, especially his refusal to back Maruca's move to Chile. The poet vividly understood that, though they were physically separated and had not been living together, his spouse's obsession would not diminish in Chile. On the contrary, he foresaw that she would spend most of her time making life impossible for him and his new partner. The facts would show that that risk was enormous and real. During at least the next ten years Maruca did not relent in her desire to recover—at whatever cost—not the love she knew was inexistent, but rather the illusion of diplomatic *status*, which was tied in her mind to the idea of marrying a Chilean consul in Batavia in 1930. He was poor, but he was a consul.

---

22 Schidlowsky, p. 326.

Pablo's weakness in dealing with his difficulties in cutting things off also contributed to Maruca's obsession. But it is worth repeating that since the actual separation the bard had fulfilled his responsibility of providing economic support to Maruca and Malva Marina as best he could. He did this even when he was in a precarious and uncertain situation, without a salary and without any hopes of returning to his job. He confessed his worries about the problems he faced and the efforts he made to send monthly sums—which were high relative to his earnings—in letters he wrote to Delia and Laura. In a letter from 1938, even Maruca admitted implicitly the general regularity with which he sent the monthly money when she complained that in the last sum two of the usual seventy-dollar payments were missing and asked that he include them in the next transfer.

7

In July 1937, having received the reply signed by Vergara Donoso, Maruca left Montecarlo for Holland with their daughter. "Maruca settled down in The Hague (Grote Hertonginnenlaan 170 was her first address), while Malva Marina was taken in by a family in Gouda, which cared for her."[23] The latter is not right. Besides, it does not explain why we suddenly find Maruca in the The Hague, in 1937, working for no less than the Ministry of the Legate of the Spanish Republic.

The explanation had a name: Pablo Neruda. With the clear objective of helping Maruca above and beyond the more or less regular monthly money he sent her, to help her with her move and to have money to live on in The Hague, Neruda appealed to José Bergamín (and via Alberti to the leaders of the Communist International [Comintern]) to find her a job as a secretary and translator in the Legate of the Spanish Republic in Holland. The first known information about this matter comes from the famous *Autobiografía de Federico Sánchez* [Autobiography of Federico Sánchez, 1977], by Jorge Semprún, who lived through the civil war years—that is, his adolescence—in The Hague. The text includes the facts which testify to its importance:

> Pablo Neruda also had that unmistakable air many years later. To tell the truth, you knew Neruda was a poet even before you knew that there was a poet named Pablo Neruda. Let me explain. In 1937, in The Hague, a Dutch woman from Java or Sumatra, who had been Pablo Neruda's wife,

---

23 Schidlowsky, p. 311.

was working for the Chancellor's Office in the Legate of the Spanish Republic, where your father was in charge of the Business Office during the civil war. And only one poet could have had a wife like that, so over the top, so like a soft and dreamy giraffe. Ten years later, when you met Pablo Neruda in person, you were not surprised to confirm the degree to which he had the air of a poet. Only a poet could have married a dreamy female giraffe from Sumatra or Java.[24]

Without alluding directly to Jorge Semprún's book, Schidlowsky verified through a different source that in 1937 Maruca's boss in The Hague was José María Semprún Gurrea, the writer's father:

> In a conversation in Berlin in February 2008, Jorge Semprún, a youngster of about 15 years of age at the time [in 1937], remembered Maruca Reyes and how he and his friends gave Maruca the nickname Giraffe because of her height. It is the first confirmation [*this is not correct: the first, as I just showed, shows up in the* Autobiography] that she had that job which was not well paid, but she needed to speak some Spanish in order to obtain it.[25]

She not only had to speak Spanish: Maruca definitely needed the help of someone influential who could introduce her to the world of the Legate in a country which, because it was at war against an internal enemy and against the German intervention, was forced to be very careful and unassuming when it came to its personnel. And she needed an influential person who would be sufficiently *motivated* on her behalf. Otherwise, how can one explain the presence and the work of Maruca in the Legate? Even Schidlowsky, unknowingly or without meaning to, provides us with a sure tip in his footnote about Jorge Semprún's father:

> José María Semprún Gurrea...attorney and a Catholic intellectual who supported the Republic. A Christian Democrat, which combined 'socialization with democracy,' State intervention and the promotion of freedom. He was a real good friend of José Bergamín, and worked intensively for the press and journal *Cruz y Raya* [Cross and Line], where he

---

24 Jorge Semprún, *Autobiografía de Federico Sánchez* [Autobiography of Federico Sánchez], p. 95.
25 Schidlowsky, p. 397.

published the complete edition of *Residence on Earth* for the first time, and that was where he surely met Neruda.[26]

Armed with these facts, it does not take much imagination to understand that when Maruca left Montecarlo she already had been offered that job that Neruda, via Bergamín and José María Semprún, had arranged for her in The Hague. Consequently, I disagree with Schidlowsky, who has Maruca arriving in Holland completely abandoned and looking for work "since the sum of money sent monthly on an irregular basis was not enough to live on with her daughter, who was ill."[27]

By contrast, I concur with Bernardo Reyes that Maruca apparently "from Montecarlo had already looked over the itinerary in detail, which is why she went to Gouda directly and to a specific family—the Jusling's—in particular." [28] She had established contact with that family through the Christian Science religious sect, whose doctrine included the rejection of medicine, surgery, blood transfusions and other types of medical procedures to tackle diseases. Hendrik and Gerdina Jusling were part of that sect, along with their children Heika, Geesje and Frederik. They took care of Malva Marina during last few years of life she had. With the sums of money she received from Pablo and what she earned in the Chancellor's office, Maruca paid the Juslings an amount for better part than a year that allowed them to hire the young woman, Neil Leys, according to Reyes,[29] whose only job was to take care of Malva Marina. Perhaps Pablo and Maruca's daughter "could not have had a better home considering the Juslings kindness and that the only acceptable option, given the lack of medical alternatives to treat Malva's illness, boiled down to prayer."[30]

Taking the historical context into account, neither is it difficult to understand why Maruca's job was not well paid, as Schidlowsky notes, nor why it might have gotten worse, for presumably the Spanish Republic's financial resources diminished during the unfavorable course of the civil war. Nevertheless, a letter Maruca sent in English, dated November 19th, 1938, reported that she still had the job (which began in 1937 according to Jorge Semprún's

---

26 Schidlowsky, p. 398.
27 Schidlowsky, p. 397.
28 Bernardo Reyes, *El enigma de Malva Marina. La hija de Pablo Neruda*, p. 202.
29 Quoted by Schidlowsky.
30 Reyes, *El enigma de Malva Marina*, p. 169.

quote) and seemed to have a good relationship with her boss, who around that time was reading the journal *Aurora de Chile* [Chilean Dawn], which Neruda sent to her from Santiago.

8

In March 1939 Neruda traveled with Delia to Paris as a consul for the government of President Aguirre Cerda to organize *Operation Winnipeg*. Some weeks after August 4th, which was the date the ship was set to sail with its 2000 Spaniards en route to Valparaíso, Neruda traveled to The Hague to visit Maruca and their daughter Malva Marina. There is no information available about this encounter.

The poet and Delia stayed in Paris until the beginning of December. Before returning to Chile, in November 1939, Neruda traveled to Holland again, where he saw Malva Marina for the last time. War had not yet impacted the country. Maruca wrote Morla Lynch many years later that on that occasion Neruda promised her financial support during the period of difficulties that would likely be unleashed by the war in Europe.

The difficulties would be much more than he could have imagined.

Among the many documented contributions to the biography of Neruda, one of the most noticeable ones in David Schidlowsky's work is the tracing of Pablo and Maruca's trying and complicated itinerary as a couple living at a distance in the years preceding Malva Marina's death (March 1943) and in the following years. The following summary of that itinerary is traced over hundreds of pages in Schidlowsky's monumental book, which was of great help to me.

The outbreak of the war managed to complicate the problems. With the German occupation of Holland in May 1940 Maruca's situation became more and more difficult and it also became thornier for Pablo to send financial help to his ex-wife. "There is a stormy exchange of letters, pleas, telegrams and messages which lasted years."[31] Neruda got in touch with Tobías Barros Ortiz, the Chilean ambassador in Berlin, to help resolve the unexpected difficulties he was having sending money to Maruca. There were problems at the end of

---

31 Schidlowsky, p. 460.

June, and in August two checks for one hundred dollars were returned to the ambassador because they could not be cashed in Holland nor in Germany.

War meant the rejection of the dollar and other Western currencies in occupied territories, but Pablo had a great interest in fulfilling his promise of economic support, it was a way to calm Maruca and keep her at a distance. She continued to ignore the separation and continued to believe in the validity of their marriage. War made the situation even worse. In 1941 ambassador Barros wrote to Neruda "that he was able to send three monthly payments to Maruca Reyes, his wife. But she demanded a fourth which was outstanding. It seems as though Maruca and their daughter's situation began to stabilize, at least economically."[32]

In January 1942 Neruda filed the paperwork for divorce in Mexico—where he was the consul—in order to marry Delia. On November 4th that year the Ministry sent Neruda a telegram reiterating that Maruca wanted to travel to Mexico to be with her husband. Two days later Pablo cabled a response, declaring that despite the divorce he would continue to send her monthly sums.

In February 1943 Neruda and Delia traveled to New York with permission due to the poet's health problems (and he really was very ill in Mexico): "Enfermo en Veracruz, recuerdo un día / del Sur, mi tierra..." [Ill in Veracruz, I remember a day / in the South, my homeland...]. But the main reason for the trip was his stellar participation in the antifascist soirée *Noche de las Américas* [Night of the Americas], beside Vicente Lombardo Toledano, the Mexican labor leader.

Just before leaving for New York, Neruda received—via the Chilean Embassy in Washington—a telegram sent from Berne by Morla Lynch: "Mrs. Neruda notifies from Holland that their little child died quietly March 2nd [1943]. Please inform her father. Would like to meet with her husband as soon as possible."[33] Back in Mexico, Neruda responded through ambassador Schnake, specifying that despite the divorce decree he would continue sending monthly support for Maruca to Switzerland.

On May 23rd Morla Lynch informed the ministry once again that Mrs. Maruca Reyes, who had a Chilean passport and was Dutch citizen, would like

---

32 Schidlowsky, p. 485.
33 Schidlowsky, p. 548.

to return to Chile. According to Schidlowsky's detailed explanation,[34] ambassador Barros Ortiz was willing to repatriate Maruca as part of an exchange of diplomats and their families agreed upon by Chile and Germany. Ambassador Schnake transcribed Neruda's curt reply: "Although I appreciate ambassador Barros' interest, I regret to say that I do not want my ex-wife to return to Chile and I will suspend my monthly support if she does so."[35]

The following line in Schidlowsky's book includes the following final judgment: "This biography of Pablo Neruda reaches here one of its most inhumane and lamentable moments. One should not forget that Neruda left his wife or ex-wife in Holland, without money, with little hopes of receiving her monthly support, [and] in a country under a brutal German Nazi occupation."

Neruda, who by that time planned on leaving the diplomatic corps and living in Chile, insisted that his financial support was the only possible relationship he could have with Maruca. After the Battle of Stalingrad, the situation in countries occupied by the Nazis became aggravated, but Neruda managed to send his ex-wife the sum of $335 dollars in December 1943 through a commercial operation tied to the Corporación de Ventas de Salitre y Yodo [Corporation of Nitrate and Iodine Sales] in Lisbon. In those years the interest and help of the Ministry of Foreign Relations, and of diplomats like Morla Lynch, Barros Ortiz and Schnake in establishing communication lines between Neruda and Maruca were significant.

From December 1943 to mid 1945, the end of the war, those communication lines did not work. In July that year Morla Lynch notified Neruda that Maruca had moved to Brussels and that she had reiterated her desire to "meet with her husband who had not been able to send her any sum of money since December 1943."[36] Morla added that she had some funds available, which were about to expire, alluding probably to the money Neruda had sent, which she had put away for Maruca. Likewise, in March 1946 she declared that she had 1630.60 Swiss Francs.[37]

---

34 Schidlowsky, pp. 552–554.
35 Schidlowsky, p. 553.
36 Schidlowsky, p. 642.
37 Schidlowsky, p. 662.

In August 1945 Neruda reconfirmed his intent to continue helping Maruca in Brussels, where she lived "in unknown conditions"[38] until 1948, when the government of Gabriel González Videla asked her to travel to Chile in March to use her in its pursuit of Neruda by bringing to light his ostensible bigamy. Apparently, Maruca did not understand the situation well and even had some meetings regarding the matter with Margarita Aguirre (daughter of the General Consul of Chile in Buenos Aires, 1933–1934, and later a friend and biographer of Neruda) whom she had met when she was a child on the 20th floor of the Safico Building.

The attorney Fernando Silva Yoacham, representing Neruda, who was then in hiding, managed to come to an agreement with Maruca which involved her accepting the end of the conjugal relationship with the poet in exchange for two considerable sums of money, one in cash and the other to be paid in six installments. Before this agreement, and since her presence in Chile had not been useful to the political plans the government had with regards to Neruda, Maruca was practically abandoned by those who had brought her to the country, and so the poet himself arranged to help her economically while in hiding in 1948 until the beginning of 1949.[39]

Maruca continued to live in Chile until, in October of 1957, she received a Dutch passport from the embassy in Santiago and was able to return to The Hague, where she settled in January 1958. There are records of her addresses until 1961, after which time there is no trace of her whereabouts. "We only know that she lived most of the rest of her life without stable employment and received help from the Dutch State."[40] She died in The Hague on 27 March 1965. Some months later Neruda managed to obtain his first wife's

---

38 Schidlowsky, p. 729.
39 Translator's note: Neruda was in hiding from the government of President González Videla who, despite winning with the support of the Democratic Alliance—which included the Radical Party (a liberal party), the Socialist Party, the Socialist Workers Party, the Democratic Party and the Communist Party—in 1946, two years later bowed to pressure from President Truman and his Truman Doctrine and declared the Communist Party illegal. Neruda, a senator with the Communist Party, delivered the blistering speech "Yo acuso" [I accuse] in congress and then went into hiding. He was taken in by different households throughout in Chile until he was able to cross the Andes mountains on horseback into Argentina in 1949.
40 Schidlowsky, pp. 971–972.

death certificate. The versemaker "was interested in legalizing his relationship with Matilde Urrutia."[41]

9

Even today Neruda's matrimonial matters have the strange virtue of unleashing in Chile severe moral judgments. David Schidlowsky's book, so valuable with respect to different aspects of Neruda's life, includes—among other denunciations of Neruda's garden variety of sins—a paragraph that ends like this: "Neruda's relationship with his wife ended up being one of the saddest and most embarrassing chapters in the poet's life."[42]

In the Chilean literary terrain, Neruda seems to monopolize almost all of the inquisitional energy circulating about. I know of no other poets or narrators (except Gabriela Mistral) whose private lives have attracted anywhere near the scrutiny visited upon Neruda's life. He is accused of abandoning Maruca. That is not true, or at least it is not *all* there is to it. I have demonstrated that—within his human limits, and historical and private circumstances that were objectively very difficult—Neruda was quite responsible and did as much as he could to help her, except agree to be her partner again.

Maruca's obsession made his forced return to Chile not only a relief but also a vital necessity. That fixation made a commonly agreed upon and friendly agreement between Maruca and Neruda and her return to Chile, with their child, impossible. Her letters to Laura and doña Trinidad (quoted above) makes one think that our poet must have made a false promise to her, besides making one think about his weakness in terms of reaching a definitive solution with regards to the breakup of their marriage.

Yet the moral cases against Neruda accuse him above all—and without taking into account all the above—of having abandoned his daughter. The bard did not abandon his daughter: what he did was separate from Maruca, but—motivated by Malva Marina—he continued to help her in extremely difficult circumstances.

The "enigma" that some have invoked does not exist in the case of Malva Marina—what could it possibly be?—but rather in her father's relationship with her. We can only conjecture based on certain evidence. From the moment the irreversibility of his daughter's illness was confirmed, Neruda

---

41 Schidlowsky, p. 1134.
42 Schidlowsky, p. 311.

stopped *naming her*. For some time, his letters referred to her as *our child* or *our girl*; later she disappeared from his writings. As I understand it, that did not mean he was indifferent or had forgotten her. Silence was always very eloquent in Neruda (as Jorge Edwards reaffirmed in *Esclavos de la consigna* [Slaves to the Slogan]). And all the more so in the case of a *name*, because we are well aware of the importance Neruda attributed to *naming* in his life-poetry (as witness the case of Josie Bliss). My hypothesis is that the omission of Malva Marina's name was a display of the poet's mourning, for the illness made it impossible for him to communicate verbally and emotionally with his daughter. The geographic separation, and his distancing from Maruca, did the rest.

In an interview with the attorney Aída Figueroa, a confidant who knew Neruda very well, made a valid claim, similar—to my mind—to what I detailed above in this chapter about the relationship with Malva Marina:

> Pablo never mentioned her in the 25 years I knew him. My view is that he was not one for mourning, suffering, pain. He always said, "You have to live life cheerfully." He always remarked that his daughter was precious, and the truth is that they were all horrified when they saw her, but always the optimist, he thought his child was going to get better [see the testimony of Aleixandre above]. When he realized that that was not the case, he separated from that pain and never mentioned her again.[43]

Another indication, to which I have already referred, is present in the fish with armillary rings that Neruda asked Miguel Prieto to design in Mexico as the epicenter of his *ex libris* which was destined to appear on the cover of the first edition of *Canto general* (1950) and later to become the poet's logo for the cover of the Losada editions of his books and for the blue flag that flew over his house in Isla Negra. Since Miguel Prieto had designed the small fish that appeared on the bottom of the announcement with which Pablo and Maruca made known Malva Marina's birth in Madrid in August 1934, and since Neruda never explained why he chose the fish for his personal and publication logo (nor did he ever reveal who had designed it), I am certain that that logo with the fish and the silence that surrounded it, as well as the omission of the *name*, were his secret way of paying an intimate tribute and conferring everlasting life to his daughter.

---

43 Inés María Cardone, *Los amores de Neruda* [Neruda's Lovers], p. 122.

A Mortal Sin

Stalinist

"Stalin,
con su paso tranquilo,
entró en la Historia acompañado
de Lenin y del viento."

[Stalin / with his quiet steps, / went down in History accompanied by Lenin and the wind.]

"En su muerte" [Upon his death],
Las uvas y el viento [Grapes and the Wind]

"Y aquel muerto regía la crueldad
desde su propia estatua innumerable:
aquel inmóvil gobernó la vida."
[And that deceased man ruled with cruelty / from his own innumerable statues: that immobile one governed life.]
"El episodio" [The Episode], *Memorial de Isla Negra [Isla Negra]*

I

IN THE BEGINNING WAS the anarchist poet. José Santos González Vera, a writer and leader of the Federación de Estudiantes de Chile [FECH; The Student Federation of the University of Chile] who arrived in Temuco (capital of the southern province of Cautín) looking for a place to live, provides proof of his early backing of the cause. Doctor Juan Gandulfo had indicated that he should contact a student named Neftalí Reyes: "Shortly after my arrival in Temuco in July 1920, I went to wait for him by the door of the high school, where he was in his senior year. He was a very thin young man, with a pallid earthy color, with a big nose. His eyes were two small, dark points, and his face, like a sword. Under his arm he clung to *La sociedad moribunda y la anarquía* [The Moribund Society and Anarchy], by Jean Grave."[1]

This account conjures up an image of a young man who was 16 years old and who was already a studious follower of anarchism via that important book of 1892 (for which the author had been condemned to two years of prison, accused of promoting fires, robberies, assassinations, pillaging, as instruments to achieve social justice). And who, simultaneously, was already an activist tied to the university anarchists of the FECH and correspondent and contributor to the publication *Juventud* [Youth]. A year later in that magazine he published a fiery text calling on his *comrade poets* to fight for Joaquín Cifuentes Sepúlveda, who was serving time for homicide in a jail in Talca, "delito que no cometió" [a crime he did not commit]:

> Y aunque lo hubiera cometido. Era
> un poeta. Decidles a los jueces
> el aleteo de sus versos hondos...
> los paisajes enormes de la tierra
> que los jueces no miran. Pobres almas
> de estampilla de impuesto! Y si no saben
> todavía del cielo ni del verso,
> incendiadles sus casas,
> robadles sus mujeres,
> y que la dinamita milagrosa
> fecunde las entrañas de la tierra,
> reviente las murallas de la cárcel!
> Que los mismos gusanos que comieron
> la carne de Domingo Gómez Rojas
> vayan comiendo carne de juzgado!

[And though he might have committed it. He / was a poet. Tell the judges about / the fluttering of his profound lines... / the enormous landscapes of the earth / that the judges ignore. Poor tax stamp / souls! And if they do not know / yet of the sky or the poet's line, / burn their houses, / kidnap their wives, / and let miraculous dynamite / fertilize the bowels of the earth, / blow out the walls of the jail! / Let the same

---

1 José Santos González Vera, "Testimonio" [Testimony] in *Aurora*, p. 230.

worms which ate / Domingo Gómez Rojas' flesh / eat the flesh of the court!²

Jean Grave's lesson was very evident in these poetic lines, addressed to his *comrade poets*. The text in prose "Empleado" [Employee], from the same period, refers to a first-person subject (*we*)—clearly "we, anarchists"—whose exemplary discourse was addressed to a worker who is not conscious of his working conditions:

> And the thing is you do not know you are exploited. That they have stolen your happiness, that for the dirty money they gave you, you gave the portion of beauty that fell on your soul... Perhaps you feel weak. No. Here we are, those of us who are not alone, who are your equals; and like you, exploited and in pain, but we are rebels.
>
> And do not think that you need to read Marx to know this. It is enough to know that you are not free, that you want to be free, that you will break free, through love or force—what does it matter?—the chains that hold you down and debase you...³

In the poem lauding Joaquín Cifuentes Sepúlveda, the discourse was collective, the speaker was addressing his brother poets in anarchist language. In "Employee" the anarchist militant—who at the age of 17 mentions Marx here for the first time—was writing to an addressee from his superior condition of having a more developed social consciousness. In both cases he showed his desire to belong to an organization, to not act like a lonely wolf. Upon arriving in Santiago in 1921, Neruda felt at ease for a while in the student environment at the Federation and in its journal *Claridad* [Clarity], for which he wrote numerous chronicles, editorial pieces and poems which evinced recognition of their quality and authority.

2

The evolution of Neruda's political activity connected to his poetry can be explained by the early affirmation of his persona. He knew what he wanted

---

2 Neruda, "A los poetas de Chile" [To the Poets of Chile] (1921), in *Poesía completa* [Complete Poetry], pp. 422–423.
3 Neruda, "Empleado" [Employee], originally published in *Claridad*, 29, 8/13/1921.

and searched for it calmly and surely. The editor Carlos George Nascimento remembered his first encounter with the young poet that way, at the beginning of 1924:

> At the time I was still a novice editor more or less. I had published Eduardo Barrios' *El hermano asno* [The Brother Ass], and he told me: "An easy going, modest, young man who goes by the name *Pablo Neruda* is going to come talk with you. He is going to be a great poet. He is going to be much talked about some day. Do not lose sight of him." And I did not lose sight of him. He had something about him, I cannot quite explain it. He was very thin and pallid, he hardly spoke, but he was always so easy going and sure of himself, so much so that he won me over and to such a degree that I had to publish the book [*Twenty Love poems*] the way he specified: a big format, square, which was not cheap at all because a lot of paper was wasted. But you see now, so thin and quiet, he got what he wanted.[4]

The *Twenty Love Poems* were an instant success, which surprised Nascimento, despite Alone's and Mariano Latorre's unfavorable critiques.[5] Though it was not the book Neruda would have liked to launch his fame, he jumped in the ring to defend it from those attacks with a short text of great interest because of what it revealed about the author:

> I have only sung about my life and the love of some very dear women, like someone who greets another yelling in the closest part of the world. I tried to add ever more expression to my thoughts, and I won a battle or two... Honorable and unknown folks—not employees and pedagogues who detest me personally—have shown their cordial approval decidedly, from afar... I never tired of any discipline, because I did not have

---

4 Quoted in Teitelboim, *Neruda*, p. 118.
5 In *La Nación* [The Nation], 8/3/1924 and *Zig-Zag*, 8/16/1924 respectively. Translator's note: Alone was the pseudonym for Hernán Díaz Arrieta (1891–1984), Chile's most prolific critic at the time, who wrote for the newspaper *El Mercurio*, and a writer who won the National Prize for Literature in 1959. His best-known works are *Historia personal de la literatura chilena* [A Personal History of Chilean Literature, 1954], *Aprender a escribir* [To Learn to Write, 1956] and *Pretérito, imperfecto* [Preterite, Imperfect, 1976]. He was very religious and a staunch conservative. Mariano Latorre (1886–1955) was a Chilean naturalist writer who won the National Literary Prize in 1944. His most significant book was *Zurzulita* (1920).

any: used clothing which fit others was too small or big for me, and I recognized it without having to look at it..."[6]

Instead of underlining the obvious personal and erotic intimacy, Neruda exhorted readers to find in these love poems a new way of capturing reality, "like someone who greets another yelling in the closest part of the world." Something truly important had taken place. By criticizing his break with the poetics of *The Book of Twilights*, Alone's and Latorre's reviews allowed Pablo to understand that his new book, above and beyond its successful reception and unexpected popularity, amounted to a return to degree zero, the beginning of a new writing phase which was not subordinated—like his 1923 book—to traditional literary models. It was *modern* writing in the end, but within his own writing style. To sing to his lovers meant embracing with unusual enthusiasm "the closest part of the world."

With his *Twenty Love Poems* Neruda's mythic South was born, the South tied to his childhood as a fecund, lively and active literary space, much like Macondo, Comala and Santa María in the narratives of García Márquez, Rulfo and Onetti or like Yoknapatawpha County in Faulkner's works. Two years later, in *El habitante y su esperanza* [The Inhabitant and his Hope] Neruda named another fictional space—Cantalao—as the nucleus of the mythic space which had emerged with *Twenty Love Poems* and which had been intricately tied to his love and poppy-filled back yard in Puerto Saavedra.

Paradoxically, that geographical and poetic fiction became the bridge that led Neruda to the elaboration of his portrayal of reality via his sojourn in *Residence on Earth*, from Chile to the Orient, to Spain. During that journey, his song to his beloved Josie Bliss gave a name to the title *Residence on Earth*, "like someone who greets another yelling in the closest part of the world," taking in the geographic and historical totality.

3

At the beginning of 1930, Albertina Azócar's refusal to travel from Brussels to Ceylan (Sri Lanka) was a terrible private catastrophe for Pablo.

---

6 Neruda, "Exégesis y soledad" [Exegesis and Solitude] in *La Nación* [The Nation], 8/20/1924.

...and we arranged her arrival, we were going to get married, and for a while I lived for her arrival... And she was not able to make the trip, or at least at that time, due to reasonable circumstances perhaps, but I was sick in bed for a week, with a fever and without appetite, it was as though they had burned me from within, a terrible pain. All this happened without my being able to tell anybody about it, and thereby feel alleviated, it has been buried along with the other days. To hell with that story![7]

Around that time, Neruda read "kilometers of English novels" which his friend Lionel Wendt sent him, among them the rare first edition of *Lady Chatterly's Lover*, by D.H. Lawrence. Printed in Florence, he thought its initial paragraph had been written to rescue him from that fatal moment:

Ours is essentially a tragic age, so we refuse to take it tragically. The cataclysm has happened, we are among the ruins, we start to build a new little habitat, to have some new hope. It is rather hard work: there is now no smooth road into the future: but we go round, or scramble over the obstacles. We've got to live, no matter how many skies have fallen.[8]

But reading Lawrence, and also Joyce and T.S. Eliot not only helped Pablo find the road to renew his life: it also motivated him to write the last texts in Wellawatta, in particular "Ritual de mis piernas" [Ritual of my Legs]. This period of sexual solitude, intensified by Albertina's refusal, was articulated in this poem where the speaker celebrates himself as a "part of nature" while rationalizing his critique of the surrounding and hostile society. The poem focuses on the I's natural condition while gradually describing his own legs, celebrating his muscles, his knees, his calves, his ankles and his feet. His muscles:

Como tallos o femeninas, adorables cosas,
desde las rodillas suben, cilíndricas y espesas...
son allí la mejor parte de mi cuerpo:
lo enteramente substancial, sin complicado contenido
de sentidos o tráqueas o intestinos o ganglios...

---

7 Neruda, Letter to Héctor Eandi, 2/27/1930.
8 Translator's note: Quoted from D.H. Lawrence, *Lady Chatterly's Lover*, thirtieth edition (New York: The New American Library, 1959), p. 5.

[Like stalks or feminine and adorable things, / they rise to the knees, cylindrical and thick... / they are the best part of my body: / what is completely substantive, with no complicated thematics / of senses or tracheas or intestines or ganglions...]

In this encompassing, live synecdoche (the parts standing in for the whole: his legs representing his entire body) the text inserts a rational, critical discourse mapping cold counterpoints which are interspersed in the development of a passionate description of the parts of his legs:

Las gentes cruzan el mundo en la actualidad
sin apenas recordar que poseen un cuerpo y en él la vida,
y hay miedo, hay miedo en el mundo de las palabras que
    designan el cuerpo,
y se habla favorablemente de la ropa,
de pantalones es posible hablar, de trajes,
y de ropa interior de mujer (de medias y ligas de "señora"),
como si por las calles fueran las prendas y los trajes vacíos
    por completo
y un oscuro y obsceno guardarropas ocupara el mundo.

[People cross the world nowadays / without even remembering they possess a body and in it, their life, / and there is fear, there is fear in the world of words that / designate the body, / and they talk favorably about clothes, / of pants one can talk, of suits, / and of women's undergarments (of ladies' hose and clips), / as if the clothing and empty suits ambled / on their own / and a dark and obscene armoire were the world.]

This "Ritual of Legs" was the anarchist poet's last important text written along naturalist lines. But at the same time Neruda was able to become fast friends with Lionel Wendt (1900–1944), a multifaceted creole intellectual who had studied in the colonial metropolis, who was a musician and also a critic of art, literature and film: a tireless cultural activist. And, above all, he was a leftist activist. Neruda saw in Wendt the type of intellectual communist that would lead him away from anarchism and who would open up his Marxist horizon. From there on, his political reflections tended to put that perspective (the anarchist one) to the test. The seeds of the communist poet sprung forth in Ceylon [Sri Lanka].

4

When Neruda returned to Chile in 1932, the national Communist Party was going through a hard time, although its ties to the Moscow-centered International conferred it universality and prestige due to Soviet economic success, in contrast to the crisis of 1929, which was still plunging the West (and especially Chile) into the abyss of fear, misery and dissatisfaction.

Had Chilean communism not been, like most of the communist parties in the world at that time, immersed in the most close-minded sectarianism—preoccupied more about the purity of its rank and file [and its alignment with the Stalinist line of the Soviet CP after the internal triumph of that line over the "opposition"], maybe it would have been capable of capitalizing on the discontent and becoming the political great reference point for the country.[9]

That Chilean CP could hardly attract a figure like Neruda. His true and cautious political evolution, which he pursued with growing interest, made itself known in 1932 with his own silence on the topic because he did not feel ready to publish his own personal reflections, but he did write about them privately in an extraordinarily interesting letter to his friend Eandi:

I do not feel the anguish for what is going on in the world.

I am just reintegrating myself into Western life, I like enjoying the pleasures which I denied myself for years.

A wave of Marxism seems to be haunting the world, letters I receive from my Chilean friends hound me to take that position. The truth is, now one can only be a communist or an anticommunist. The rest of the doctrines have been collapsing or have collapsed. But that is for those who are *political*, that is [for those who] exist civilly.

---

9 Olga Uliánova, "Entre el auge revolucionario y los abismos del sectarismo: el PC chileno y el Buró Sudamericano de la Internacional Comunista en 1932–1933" [Between the Revolutionary Rise and Abyss of Sectarianism and the South American Bureau of the Communist International in 1932–1933] in Rolando Álvarez et al., *Fragmentos de una historia. El Partido Comunista de Chile en el siglo XX...1912–1994* [Fragments of a History: The Chilean Communist Party in the 20th Century...1912–1994], p. 53.

> I was an anarchist years ago, editor of the anarcho-syndicalist newspaper *Claridad* [Clarity], where I published my ideas and things for the first time. And I am still left with the anarchists' lack of faith regarding the State, regarding impure politics. But I think my point of view, as a romantic intellectual, is of no consequence. One thing is for sure: I loathe proletarian art, proletarian liturgy. Systematic art can have no purchase, in any period of history, except in the case of minor artists. Here we have been invaded by odes from Moscow, armored trains, etc. I continue to write about dreams.[10]

The first paragraphs declared Neruda's frivolous lack of interest in the critical international state of affairs, justified by his current hedonism in Santiago. With his friends and modest bohemian life, he tried to make up for his privations and abstinence during his exile in Asia. But it was only a masked caution with regards to an issue that in reality was very important to him. A scarce two weeks before, on February 17th, 1933—when he wrote the letter—Adolf Hitler had become Chancellor of the Reich in Germany. Neruda's indifference with respect to such a startling fact (although distant) was not credible; rather he was awaiting his compass' signal. Waiting for what?

A "wave of Marxism seem[ed] to be haunting the world" and was reaching the poet with his friends' invitations and insistence. In reflecting on that, Neruda said that "one can only be a communist or an anticommunist," which was not so, because in 1933 he could not declare himself an anticommunist. But neither was he capable yet of accepting or rejecting the alternative. For the time being he eluded the dilemma by proclaiming that he had no civil presence, he was no political being: he was covering up the absence, the interior conflict, he was unable to hide.

I was an anarchist years ago: for the first time in Neruda's writings, he placed his anarchist militancy in the past, in a vague "years ago" which we could place in Wellawatta in 1930, as we noted, and affirmed his decision to remain in an irrelevant limbo of a "romantic intellectual." It is followed by the important *one thing is for sure*, which showed his good measure of reserve with regards to Marxism, a reserve that was aesthetic in nature: "I loathe proletarian art, proletarian liturgy" (a problem he resolved later, in Spain). Consequently, for the moment, he aimed to keep *writing about dreams*.

---

10 Neruda, Letter to Héctor Eandi, 2/17/1933.

5

Spain, fall of 1934. The Asturian revolution in October and love in the times of the Correos Brewery: two factors that, united, were decisive in the education of this communist poet.

Delia del Carril and Pablo Neruda needed each other, without knowing so. In January of 1934 Delia moved to Madrid after several years in Paris. The latter years of that period were focused on her introduction to Marxism with the support of Louis Aragon and Elsa Triolet. They had returned from the Soviet Union very motivated to organize and strengthen communism among French intellectuals. Delia gave all her passion and intellect to the cause. Now she lived in Madrid in a state of exaltation, full of activities and a sincere communist fervor, but she was alone, missing a partner. By contrast, Pablo, midway through the year, arrived in Madrid in the company of Maruca, but was living a phase of existential and intellectual confusion. By getting together, they brought out the best in one another.

In the fall, that union was quickly put to the test due to the grave crisis that shook the Spanish Republic, then governed by a right-wing coalition. The rivalry between the socialist leaders Largo Caballero and Indalecio Prieto, in addition to the anarchist excesses and other errors committed by the fragmented Left, played into the hands of the arrogant fascist Gil Robles, who on October 4th withdrew the support of the Spanish Confederation of the Autonomous Right (SCAR) from Samper's inefficient government. Although president Alcalá Zamora did not ask Gil Robles to form a new cabinet, and turned once again to Alejandro Lerroux, SCAR was still able to garner three ministerial posts in the government.

The immediate and violent reaction to these events in Madrid and Barcelona were quickly put down by the army in both cities. But such was not the case in Asturias, where, armed and well-organized, the working-class parties took over Oviedo, Gijón, Avilés and the mining regions of Mieres and Sama. In the downtowns they set up revolutionary soviets which issued their own currency, requisitioned trains, confiscated buildings, organized supplies and, together, managed to mobilize some thirty thousand, well-armed, workers.

By closing the Cantabrian mountain passes, this popular army blocked the advance of the strong contingent of forces sent by the government to put down the uprising. As the main points of the rebellion yielded, a ferocious retaliation was unleashed which left approximately four thousand victims (among them, one thousand dead) and enormous destruction. The success of the Asturian repression gave the young general Francisco Franco, who headed it up, the license as leader of the anti-Republican revolt of 1936.

The civil war consigned this episode in 1934—an authentic revolution—to the historical dust bin. With the uprising in Asturias drowning in blood, the repression reached Madrid, Barcelona and other cities. For Neruda the Asturian revolution and its repercussions in Madrid were a new and moving experience, whose meaning and details he understood thanks to Delia's help. As a diplomat, the poet could not openly speak about the matter, but the Asturian rebellion, the subsequent repression and, in particular, the ongoing underground reorganization of the resistance and the popular movement, in many ways and to varying degrees, are a part of almost all the final poems published in the second part of *Residence on Earth*. It took centerstage in "Estatuto del vino" [Statute of Wine], where *the men of wine* cryptically incarnate the revolutionary energy that is reborn and is reorganized after the defeat. It is highlighted too in "Apogeo del apio" [The Apogee of Celery] and "La calle destruida" [The Destroyed Street], but also, incidentally, in certain lines in "Vuelve el otoño" [Autumn Returns], "El desenterrado" [The Unburied One], "Oda a Federico García Lorca" [Ode to Federico García Lorca] and other poems.

I owe a debt to Professor Gutiérrez Revuelta (University of Houston) for having pointed out to me the presence and impact of the Asturian revolution in the poem "The Destroyed Street", which in my critical edition of *Residence on Earth*[11] referenced other poems in the book, in particular one of the three material songs, "Statute of Wine". Beneath its hermetic appearance I discovered the true point of departure for Neruda's commitment to the communist movement. Not by chance, it was also the first product of the union of Pablo and Delia.

6

Book burnings on May 10th, 1933 in Nazi Germany, a mere three and a half months after Adolf Hitler became Chancellor, shook the European cultural media to its core. No wonder: the public burning on May 10th took place simultaneously in twenty-two German cities which were

---

11 (Madrid: Cátedra, 1987). For more details, see Pedro Gutiérrez Revuelta, "El galope verde de Pablo Neruda" [Pablo Neruda's Green Gallop], *Nerudiana*, 1995.

homes to universities. Professors led the parades that preceded the flames. If the University of Freiburg was unable to join this mass burning it was because it had rained.

Eutimio Martín

Hitler's rise to power in 1933 was a violent and jarring act for the political strategizing of the Comintern, which had dismissed the direct struggle with Nazi fascism, underestimating it in the main struggle with the Social Democrats, considered to be the principal obstacle to strengthening the united front of the working class in favor of the Soviet Union and against the war. Hitler's triumph forced the communists to change their strategy. In the face of the new Nazi threat, popular initiatives of antifascist unity sprouted up and proliferated spontaneously, especially in France, where the French Communist Party was forced to change its sectarian line of *class against class*—put into effect in 1929—to the *united anti-fascist front*. In May of 1935 the Central Committee of the Comintern approved and agreed with the position of the French delegates Thorez and Marty. Consequently, the International Congress of Writers for the Defense of Culture, in June 1935 was, in fact, the first consecration of the new political stance of the Popular Front.

The Congress began on June 21st in the Palais de la Mutualité, located near the Latin Quarter in Paris. Despite the summer heat and the entrance fee, the hall was filled to the brim and speakers had to be set up outside. 230 delegates from 38 countries attended, invited in a prior announcement signed by the members of the French coordinating committee, which included Louis Aragon, Henri Barbusse, Jean-Richard Bloch, Jean Cassou, René Crevel, Paul Nizan, Romain Rolland, and the honorary presidents André Gide and André Malraux. The Latin American delegates included Raúl González Tuñón, Armando Bazán, César Vallejo and Pablo Neruda, who traveled from Madrid.

Meeting so many sacred cows of world literature and intellectual life— Aldous Huxley, Edward M. Forster, Julien Benda, Michael Gold, Waldo Frank, Heinrich Mann, among the other French guests already mentioned— was a real rite of initiation for Neruda and the confirmation of the highest purpose to which he wanted to dedicate his work now. With Alberti as mediator, he surely had undocumented conversations with the French communist writers (Aragon, Barbusse, Nizan).

That Congress in 1935 was extremely important for Neruda especially as regards his politics. There and then *he decided to dedicate this life and his work to the cause of the communists*, although not yet as a militant. Contrary to the theory advanced by Amado Alonso about Neruda's *political conversion*, by stepping over to the side of communism Neruda let go of the honest reservations that had impeded him from adopting the only political and ideological option which was of interest to him as a poet and a citizen.

7

The plan was for the Nationalist forces to enter the capital on 12 October, the day of "The Feast of Spanish Race" [Día de la Raza]. Mola had claimed that he would drink a cup of coffee that day on the Gran Vía and, although the attack on Madrid was delayed, even Franco's staff began to prepare for a triumphal entry. The seemingly inevitable capture of Madrid would not only mean a crushing psychological blow to the Republicans. It should guarantee belligerent rights, if not *de facto* recognition, from foreign powers.[12]

A. Beevor

It is well known that the Spanish civil war changed Neruda's poetry. Here I will attempt to detail exactly what it was that had a decisive impact on the poet during the few months (July-November 1936) which he experienced in the very heart of the conflict: in the capital of the Republic.

The defense of Madrid became an international cause that united Europe and the Americas, and all who were ready to confront fascism head on. The situation was desperate not only because of the forceful advance of the armies from Africa, supported as they were by Luftwaffe squadrons and the Italian Aviazione Legionaria, but also because of prevailing chaos among the Republican forces. Since the first weeks of battles *the system of militias* demonstrated that it was inefficient in practical terms, which was due to the lack of discipline. Entire detachments abandoned the front at a whim to spend the weekend in Madrid or Barcelona. "Although the workers' militias were the only possible response to the generals' rising, since few regular army units remained in formation, the anarchists, the POUM and the left socialists, including Largo Caballero, regarded the militias as a virtue rather than a

---

12 Antony Beevor, *The Spanish Civil War*, p. 129.

necessity. (...) Meanwhile the Madrid government, the regular officers, centrist politicians and the communists were advocating a conventional army as the sole means of resisting the Nationalists."[13]

On October 18th, 1936 the Republican General Staff ordered the creation of six "mixed brigades;" in doing so it took the first important step towards converting the militias into a formal army. The most significant of the six was under the command of the legendary Enrique Líster. Neruda saw this act as a sign of the growing influence of the communists in the organization of the defense of Madrid.

On October 28th, the Soviet ambassador in London declared before the Committee of Non-Intervention that his country no longer felt bound by the agreement (the pact signed on August 2nd) any more than Italy, Germany and Portugal in that regard. From that moment on, the USSR openly supported the Spanish Republic with military aid, above all with massive shipments of fighter planes (in particular the Chatos fighters, known as the Snubbed Nosed, which turned out to be superior to the Fiat and Heinkel 51 fighters). Many members of the Red Army arrived also, more or less camouflaged as volunteers for the International Brigades. It goes without saying that these solidarity troops contributed a great deal to lift the morale of the loyal troops.

And opportunely, because the night of November 6th the Republican government—with documents and archives in a long convoy of trucks—moved (or rather *fled*) to Valencia. It was clear that for president Azaña and the majority of the ministers, including Indalecio Prieto and Largo Carballero, the fall of Madrid was imminent. The capital was subsequently led by the Council for the Defense of Madrid, headed by the General Miaja, which established its headquarters in the Ministry of Finance. There Miaja and the Head of the Joint Chiefs of Staff, the lieutenant colonel Vicente Rojo, were able to count on the Soviet general Goriev's expert military advice, "the man said by many [historians] to be the real commander in Madrid, was also established in the ministry."[14]

A surprising thing occurred then. Rather than demoralizing and enveloping the inhabitants of Madrid in chaos, the government's abandonment of the capital led to a magic moment in the course of the war. An impulsive

---

13   Beevor, p. 105.
14   Beevor, p. 135.

instinct, almost primordial, to defend the city overtook the inhabitants who were under siege. The best souls of the anti-fascist Left united spontaneously and the enthusiasm of the anarchists who yelled "Long live Madrid without a government!" was channeled in an optimal way by the communists who, setting aside their routines, put into action their well-known organizational ability, even calling for the creation of local committees (which they had formerly rejected). The terror and the hate of the African troops galvanized the inhabitants of Madrid. In those days the international press announced the "last hours for Madrid" and General Franco had declared that on November 7th he would attend mass in the capital. Jesús Hernández wrote this enraged testimony of the situation:

> The city's eyes became desperate, it felt like a circle of iron almost around its neck, it understood the frenetic sting of vengeance, assassination, revenge... Was defending oneself possible? Yes, it was possible. And the communists...yelled it to all of Madrid...
>
> By day, by night, in the cafés, on the street corners, on the promenades, in the theaters, in the workshops, the agitators' megaphones drove home the idea to common folk in Madrid, in the very entrails of the city, in the veins of each of its sons and daughters, two words that the artillery, the fighter planes, the generals, the Moors, the Italian tanks could not run through: ¡no pasarán! [they will not pass!].[15]

On November 7th general Varela ordered a major attack against Madrid. By pure chance Miaja found out about Varela's plan the day before and his false maneuver in the area of Carabanchel, so that the Castejón column was surprised to encounter a wall of militia fighters in Casa de Campo, including a battalion of women, many of them poorly armed and with little military training but they were so fired up that "that day the Nationalist assault columns were held at the western edge of the city that day, a victory of great psychological importance. The African army no longer appeared invincible. Republican spirits were further raised by the deployment that evening in the Casa de Campo sector of the first of the International Brigades."[16] That November 7th, 1936 should be remembered and celebrated every year all over

---

15 Jesús Hernández, *Negro y Rojo. Los anarquistas en la revolución española* [Red and Black: Anarchists during the Spanish Revolution], p. 291.
16 Antony Beevor, *The Spanish Civil War*, p. 137.

the world as the International Day of the United Left, and for what that unity, when it is practical, is capable of achieving.

Two days later, on November 9th, Neruda left Madrid after having had experiences which were decisive in his political development. The master lesson he learned during the dramatic reality of those days was the value of organization and of discipline that a major political project needed to come out on top.

During the first half of 1937 Pablo settled in Paris with Delia, where Louis Aragon put him to work on the organizing committee of the Second Congress of Antifascist Writers, scheduled for the summer in Valencia and Madrid. Besides the salary he received, which was modest, allowing him to survive those months, Neruda learned another master lesson from the French communists: to know how to organize and follow through with public political activities, an experience that later proved to be very helpful in Chile.

8

On September 1st [1939] at 4:45 in the morning Germany invaded Poland. On September 3rd England and France, united by a pact of mutual aid with Poland, declared war on the German aggressor... A few days later another pact had been signed. It provoked big discussions on the Left worldwide, especially in the communist movement: the non-aggression pact between the Soviet Union and fascist Germany. It went down in history as the Ribbentrop-Molotov Pact. It was signed on August 23rd, 1939...

That non-aggression pact had the effect in communist circles in general, and in Neruda in particular, of encouraging them to see the recently launched world war as an imperialist war... The propaganda did not negate antifascism, but Neruda did not organize nor take part in any political campaigns against fascism at that time. That only changed when the Soviet Union was attacked in 1941. But the Ribbentrop-Molotov Pact was not attacked.[17]

David Schidlowsky

Among the accusations leveled at the Stalinist poet, the one with the least amount of attention paid to Neruda's reasons is the Nazi-Soviet pact. His

---

17 Schidlowsky, *Neruda y su tiempo*, pp. 441–442.

reasons were identical to the Soviet reasons for the pact, generally ignored when dealing with this matter. Consequently, I will attempt to sum them up here.

Since the destruction of bolshevism was one of the explicit and central objectives of *Mein Kampf*, Stalin had little reason to want to sign a pact with Hitler. Indeed, the German dictator was the one who took the initiative. Why did the Soviet leader accept the terms? It is important to note that since 1935 Stalin had been proposing in vain an alliance of antifascist forces with France and England (there was only one mendacious agreement, which in fact denied the Soviet Union the ability to use military force). During this same period those two nations practiced the blind policy of *appeasement* with regards to Hitler, which culminated in the Munich pact in 1938. That stance of appeasement led to a mocking epilogue: the Nazi occupation of all of Czechoslovakia, and not only of the inhabitants of the Sudetenland.

That personal offense forced Chancellor Chamberlain to energetically guarantee the safety of Poland. Although it had not even been included in the Munich pact as a courtesy, Stalin made a final proposal for an alliance with the governments of London and Paris *in the first days of August 1939*. By contrast, the two countries sent mid-level delegates to Leningrad who had no authorization to sign any document of import. The Franco-English message could not have been more disparaging.

Meanwhile Hitler had his invasion of Poland well prepared by the beginning of September. Although the Führer despised the possibility of a serious reaction on the part of France and England after the Munich meeting, Chamberlain's latest military guarantees with regards to Poland gave Hitler pause. Germany was not prepared for a war on two fronts. And the Soviet Union had well-founded territorial demands since 1920, when Poland took advantage of the Russian Federation's weakness and annexed the western regions of Ukraine, Belorussia and Lithuania, which were then Soviet territories. Hence, if Hitler attacked Poland, the USSR could not allow the German army—since those territories were historically a part of Russia—to come close to Minsk, Kiev and Leningrad. If that would have happened Hitler would have risked finding himself at war with Poland and concurrently with France, England and the Soviet Union. That was the situation that made it vital that the Führer sign an agreement with Stalin.

The Soviet leader was initially indecisive, but the strategic advantages of the non-aggression pact, including the secret protocol that allowed him to recuperate the western regions of Poland, were all too evident. The Russians always felt it was important not to share borders with the Germans. By signing the pact with Hitler, Stalin assured that the first countries that would test the renewed German military force would be England and France. When Chamberlain understood the mistake he had made of thinking that by stimulating Hitler's anti-bolshevism and yielding to his pretentions, and the even graver error of having rejected the alliance with Stalin, it was too late.

The Nazi-Soviet pact was signed on August 23rd. The political price to be paid was extremely high. The alliance with the aggressive Nazi regime was received with panic and consternation by communists all over the world, before the internal reasons were understood. There is a portrait of this initial situation in the pages of the Cuban novelist Leonardo Padura Fuentes' now famous book about the assassination of Trotsky:

> Ramón tried to process the information, but he felt as though something was eluding him. Comrade Stalin was signing a pact with Hitler? What Trotsky had foretold had occurred?
> "What else do they say, Caridad? What else do you they say?" he yelled, standing in front of his wife.
> "That is what they say, holy shit! A deal with the fascists!"
> [...]
> "Stalin knows what he is doing, he always does. Do not worry yourself, if he signed the agreement with Hitler, it is because he has his reasons for doing it. He did it for a reason..."
> "In Concorde and Rivoli they have burnt Soviet flags. Many people are saying they are going to leave the Party, that they feel betrayed..."
> "Caridad burrowed more into the wound."
> "The damn French cannot talk about betrayal, damnit! Ribbentrop was French kissing with them here in Paris while Franco massacred the Republicans."[...]
> "A brilliant play," said Tom and he patted Ramón on the back when he passed by him. "An incredible play..." "I have not slept in two days... Sure, and you will remember that it has been a year since European democracies accepted the silence about Hitler biting off a piece of Czechoslovakia. And now they do not want Stalin to protect the Soviet Union?[18]

---

18 Leonardo Padura, *El hombre que amaba a los perros* [The Man Who Loved Dogs], pp. 439–441.

In light of the verifiable facts about French and English foreign policy, from the civil war to the Munich pact, which sought to set Germany against the Bolsheviks, and taking into account the weakness of Soviet military power in 1939 due to the abundant purges of high-ranking officers from 1937 to 1938, the Ribbentrop-Molotov pact could be justified as a type of self-defense of the Soviet Union. Accepting Hitler's offer was also a smart move by Stalin in the long run, whose effects were resounding after the Soviet victory in World War II and its wide-ranging consequences in Europe. This is not to deny for a minute the deplorable excesses, acts of villainy and crimes committed by the Red Army and additional detachments in Poland during the pact.

In March 1939 Neruda left Chile and headed to France to organize the *Operation Winnipeg*. Beginning in April he was fully concentrated on carrying out this difficult task, until the *Winnipeg* set sail on August 4th to Valparaíso, with more than two thousand Spanish refugees who disembarked in the Chilean port on September 3rd, coinciding with the beginning of World War II.

Pablo stayed in Paris until the beginning of December, meaning he commented on the Nazi-Soviet pact with Rafael Alberti—who was also in France at the time—and with the French communists. In those months he was also in touch with friends who were leaders of the Chilean CP.

As Schidlowsky underlines, Neruda did not organize nor participate in antifascist demonstrations until 1941. The French communists as well as the Chilean comrades accepted the justification of the pact the Comintern undoubtedly disseminated, and Neruda did the same from his unofficial yet de facto position. As to be expected, the communists could not explain the reasons for the pact publicly while it was still in place.

9

He wrote an ode to Stalin! A mortal sin, a pharisee vociferously charged who was waxing nostalgic about some Europeanized dictator. A pharisee who would look for the "ode to Stalin" in vain in the table of contents of Neruda's complete works. To begin, let us examine what the accused wrote about this in his memoirs:

> Many have thought I was a committed Stalinist. Fascists and reactionaries have portrayed me as Stalin's lyrical exegete. None of this irritates

me much. Any conclusions are possible in this diabolically confusing time. [...]

This has been my position: above and beyond the darkness—unknown to me—of the Stalin era, there was the first Stalin who emerged before me as a principled, affable man, sober and hermetic, a titanic defender of the Russian revolution. Besides, this small man with a large mustache grew immeasurably during the war: with his name on its lips, the Red Army attacked and pulverized the fortress of the Hitlerian demons.

However, I dedicated only one of my poems to that powerful personality. It was on the occasion of his death. Anyone can find it in the editions of my complete works. The death of the Kremlin's cyclops had an international reverberation. The human jungle was moved. My poem captured the sensation of that earthly panic.[19]

Indeed, the only poem Neruda dedicated exclusively to Stalin was titled "En su muerte" [On his death] and included in *Las uvas y el viento* [Grapes and the Wind].[20] He had first mentioned the Soviet leader in a speech as a communist senator during a meeting on June 5th, 1946. He had dedicated it to Mikhail Ivanovich Kalinin, who had died two days before. To be precise, nonetheless, a short ode to Stalin (while he was alive still, in 1948) was included as a fragment (without a subtitle) in the poem "Que despierte el leñador" [Let the Rail Splitter Awake[21]], in chapter IX in *Canto general*, where Neruda affirmed the image of that first Stalin that he recalled in his memoirs:

En tres habitaciones del viejo Kremlin
vive un hombre llamado José Stalin.
Tarde se apaga la luz de su cuarto.
El mundo y su patria no le dan reposo.
Otros héroes han dado a luz una patria,
él además ayudó a concebir la suya,

---

19 Neruda, *Confieso que he vivido* [Memoirs], pp. 370–371.
20 Neruda, *Obras completas* [Complete Works], I, pp. 998–1004.
21 Translator's note: I take this translation from *Let the Rail Splitter Awake and other Poems* (New York: International Publishers, [1989] 2001). "Leñador" could be translated as "lumberjack."

a edificarla,
a defenderla.
Su inmensa patria es, pues, parte de él mismo
y no puede descansar porque ella no descansa.
En otro tiempo la nieve y la pólvora
lo encontraron frente a los viejos bandidos
que quisieron (como ahora otra vez) revivir
el knut, y la miseria, la angustia de los esclavos,
el dormido dolor de millones de pobres.
Él estuvo contra los que como Wrangel y Denikin
fueron enviados desde Occidente para "defender su Cultura".
Allí dejaron el pellejo aquellos defensores
de los verdugos, y en el ancho terreno
de la URSS, Stalin trabajó noche y día.
Pero más tarde vinieron en una ola de plomo
los alemanes cebados por Chamberlain.
Stalin los enfrentó en todas las vastas fronteras,
en todos los repliegues, en todos los avances
y hasta Berlín sus hijos como un huracán de pueblos
llegaron y llevaron la paz ancha de Rusia.

[In three rooms in the old Kremlin / a man named Joseph Stalin lives. / The light in his room is turned off late. / The world and his homeland do not give him respite. / Other heroes have given birth to a homeland, / he helped conceive his, /to build it, / to defend it. / His immense homeland is part of him / and he cannot rest because it does not rest. / In other times the snow and the dust / found him facing the old bandits / who wanted (as they do now) to revive / the knut, and the misery, the anguish of the slaves, / the sleeping sorrow of millions of poor people. / He was against those who like Wrangel and Denikin / were sent by the West to "defend Culture." / There those defenders of executioners / left their skin, and the USSR's wide territory. / Stalin worked night and day. / But later Germans fattened by Chamberlain / came like a wave of lead. / Stalin confronted them on all the vast borders, / in all of its retreats, in all of its advances / and until Berlin his sons, like a hurricane of the people / arrived and took with them the ample peace of Russia.][22]

---

22 Neruda, *Obras completas* [Complete Works], I, pp. 998–1004.

Since Late Antiquity and during the Middle Ages the sovereigns' panegyric was based on the topic *sapientia-fortitudo*: on the one hand, knowledge, calm, intelligence, resolution of difficulties; on the other hand, force, power, manliness, courage, military skill, strategic vision.[23] This panegyric to Stalin instinctively built on this secular tradition, but subordinated knowledge and force to a superior achievement, the *constructio*: "His immense homeland is part of him / and he cannot rest because it does not rest." The praise of the emperors of Antiquity and of the kings and feudal lords of the Middle Ages took for granted a territory or an established kingdom by a dynasty or by conquest. The maximum and basic praise of Stalin that Neruda underlined was as the tireless builder of an immense homeland, developing under siege and constant threats, in a permanent *state of exception*. That was the main feat that that calm man, who worked burning the midnight oil in the three rooms in the Kremlin, pursued.

Behind this image of the constructor that these first lines portray against a background of calm wisdom and constant work, the poem traces the Captain's rapid sequence of events as a figure who fought in the first years after the Revolution against the aristocrats, official tsarists and mercenaries who tried, under the leadership of Wrangel and Denikin, to restore the *ancien régime*. In more recent years he had skillfully led the conflict against the German invader, from the first initial shock until the final victory in Stalingrad, and lastly the Red Army's overwhelming counterattack which led them into the very heart of Berlin. These were the feats of a hero who made a man "named Joseph Stalin" a Constructor.

10

Years later, when Stalin died in 1953, Neruda wrote the elegy "En su muerte" [On his Death], which was disseminated and translated all over the world, and was included in the volume *Las uvas y el viento* [Grapes and the Wind]. A lengthy text, it was introduced by the poet's personal invocation. The poem borrows from the elegiac tradition by describing the international blow provoked by the Great Leader's death:

---

23 For more details, see Ernest Robert Curtius, *Literatura europea y Edad Media latina* [European Literature and the Latin Middle Ages], pp. 252–256.

> Camarada Stalin, yo estaba junto al mar en la Isla Negra,
> descansando de luchas y de viajes,
> cuando la noticia de tu muerte llegó como un golpe de
>   océano.
>
> Fue primero el silencio, el estupor de las cosas, y luego
>   llegó del mar una ola grande.
> De algas, metales y hombres, piedras, espumas y lágrimas
>   estaba hecha esta ola.
> De historia, espacio y tiempo recogió su materia
> y se elevó llorando sobre el mundo
> hasta que frente a mí vino a golpear la costa
> y derribó a mis puertas su mensaje de luto
> con un grito gigante
> como si de repente se quebrara la tierra.
>
> [Comrade Stalin, I was next to the sea in Isla Negra, / resting from struggles and from trips / when the news of your death arrived like a blow from / the sea. // First there was the silence, the stupor of things, and later / an enormous wave came barreling in from the sea. / It was made of / seaweed, metal and men, stones, foam and tears. / It collected its material from history, space and time / and it rose weeping over the world / until before me it crashed on the coast / and a message of mourning fell at my doorstep / like an enormous cry / as if the earth had cracked suddenly.]

The following short line, "Era en 1914" [It was in 1914], gives an abrupt beginning to the body of the poem, focusing as it does on the prerevolutionary period in the capitalist world, a time of injustice and violence:

> Desde Hong Kong a Chicago la policía
> buscaba documentos y ensayaba
> las ametralladoras en la carne del pueblo...
> Olor a invierno y sangre
> emanaba de Europa
> como de un matadero abandonado.
> Mientras tanto los dueños
> del carbón,
> del hierro

del acero...
los senadores norteamericanos,
los filibusteros
cargados de oro y sangre
de todos los países,
eran también los dueños
de la Historia.

[From Hong Kong to Chicago the police / searched for documents and tried out / their machine guns on the flesh of the people... / A scent of winter and blood / emanated from Europe / like an abandoned slaughterhouse. / Meanwhile the owners / of the coal, / the iron / and steel... / the North American senators, / the filibusterers / made off with the gold and the blood / from other countries, / and were also the owners / of History.]

This is followed by the middle of the elegy in which Lenin is represented as a hero who changed this degraded world ("Cambió la tierra, el hombre, la vida. / ... / Nació una patria / que no ha dejado de crecer" [The earth, man, life changed. / ... / A homeland was born / which has not stopped growing]) and Stalin as his successor: "Lenin dejó una herencia / de patria libre y ancha. / Stalin la pobló / con escuelas y harina, / imprentas y manzanas" [Lenin left an inheritance / of a free and wide homeland. / Stalin covered it with schools and flour, / printing presses and apples]. These lines confirm and reiterate the theme of construction:

Stalin desde entonces
fue construyendo...
Los minerales
acudieron,
salieron
de sus sueños oscuros,
se levantaron,
se hicieron rieles, ruedas,
locomotoras, hilos
que llevaron las sílabas eléctricas
por toda la extensión y la distancia.
Stalin
construía.

> [From then on Stalin / went about building... / The minerales / came together, / emerged / from their dark dreams, / arose, / became railroad tracks, wheels, / locomotives, wires / that carried electric syllables / throughout the expanse and distance. / Stalin / built.]

The next part completes the main body of the poem with two stanzas about the exaltation of Stalin's pacifist and constructive legacy, elaborated in rather weak rhetoric. Nonetheless, in this regard the affinity between Neruda's elegy and the obituary Isaac Deutscher wrote of Stalin might be surprising and unexpected:

> In the arc of the three decades, the face of the Soviet Union has been completely transformed. The nucleus of Stalin's historical action consisted in finding a Russia which tilled the soil with wooden plows and left it winning the arms race. He raised Russia to the level of the second most industrial power in the world. And it was not only the pure and simple matter of material progress and organization. Those kinds of results would have been impossible to obtain without a vast cultural revolution which sent everyone in that enormous country to school to get a very complete education. [24]

II

This is not the place to reexamine the origin and the effects of Nikita Khrushchev's revelations during the XXth Congress of the Communist Party of the Soviet Union (February 1956) about the crimes and abuses the Stalin regime committed, nor is it the moment to examine the phases those denunciations went through until *Pravda* published, in June, an unsigned article from Peking (no doubt written by Mao Tse Tung in person) in which Stalin's successes were considered to outweigh his errors.[25] "To put it in the simplest of terms, the October revolution created the communist movement on a global scale, the XXth Party Congress destroyed it," summed up the Marxist

---

24 Domenico Losurdo, *Stalin. Storia e critica di una leggenda nera* [Stalin: Story and Critique of a Black Legend], p. 12. Translator's note: Deutscher (1907–1967) was a Trotskyist known for his biography of Trotsky, among many other works.
25 Roy A. Medvedev and Zores A. Medvedev, *Stalin sconosciuto. Alla luce degli archivi segreti sovietici* [Translator's note: translated into English from the Russian as *The Unknown Stalin*], p. 124.

historian Eric Hobsbawm.[26] Of course, the simplification of the subsequent history and the enemy's always active political strategy—in Latin America against Cuba in 1959, against Chile in 1973 and against Venezuela today—demand some nuance. And, indeed, the interminable case against Neruda's sins is directly or indirectly rooted in anticommunism.[27]

Returning to 1956 from one of his trips, Jorge Edwards remembers that Neruda

"disembarked from the boat in the port in Montevideo and could not answer the questions the press posed because he was absolutely aphonic. His aphonia prolonged for weeks, later disappeared, and reappeared over the years that followed. It was a curious psychosomatic malady which robbed him of the ability to speak in the most opportune or inopportune time, depending on how you look at things. I never thought this was a simple comedy, as the cynics claimed all over, but rather as the product of anguish, of an internal conflict that was much more serious."[28]

Neruda's reaction was silence (eloquent as always). He did not claim he had been betrayed or deceived. Although the shock might have been harsher for him than for other communist writers, he continued to be an active member of his party until the day he died—September 23rd, 1973—a few days after his friend the president Salvador Allende.

To be sure, there were changes in terms of his worldview, but they did not affect his presence in public but rather his poetry. He changed his poetry, not his party affiliation. Neither the Khrushchev report nor the Soviet tanks in Budapest led Neruda to take dissident positions in 1956, but it did involve recalibrating the historical optimism that had suffused the prior cycle of his

---

26 Quoted by Greg Dawes, *Multiforme y comprometido. Neruda después de 1956* [Multifarious and Committed: Neruda after 1956], p. 21.
27 Regarding how Neruda and some of his communist friends reacted to the crisis provoked by the XXth Party Congress, I refer the reader to *Multiforme y comprometido. Neruda después de 1956* [Multifarious and Committeed: Neruda After 1956], by Greg Dawes, a professor at North Carolina State University, Raleigh, North Carolina. His "Palabras iniciales" [Opening Words] include information about Ilyá Ehrenburg, Nazim Hikmet, Paul Robeson, Howard Fast, Volodia Teitelboim and others, before analyzing intelligently and in detail Neruda's case via his life and works. From a perspective that is like Dawes', I will attempt to condense my age-old reflections here.
28 Jorge Edwards, *Adiós poeta*, p. 66.

work, from "Alturas de Macchu Picchu" [Heights of Macchu Picchu] (1946) to *Nuevas odas elementales* [New Elemental Odes, 1956].

The *Tercer libro de las odas* [Third Book of Odes, 1957] was a very different book of odes: it was more of a transitional book to the radical metamorphosis of language, the imaginary and the style that was later apparent in *Extravagaria* (1958). The latter chapbook, which included illustrations, appeared in connection to the poet's new life with Matilde Urrutia. Together they had taken a long trip through Asia and Europe in 1957: a sentimental cruise, but really a pilgrimage to the places where Neruda had lived before he met the redhead, especially Rangoon, Colombo and other cities in Asia.

It was a sudden and decisive innovation with regards to his self-representation: with the *Third Book of Odes* and above all with *Extravagaria* the triumphant and totalizing figures disappeared (the Captain, the Invisible Man) that the "Yo soy" [I am] in *Canto general* had passed on to *Los versos del Capitán* [The Captain's Verses], *Odas elementales* [Elemental Odes] and *Las uvas y el viento* [Grapes and the Wind]. Moreover, the univocality of "I am," so arduously won, disintegrated unexpectedly, as much in the vertical autobiographical sense (the "muchas vidas" [many lives] of the poet) as in the horizontality of the present ("muchos somos" [we are many]).

The shock of 1956 and the poet's personal autumn (in 1954 he would have turned 50) were textualized, then, as a break and dissolution of the self incorporated on different levels: the abandonment of certainty, the acceptance of uncertainty and paradox, and the desertion of the oracular and the didactic emphases in the *Elemental Odes* and *Grapes and the Wind*. In fact, the bard renounced his earlier pretensions to be serious, untouchable or privileged, and opened up an ample space for irony, humor and even irreverence which would have been unthinkable in *Canto general*.

12

His ideological and militant priority ceased to govern the elaboration of such books as *Extravagaria, Navegaciones y regresos* [Navigations and Returns], *Cien sonetos de amor* [One Hundred Love Sonnets], books that were ruled by his love for Matilde who, paradoxically, as Greg Dawes notes, was the person most responsible for leading Neruda to reformulate his political stance in *Canción de Gesta* [Song of Protest, 1960]: "It was the shared passion that drove him to write this book of poetry dedicated to the Cuban revolution with a rekindled, but somewhat tenuous collective passion. Without abandoning for a moment nor at any moment the cause of the Soviet Union and the project of the Socialist Bloc, he explores the recent phenomenon of the Cuban revolution as a type of socialist alternative, a Latin American formulation of socialism."[29]

An event of that historical and political magnitude could not be relegated to the realm of occasional pieces. But how could he write verse about the Cuban revolution without falling into the rhetorical trope, the exaltation of the leader? Burnt by the Stalin experience and the cult of personality as it was called, Neruda did not want—and the truth is he could not, he was not up for it—write along the lines of *Canto general* or *Grapes and the Wind*, but he could not hold back his enthusiasm.

Consequently, *Canción de gesta* reflected the transaction between a light and a solemn tone: "*canción* de gesta" [present *epic poem*] not "*cantar* de gesta" [archaic *epic poem*], which might have sounded too archaic and serious.[30] Neither was *canto* because it would have evoked *canto general* and the style he had left behind. *Song* was synonymous with levity since the times of *Residence on Earth* and adapted itself better to the emerging *guajira* revolution: lively, abundant in Afro-Latin American colors and rhythm.

In keeping with that, Pablo rejected the grand solemnity and the epic tone in *Canto general* and *Grapes and the Wind* in favor of a tone which was deliberately traditional, archaic and popular. His different intentions could be discerned in particular—and with typical Nerudian subtlety—in the metric form which was constant throughout the book: the hendecasyllablic *romance*.[31] It is a brilliant exercise in Major Art versification, sustained and

---

29 Dawes, p. 26.
30 Translator's note: *Song of Protest* is the title used by translators to English and it is misleading. A more accurate translation would be *Present Epic Poem*. Neruda uses "canción" (song) in this context instead of "cantar" (an archaic epic poem in Spain, for example, *Cantar de Mío Cid Campeador*) to indicate that it is a present popular composition in line with the Spanish tradition. The tone is popular in Neruda's book, but the form is archaic (the distich). The book refers to his positive view of the Cuban revolution. Heretofore, the translation will appear in Spanish.
31 Translator's note: *Romance* is a traditional metric form in Hispanic literature that dates from the Medieval period. It consists of an indeterminate number of lines using the same number of metric syllables, generally eight-syllable lines. The rhyme is assonant in the even lines; the odd lines do not rhyme. Throughout *Canción de gesta* Neruda uses the hendecasyllable and not the more common eight-syllable line, like the *Romancero gitano* [Gypsy Ballads, 1928] by García Lorca.

monochord like the Medieval troubadour's: it was a solid yet light versification; rigorous and yet popular. Another contrast with the previous archaic form was marked subtly by the case of the invocation of the Hero (poem XIX, "A Fidel Castro" [To Fidel Castro])

> [...]
> esta es la copa, tómala, Fidel.
> Está llena de tantas esperanzas
> que al beberla sabrás que tu victoria
> es como el viejo vino de mi patria:
> no la hace un hombre sino muchos hombres
> y no una uva sino muchas plantas:
> no es una gota sino muchos ríos,
> no un capitán sino muchas batallas.
>
> [this is the glass, take it, Fidel. / It is full of so many hopes / that when drinking it you will know your victory / is like the time-tested wine of my homeland: / it is not made by one man but rather by many / and not by one grape but rather by many plants: / it is not a drop but rather many rivers, / not a captain but rather many battles.]

It does not take much discernment to understand the underlying cautionary tone, particularly as regards *a captain*, which evokes the image of the mustachioed and monumental Captain who had been given that name by Nicolás Guillén and by Neruda himself. I believe that the good faith and hopeful admiration with which Neruda—nearing the age of 60—wanted to cautiously warn a young Fidel about the dangers of revolutionary power, were misinterpreted. The Cuban leadership failed to grasp—and still fails to grasp—that Neruda was undergoing a metamorphosis as a poet and at that moment he was looking to recuperate his utopian dreams: from a personal point of view, he was very interested in seeing that the singularity of the revolution did not go by the wayside.

The book then concludes suddenly with the poem "Meditación sobre la Sierra Maestra" [Meditation on Sierra Maestra], an epilogue that seems disconnected from the book's objective as it underlines his subjective reflections. It was a reaffirmation of History and collective combat, but no longer in the vein of an intercontinental Soviet-inspired revolutionary utopia, but rather a project that underscored its Latin American and Third World vision. In other words, it underlined the fragmented or local nature of the *barbudos'* [bearded ones] revolt. Of note is the fact that Neruda placed an autobiographical synopsis in this brilliant epilogue which approached the idea of a new systematization of memories, which was very different from the autobiography with which *Canto general* ended. It is important to read the poem as a significant step towards the crucial themes taken up in *Memorial de Isla Negra* [Isla Negra].

13

In 1946 Neruda wrote the poem "El pueblo" [The People], later included in Chapter XI in *Canto general*. It was a short text from which I will quote a few lines:

> Paseaba el pueblo sus banderas rojas
> y entre ellos en la piedra que tocaron
> estuve, en la jornada fragorosa
> y en las altas canciones de la lucha.
> Vi cómo paso a paso conquistaban.
> Sólo su resistencia era camino,
> y aislados eran como trozos rotos
> de una estrella, sin boca y sin brillo.
> Juntos en la unidad hecha silencio
> eran el fuego, el canto indestructible...

   [The people ambled about with red flags / and among them on the stone they touched / there was I, on the noisy workday and in the lofty songs of struggle. / I saw how they triumphed little by little. / Resistance was their only road, / and they were isolated like shattered bits / of a star, without a voice and without any sparkle. / United in silence / they were fire, the indestructible song...]

In this text the poet-senator wrote from the point of view of someone who had a full and formidable knowledge of the image of *the people*, with whom he clearly identified. That was a correlative image of a poet who saw himself marching ahead toward his triumphant self-representation as the Captain, toward the height of the victorious *Yo soy* [I am]. To the extent that that road was seen as linked to the horizontal triumph of the Soviet socialist project, the bard faced the consequences of Khrushchev's denunciations in 1956 like a personal catastrophe, like the disastrous fall *of an idealized image of himself* which for the longest time informed his pride and his own mistaken views. In various poems in *Extravagaria*, like "A callarse" [Let us be quiet] and "No tan alto" [Not so high], the acknowledgment of the error was apparent. *Extravagaria* was the book that revealed Neruda's personal reaction under shock, with no explicit judgments regarding what had happened, but with such radical changes in terms of his style, themes and images, that they alone signaled the deep lesions of his trauma. But they were, above all, a clear indication that the wound that was open in the personal and poetic domains was as severe as in the ideological and political spheres. Ergo, Neruda did not cry betrayal or treason; ergo he never abandoned his party. The task he set before himself in the coming years was not a typical self-criticism following the communist tradition, but rather the sincere reformulation of his own poetic and personal project, which included his own role in the party.

From *Extravagaria* in 1958 to *Plenos poderes* [Fully Empowered] in 1962, Neruda's postmodern books offered more indications of the slow but firm reflections underway about Khrushchev's revelations and, at the same time, a reformulation of the ideological basis of his political commitment.

In March 1962, during the XII Congress of the Communist Party in Chile, Pablo Neruda—an active member of the Central Committee—in an unusual move, read his yet unpublished poem "El pueblo" [The People], which would be included that year in *Plenos poderes* [Fully Empowered]. It might have seemed like an extravagance on the part of a party leader particularly in an assembly which rarely entertained literary fantasy. But it was a deliberate and pertinent move. Neruda wanted to affirm his political recovery after the crisis of 1956, proposing as he did so (implicitly) a critical rereading of the poem from 1946.

In "The People" in *Fully Empowered* the poet and political leader humbly tried, and in a sense for the first time, to sketch out a personal view of that agent called the *people*, which distanced itself from his former communist rhetoric. It was an attempt on his part to design a blueprint based on his experience with miners, fishermen, and workers in many trades. It was image of what the people were and really meant to him, without presuming any prior and superior intellectual knowledge of its identity. It is noteworthy that the image of the people in this poem is not the abstract collective image or mass of 1946, but rather a single mythic figure—anonymous and changing—which incarnates the people with their infinite and totalizing variety. It is a long and great political text from which I cite the beginning:

De aquel hombre me acuerdo y no han pasado
sino dos siglos desde que lo vi,
no anduvo ni a caballo ni en carroza:
a puro pie
deshizo
las distancias
y no llevaba espada ni armadura
sino redes al hombro, hacha o martillo o pala,
nunca apaleó a ninguno de su especie:
su hazaña fue contra el agua o la tierra,
contra el trigo para que hubiera pan,
contra el árbol gigante para que diera leña,
contra los muros para abrir las puertas,
contra la arena construyendo muros
y contra el mar para hacerlo parir.

Lo conocí y aún no se me borra.

Cayeron en pedazos las carrozas,
la guerra destruyó puertas y muros,
la ciudad fue un puñado de cenizas,
se hicieron polvo todos los vestidos,
y él para mí subsiste, sobrevive en la arena,
cuando antes parecía
todo imborrable menos él.

En el ir y venir de las familias
a veces fue mi padre o mi pariente
o apenas si era él o si no era
tal vez aquel que no volvió a su casa
porque el agua o la tierra lo tragaron
o lo mató una máquina o un árbol
o fue aquel enlutado carpintero
que iba detrás del ataúd, sin lágrimas,
alguien en fin que no tenía nombre,
que se llamaba metal o madera,
y a quien miraron otros desde arriba

sin ver la hormiga sino el hormiguero
y que cuando sus pies no se movían,
porque el pobre cansado había muerto,
no vieron nunca que no lo veían:
había ya otros pies en donde estuvo...

[I recall that man and two centuries / have passed by since I saw him, / he did not ride a horse nor ride in a carriage: / he undid / distances / with his pure feet / and he carried no sword, no armor / but rather nets, an axe or a hammer or a shovel on his shoulders, / he never beat anyone of his species: his feat was against water or the earth, against the wheat so that there would be bread, / against the imposing tree so that it would provide logs, / against the walls to open doors, / against the sand constructing walls / against the sea to make it give birth. // I met him, and I cannot forget him. // The carriages fell to pieces, / war destroyed the doors and the walls, / the city was a handful of ash, / all the clothing turned to dust, / and he survives in my mind, he survives on the sand, / when all seemed indelible / except him. // In the comings and goings of families / at times it was my father or my relative / or it was not him / maybe someone who did not return home / because the water or the earth swallowed him / or a machine or tree killed him / or it was that grief struck carpenter / who followed the coffin, without shedding a tear, / someone, well, who had no name, / who was called metal or wood, / and whom others looked down on / without seeing the ant but rather the anthill / and who when his feet no longer moved, / because the poor weary soul had died, / they never saw that they did not see him: / there were already other feet walking where he had been...]

14

1964. Neruda celebrated his 60th birthday in various ways and worked assiduously on Salvador Allende's third presidential campaign. On precisely July 12th Gonzalo Losada turned in the edited version of the fifth and last volume of *Memorial de Isla Negra* [Isla Negra] (a gift the poet gave himself to celebrate his own birthday) and in September the Theater Institute at the University of Chile staged his translation of *Romeo and Juliet* to celebrate Shakespeare's 400th birthday on October 10th.

That fifth volume of *Isla Negra* was subtitled *Sonata crítica* [Critical Sonata], which represented a return to the term *sonata* that Neruda had used in *Residence on Earth*. It was used for poems based on experiences he had left behind however tormenting, which is the case here with "El episodio" [The Episode]. It is a long poem that summed up and ended his critical and personal reflections which he had been developing since the *episode* in 1956.

From the title of the poem on, Neruda want to clearly establish that the Stalin regime, with its crimes, abuses and treachery that Khrushchev had denounced,[32] constituted a long and terrible phase of a much larger historical and political movement which was self-critical and had the will to overcome the *episode*. His intention in using the term *episode*, then, was not to downplay the gravity of what had happened, but rather to reply to those, like his enemies, who could not have cared less about the courage and the fate of the communist movement and who pressured Neruda for years with questions and temptations designed to distance him from his party.

Given the limitations of space, I cannot here carry out a detailed analysis of a poem which is as long as it is crucial and decisive, and which, furthermore, can stand on its own and needs no commentary. Consequently, I urge the reader to read it in its entirety. Nevertheless, I will share here some observations about some of the passages I have chosen. In the introduction:

Hoy otra vez, buenos días, razón...
Hoy otra vez, aquí me tienes, compañero:
con un sueño más dulce que un racimo
atado a ti, a tu suerte, a tu congoja.
Debo abolir orgullo, soledad, desvarío,
atenerme al recinto comunal y volver
a sostener el palio común de los deberes.

[Today, once again, good morning, reason... / Today, once again, here I am, comrade: / with a dream that is sweeter than a bunch of grapes / tied to you, to your fate, to your anguish. / I need to abolish pride, loneliness, delirium, / live within the communal domain and hold fast / to the task of common goals.]

---

32 Khrushchev had revealed lies and misinformation of which the poet and the world were unaware at that point.

Clearly, the bard stepped away for a time in order to then forge a new self in place of the old self (*Yo soy* [I am]), wounded and in pieces. To do so he had to "abolish pride, loneliness, delirium." Only then could he become fully empowered.

> Qué pasó? Qué pasó? Cómo pasó?
> Cómo pudo pasar? Pero lo cierto
> es que pasó y lo claro es que pasó...
> Ay la sombría bandera que cubrió
> la hoz victoriosa, el peso del martillo
> con una sola pavorosa efigie!
> Yo la vi en mármol, en hierro plateado,
> en la tosca madera del Ural
> y sus bigotes eran dos raíces,
> y la vi en plata, en nácar, en cartón,
> en corcho, en piedra, en cinc, en alabastro,
> en azúcar, en piedra, en sal, en jade,
> en carbón, en cemento, en seda, en barro,
> en plástico, en arcilla, en hueso, en oro,
> de un metro, de diez metros, de cien metros,
> de dos milímetros en un grano de arroz,
> de mil kilómetros en tela colorada.
> Siempre aquellas estatuas estucadas
> de bigotudo dios con botas puestas
> y aquellos pantalones impecables
> que planchó el servilismo realista.
> Yo vi a la entrada del hotel, en medio
> de la mesa, en la tienda, en la estación,
> en los aeropuertos constelados,
> aquella efigie fría de un distante:
> de un ser que, entre uno y otro movimiento,
> se quedó inmóvil, muerto en la victoria.
> Y aquel muerto regía la crueldad
> desde su propia estatua innumerable:
> aquel inmóvil gobernó la vida.
>
> [What happened? What happened? How did it happen? / How could it happen? But it is / true that it happened, and it is clear that it happened... / Oh somber flag that covered the victorious sickle, the

weight of the hammer / with only one dreadful effigy! / I saw it made of marble, silvery steel, / the rough wood of the Urals / and his thick mustache was two roots, / and I saw it made of silver, mother of pearl, cardboard, / cork, stone, zinc, alabaster, / sugar, stone, salt, jade, / coal, cement, satin, mud, / plastic, clay, bone, gold, / a meter long, ten meters long, one hundred meters long, / two millimeters in a grain of rice, / a thousand kilometers of red cloth. / Always those plastered statues / of the mustachioed god with his boots on / and with those impeccable trousers / that ironed servile realism. / I saw that frigid effigy of a distant person / at the entrance of a hotel, in the middle / of a table, in a store, in a station, / in starry airports: / a being who, at one moment or another, / became immobile, dead with the victory. / And that dead person reigned cruelly / from his own countless statues: / that immobile one governed life.]

Neruda based his critique of Stalinism on what he had verified personally during his trips to the USSR, on what he had seen without seeing: the cult of personality beneath the countless statues and the effigies, and only alluded in a general way to the crimes, the executions, the purges and other forms of oppression. But I suspect that the focus on the statues, the cult of personality centered on Stalin, was also, concurrently, a secret way of carrying out a self-criticism with regards to the statue-like figures with which his poetry portrayed his own development up to 1956, as I have noted already. The "Yo Soy" [I am] of *Canto general*, the Captain and his verse, the Invisible Man of the elemental odes, and other permutations sooner or later would have led Neruda to a dead end, to become an immobile statue in his own right. Those figures disappeared abruptly and forever beginning with *Extravagaria*, without an explanation from the author.

In the middle of "The Episode" there is a section titled "El dolor" [The Grief] about how the role of the leader was altered, and another titled "Nosotros callábamos" [We kept silent], where the poet recognized that the communists kept silent when faced with the indications and denouncement of what was happening in the USSR under Stalin, until truth imposed itself and things were rectified.

Saber es un dolor. Y lo supimos:
cada dato salido de la sombra
nos dio el padecimiento necesario:
aquel rumor se transformó en verdades,

la puerta oscura se llenó de luz
y se rectificaron los dolores.
La verdad fue la vida en esa muerte.
Era pesado el saco del silencio.
Y aún costaba sangre levantarlo:
eran tantas las piedras del pasado.
Pero fue así de valeroso el día:
con un cuchillo de oro abrió la sombra
y entró la discusión como una rueda
rodando por la luz restituida
hasta el punto polar del territorio...
Y aquel camino duramente errado
volvió, con la verdad, a ser camino.

[To know is to suffer. And we knew it: / every fact that emerged from the shadows / gave us the necessary suffering: / those rumors became truths, / the dark door shone with light / and the suffering was rectified. / The truth was life in that death. / Silence's sack was weighty. / And lifting it was a bloody struggle: / there were so many stones in our past. / But that is how that valiant day was: / a golden knife cut through the shadows / and discussion began like a wheel / rolling through the restored light / and reached the polar extremes of that territory... / And that road riddled with errors / came into view, with the truth, and became a road again.]

15

After this period, Neruda ended his years of reflection about the episode with two solemn and unequivocal reaffirmations: one was political, the other personal. The first was called "Los comunistas" [The Communists] and it relied on the first-person plural:

Los que pusimos el alma en la piedra,
en el hierro, en la dura disciplina,
allí vivimos sólo por amor
y ya se sabe que nos desangramos
cuando la estrella fue tergiversada
por la luna sombría del eclipse.
Ahora veréis qué somos y pensamos.

Ahora veréis qué somos y seremos.

[Those of us who put our soul into stones, / into steel, and hard discipline, / lived there only for love / and it is well-known that we lost blood / when the star was twisted / by the somber moon's eclipse. / Now you will see who we are and what we think. / Now you will see who we are and who we will be.]

This personal reaffirmation in 1964—which he held until his death—was his definitive response to his open and covert enemies: "Todos ellos quisieron que bajara / de la altura de mi abeja y mi bandera / y que siguiendo el signo del crepúsculo / declarara mi error y recibiera / la condecoración del renegado" [All of them wanted me to step down / from the heights of my bee and my flag / and follow the sign of dusk / and declare the error of my ways and receive / the honor of being a renegade]:

Así el poeta escogió su camino
con el hermano suyo que apaleaban:
con el que se metía bajo tierra
y después de pelearse con la piedra
resucitaba sólo para el sueño.

Y también escogió la patria oscura,
la madre de frejoles y soldados,
de callejones negros en la lluvia
y trabajos pesados y nocturnos.

Por eso no me esperen de regreso.
 No soy de los que vuelven de la luz.

[And so the poet chose his road / with his brother whom they beat: / with the one who submerged himself beneath the earth / and after struggling with the stones / resuscitated only to sleep. // And he also chose his dark homeland, / mother of beans and soldiers, / dark, rainy alleys / and heavy and nocturnal work. // So do not wait for my return. / I am not the kind who returns from the light.]

16

A personal testimony. I was one of the eight people who with Matilde held a vigil for Neruda in the large room in La Chascona the night of the 24th and

25th of September 1973.[33] The house had been outrageously vandalized. They had not stolen anything. There was only the will to destroy. Broken windows, a grandfather clock disemboweled, paintings slashed with knives, so many objects and curiosities on the floor or thrown into the channel, there was no cup or glass from which to drink water, no beds, the mattresses had been gutted. Nor was there any light, which is why we had a candlelight wake, like an authentic and poor man's wake in the South. Wrapped in blankets, we spent that cold night around Pablo's cadaver.

Besides Matilde: Laurita Reyes, Elena Nascimento, Aída Figueroa, Enriqueta de Quintana, Juanita Flores, a couple who were Matilde's relatives and whose names escape me, and I were there for the wake. Nobody else. At nine in the morning, we faced the sadness of having to remove the poet's body crossing over the water that had flooded the entry way and the first floor. When we managed to remove the casket on to Chucre Manzur street, a group of people was waiting, and they joined our funeral procession to the cemetery.

I stayed behind to lock the house up, and on La Paz Avenue I joined the funeral procession, which had grown a lot, in a part of the procession which included mainly teachers, writers, artists and other intellectuals. I have to confess that I was fearful when the people around me started singing "The Internationale", almost all with their fists in the air, even those who had never even given a thought to being communists, Pablo's writer friends or admirers or just simple people. Maybe they thought that there was no better way to express what they felt. On both sides of the procession, soldiers armed with cocked rifles or machine guns lined the street.

Francisco Coloane's booming voice spread across the procession regularly with "Comrade Pablo Neruda" to which we responded "Present, now and forever!", but suddenly the invocation changed to "Comrade Víctor Jara!", and all of our voices cracked because it was the first time that Víctor's name was being shouted in public, which was the equivalent of denouncing an assassination which the newspapers and media in general had not reported on: "Present, now and forever!", we answered as best as we could. Shortly thereafter a silence overtook us and right away, as if recovering, Pancho's booming voice yelled at the top of his lungs and enunciating every word: "Comrade... Salvador...Allende!"

---

33 Translator's note: The author is referring to Neruda's house in the Bellavista neighborhood in Santiago, which is where the Pablo Neruda Foundation is located today.

Our response was something like a hoarse shout, broken, distorted by the emotions and the terror and also by the determination to let everybody hear us: "Present...now and forever!" I was walking on the outside flank of the procession. I closed my eyes, waiting for a burst of gun fire less than two meters away from me; at no other point in my life did I think that my time was up as then. For much less than what we had just done people had been assassinated, disappeared, jailed, tortured. Maybe the presence of foreign journalists saved us. The curious thing is that at that moment we got over our fear, because there was nothing more to do, we had gone beyond the bounds, and so, singing loudly, all of us crying, we entered the General Cemetery.

That was the communist poet's last battle. It was the first public demonstration against the dictatorship. For years, the only one in which people yelled the name of President Allende, and with soldiers surrounding us. It was Neruda's posthumous battle and, like the legend of The Cid, he won.

An Additional Sin

Bourgeois

O N JUNE 30th, 1969, in front of the cameras of the University of Chile's Channel 9, Pablo Neruda, poet and presidential candidate of the Republic, was interviewed by four well-known journalists at that time, of different political stripes: Julio Lanzarotti, Augusto Olivares, Emilio Filippi and Carlos Jorquera. The last question was:

EMILIO FILIPPI: *Some young people on the Left accuse you of being bourgeois, of living very comfortably and of watching the revolution go by with the eyes of a poet. What do you think of those charges?*

PABLO NERUDA: They have accused me of so many things in my life that another accusation does not bother me much. I have a political position, I belong to a party, and I have intensely experienced every political campaign my party has had in our country. During the last election campaign, I covered the map from San Felipe to Aysén talking to folks on the roads, in the marketplaces, the plazas and the schools. Is that what a bourgeois poet does? Is that sitting very comfortably and watching the revolution go by? To those who accuse me: let us compare. What do they do and what do I do? Am I not committing myself consciously and with all my energies, and my life, and most of my work to the cause of political and social change in my country?

As far as my commitment is concerned, can you not understand that a committed poet like me has had to face the other side's many attempts to entice or corrupt me? And where are my betrayals? Let us be clear then. It is easy—especially for the youth—to say that we are old, that we have become bourgeois. Okay, I would ask them to do all that I have done and continue to do in the literary and political terrains. I am 65 years old. If they can show an example of another poet who at my age is doing what I am doing, then please come forward![1]

---

[1] From the interview published in *El Siglo* [The Century], Santiago, 7/13/1969. Translator's note: *El Siglo* is the newspaper of the Chilean Communist Party.

'Archives' on Josie Bliss

(1928)

Neruda and generations of critics analyzing his life and work have filled reams of paper with descriptions of Josie as exotic, passionate, animalistic and homicidally jealous. Behind all these descriptions, however, is an absolute void: we lack not just the archival evidence to corroborate this particular version of Josie, but the evidence to suggest that there was ever any Josie at all.

Roanne Kantor, 2014: 60

Josie Bliss may not have existed at all, except in Neruda's writings and a few anecdotes he told friends later on.

Perhaps Neruda invented her evocative name to embellish his story... To this day no one knows her real name, and there is no official trace of any "Josie Bliss" [...] no one has come forward with any proof of her existence. There are no photographs. And while it is not surprising that he wouldn't mention her in any of his letters to his sister and mother, it is puzzling that someone who took up so much of his emotional time and energy didn't even once appear in all the frank correspondence he had with Héctor Eandi.

Mark Eisner, 2018: 163–164. (In the following paragraph after this passage, Eisner quotes Kantor's paragraph included above.)

The Main Archive

I KNOW A MAN IN Santiago who some 15 years ago brought me an *archive* proving that Josie Bliss existed in Rangoon in 1928. His name is Manuel Basoalto and in 2014 he directed and produced the film *Neruda*, about the fugitive poet from the henchmen of Gabriel González Videla (it came out before Pablo Larraín's on the same topic). We have been long distance friends, and I have seen him two or three times since then. He is a very active man, always wrapped up in some project or another, and extremely elusive: he frequently changes his emails, and it is almost impossible to find his telephone number and know where he lives. If you happen to run into him, if you are lucky, you will be able to exchange a few phrases with him when he suddenly slips away near a wall and turns the corner, as if someone were after him. Darío Oses can back up my view of Manuel Basoalto's behavior, who, besides was related to Neruda on his mother's side—Rosa Basoalto.

One morning before 2006 (maybe in 2002 or 2004) I ran into him at *La Chascona*, the main office of the Neruda Foundation. Strangely, he stopped to tell me about some of his projects and to show me a block of twenty or thirty aged pieces of paper—from a registry for internal use only from the local YMCA in Rangoon, as Olivares notes—with single-spaced typewritten text. They were the remains, maybe the only ones left, of the infinite reams of paper (yet these were real) that Álvaro Hinojosa placed in the portable typewriter carriage, page after page, day after day for many years, a record of his notes on the typewriter that accompanied him to Rangoon in 1927. Neruda remembered that his friend's bible was Joyce's *Ulysses*, which he read and reread continually hoping to imitate it someday. When they disembarked in Rangoon and they settled in a hotel room, Neruda went out to see the port[1] and left Álvaro feverishly typing his diary of the arrival.

The sheets Manuel placed in my hands—for fifteen or twenty minutes—contained fragments of the notes about the friends' time in Rangoon. More precisely, about the days leading up to their parting of ways and Álvaro's trip to Calcutta, where—in all likelihood—he wrote those notes using the rest of the paper from Rangoon. I knew about those passages thanks to what Edmundo Olivares had transcribed. It begins this way: "Things were getting definitely bad because Mamea was younger than I had imagined. I could pick her up, but not easily."[2] *Mamea* was obviously Álvaro's Spanish transcription of the name of his own Burmese lover. But the passage Olivares transcribed did not include the corresponding transcription of the "hidden Burmese name" of Pablo's lover.

Identifying that missing name was a long sought-after dream I pursued in my work and came about thanks to the pages Manuel showed me—noting that he was in a hurry (for a change)—and which I frenetically searched until I found the passage Olivares transcribed. It was hard to believe that the name Josie would not be nearby. And, indeed, as I imagined, the names of the two

---

1 "Rangoon 1927" in *Isla Negra*.
2 Olivares, *Pablo Neruda. Los caminos de Oriente* [Pablo Neruda: His Trail in Asia], 2000, pp. 151–152.

lovers (Álvaro's and Pablo's) appeared together on the same page, if not in the previous paragraph, and, bowled over, I memorized Josie's forever, which in Álvaro's writings was *Mañoté*. There were Mamea and Mañoté.

Álvaro alluded to Mañoté as his girlfriend's friend, who was also on the young side, but had a difficult and dominating character and treated Pablo almost as though he were a "slave" (that is how he put it, literally on that page). Although Álvaro was surely exaggerating because he was in a bad way with his travel companion and about to leave for Calcutta, it is believable that our poet behaved in a submissive way vis-à-vis Mañoté. First, because he never raised his voice and argued with women (I was a witness to this in the case of more than one conflict he had with Matilde, when I was guest or lodger at Isla Negra), and also because he received from Mañoté incomparable sexual gratification, besides lodging and the delicious Burmese meals she made which he would recall with particular delight. One could object that Pablo had no alternative, given his terrible financial situation of going without a paycheck for almost six months. But if he accepted his difficult partner's behavior for several months it was because he was truly in love with her. And for the first time he was living out the dream—which was not at all radical— of domestic bliss (pardon the pun) he had yearned for all his life: to enjoy the company of a beautiful woman and an expert in the kitchen and in bed. Consequently, I am convinced that Mañoté and Matilde Urrutia were, among the many women with whom Neruda had spent time, the ones he loved most during his lifetime.

Unfortunately, Manuel did not want to lend me those papers (I do not know how he got them nor what has happened to them), but I swear on my word that that *archival record* exists, that I had those copies in my hands and that I examined some of them for too short a time but it was sufficient enough to affirm without a shadow of a doubt that Álvaro Hinojosa wrote what I read.

Josie Bliss' Elusive Burmese Name

In the spring of 2002 or 2004 I returned to Italy obsessed with the name *Mañoté* in Hinojosa's papers. A colleague at the University of Sássari, with whom I talked about the matter, lent me his edition in Italian of George Orwell's *Burmese Days*—which was out of print—with helpful notes by Giovanna Caràcciolo, among them very interesting notes about names in Burma.[3]

---

3 (Milan: Longanesi, 1975).

I deduced that Orwell could well have transcribed the name *Mamea* from the form *Ma May* (Ma Hla May in *Burmese Days*) and the name *Mañoté* from the name *Ma Nyo Teh*, which I came up with.[4] For the first time Josie Bliss' elusive Burmese name took on an at least approximate printed form. And thanks to Álvaro's papers it documented the existence and identity of a woman Neruda declared to have loved in Rangoon ("I fell in love with a native of Burma").

I recently read the article "Josie Bliss, la amante birmana de Pablo Neruda" [Josie Bliss, Pablo Neruda's Burmese Lover],[5] which includes some paragraphs concerning Josie's possible name. The author went to Myanmar (formerly Burma) and personally inquired about the information she reported. Dr. Enrique Robertson informed her of the name *Mañoté*. He found that information in my 2006 or 2014 books[6], where it appeared for the first time. I quote a few paragraphs from Eda Cleary's article:

> In the name system in Burma last names do not exist. Everyone has a name based on the day and time they were born. Sometimes words are added to the names which denote the wishes of the parents of the child at birth or describe his or her appearance. All women under the age of 30 are given the prefix *Ma*, which means something like "Miss."
>
> This gives the first hint with regards to the name *Ma-ño-té*. *Ño* follows. In consulting with the Burmese, *Ño* might correspond to *Nyo*, which means "brown" and which would confirm the thesis that Josie was from Mandala where people generally have a darker pigmentation than in other parts of the country.
>
> We are left with the last part of her name: *Té*. In Burmese *Thein* means "rich" and also "Friday" in its the transcription as in *Thinn*. Armed with this information we can interpret the Chileanism *Ma-ño-té* as *Ma Nyo Thein* in Burmese, which would mean 'a young woman born on a Friday with brown pigmentation and who is going to be rich.' Josie was probably called *Ma Nyo Thein*.

---

4 For more details, see Hernán Loyola, *Neruda. La biografía literaria* [Neruda: The Literary Biography], pp. 340–341.

5 In *El Mostrador*, 9/4/2015. Translator's note: *El Mostrador* is an important online newspaper in Chile.

6 Translator's note: the author is referring to *Neruda. La biografía literaria* [Neruda: The Literary Biography] (Santiago: Editorial Planeta Chilena / Seix Barral, 2006) and *El joven Neruda 1904–1935* (Santiago: PenguinRandomHouse / Lumen, 2014).

Naturally, I was very glad to verify that my hypothesis in 2006—*Ma Nyo Teh*—was not far off from this second attempt in 2015, formulated in the place where the events happened. It is unfortunate that Eda Cleary treats the Josie Bliss case with ill will and prejudices against Neruda, which are similar to Roanne Kantor's and Mark Eisner's, and, like their studies, lacks a more informed reading of and information about *Residence on Earth*.

Archival Records

The parable of the love story, passion and flight of Neruda, with regards to Josie Bliss was recorded in a series of poems in *Residencia on Earth* (volume 1) which, were deliberately placed as an anti-chronological story (as explained above) and avoided an open narration of that love affair. The idea was to encourage the reader to take in the independent poems and not the corresponding episodes associated with mounting erotic passion, which would lead to a final *dénouement* consisting of the breakup and his escape. It is absolutely crucial to recognize that Neruda was incapable of writing a novel according to the conventions of his time. His only achievement on that terrain, *The Inhabitant and his Hope* (1926), was really a sequence of poetic episodes in prose.

Yet at the same time his poetic work was always, in the end, a cryptic autobiographical narration in verse, particularly in *Residence on Earth*, until he penned *España en el corazón* [Spain in the Heart, 1937–1937] and began his great project *Canto general de Chile* [Chile's General Song, 1938] which introduced History into his writing. Based on that notion, I plan to quickly analyze the texts from *Residence on Earth* (volume 1) having to do with Josie Bliss as if they were personal documents, in other words, as a grouping of archival records, but without sidestepping their poetic virtues. Deciphering this hermeneutic will allow the reader to confirm how the sequence of these poems (which the book placed deliberately in an anti-chronological order) showed the presence of his Burmese lover in the development of the poet's writing plans, and, in passing, certified her existence.

According to the order in which they were composed, the texts of interest are: "La noche del soldado" [The Soldier's Night], "Juntos nosotros" [Together], "Sonata y destrucciones" [Sonata and Destruction], "El joven monarca" [The Young Monarch], "Entierro en el Este" [Burial in the East], "Diurno doliente" [Daytime Suffering], "Tango del viudo" [The Widower's Tango] and "Arte poética" [Ars Poetica]. The last two were written in

Calcutta, the rest in Rangoon and all between May (or June) and December 1928.

A Love Archive

Pablo met Josie when Álvaro and he returned from the sojourn that took them to Tokyo during the first few months in 1928. Back in the heat and tedium of Rangoon—probably some day in April—the uninhibited Álvaro met up with Mamea and Mañoté on the street or in some bar o tea salon, and somehow learned that they spoke English. Pablo was timid and would not have dared approach them. They invited them to have a drink and that is how it all began.

No matter how they met exactly, Josie Bliss' presence became more significant and made it more difficult for Pablo to continue living with Álvaro, as the latter noted in his papers.[7] A return to poetry meant that Pablo needed the sexual and sentimental life that the unexpected Josie was willing to give him, but Álvaro, even more than normal, made life impossible for him at that moment.[8] Until, I assume around the end of April or the first half of May 1928, when his traveling companion left en route to Calcutta. At that point Pablo was able to resume his writing and life as he wished:

> Yo hago la noche del soldado, el tiempo del hombre sin melancolía ni exterminio, del tipo tirado lejos por el océano y una ola, y que no sabe que el agua amarga lo ha separado y que envejece... Por cada día que cae, con su obligación vesperal de sucumbir, paseo, haciendo una guardia innecesaria, y paso entre mercaderes mahometanos, entre gentes que adoran la vaca y la cobra, paso yo, inadorable y común de rostro...
>
> Entonces, de cuando en cuando, visito muchachas de ojos y caderas jóvenes, seres en cuyo peinado brilla una flor amarilla como el relámpago. Ellas llevan anillos en cada dedo del pie, y brazaletes, y ajorcas en los tobillos, y además collares de color, collares que retiro y examino, porque yo quiero sorprenderme ante un cuerpo ininterrumpido y compacto, y no mitigar mi beso.

---

7 Olivares, pp. 151–152.
8 For more details, see Neruda, *Confieso que he vivido* [Memoirs], pp. 94–95.

[I play the soldier's night, a time in which a man feels no melancholy or extinction, like a guy who is far afield from the ocean and a wave, and does not know that the bitter water has separated him and made him age... With each falling day, with its unusual obligation of succumbing, I walk, acting like an unnecessary guard, and I wander through Muslim markets, among people who adore cows and cobras, I pass by, unadorable and a common face...

Then, once in a while, I visit young women with fresh eyes and hips, beings in whose hair a yellow flower flashes like lightning. They wear rings on every toe on their feet, and bracelets, and bangles on their ankles, multicolored necklaces which I remove and examine, because I want to be surprised by an uninterrupted and compact body, and not mitigate my kiss.[9]

"The Soldier's Night" represented Neruda's process of falling in love followed by an anguished sense of being disoriented and lost in the horizon— which the passage above suggests with the use of verbs connoting movement without any end in mind (I *walk, pass by, cross, wander from one place to another*) which Pablo tended to use for that purpose, such as in the last stanza of "Walking around"—in a strange reality that the versemaker crossed full of interest, searching for a way out of his creative paralysis, of the Soldier's senseless watch.

The word *entonces* [then] connected this discourse of straying to a sequence of erotic encounters, whose explicit images were an important novelty in Neruda's poetry, as was the use of the plural in place of the singular, a recurring synecdoche in *Residence on Earth* (especially in titles of such poems as "*Enfermedades* en mi casa" [Illnesses at Home] or "Melancolía en *las familias*" [Melancholy in Families]). Here the "young women with fresh eyes and hips" are, in truth, only one: the plural form allowed Neruda to introduce into the highest level of his poetry, in disguise, a particular and unique woman who unquestionably was Josie Bliss. That type of strategy went along with his reticence at that time to identify and especially *name* people who were alive and with whom he shared an intense emotional bond (whether by way of love with a woman or a friendship) in his best poetry, destined to survive the test of time. Written when the Andalusian was alive in 1935, the "Oda a Federico García

---

9 Neruda, "The Soldier's Night" in *Residence on Earth*.

Lorca" [Ode to Federico García Lorca] was a rare and significant exception. It was a "safety standard" in his poetry, that explains why he never named Josie nor wrote anything about her, not even in his letters to his loyal friends Eandi or González Vera. It was not due to the presumed inexistence of that woman, as Kantor, and likewise her subaltern Eisner, imagine.[10] We will get to a subsequent confirmation of my hypothesis later, dealing with when Pablo not only named his lover but also put her in a privileged place: nothing less than in the title "Josie Bliss" of the final poem of *Residence on Earth*. For the moment let us return to "The Soldier's Night":

> Yo peso con mis brazos cada nueva estatua, y bebo su remedio vivo con sed masculina y en silencio. Tendido, mirando desde abajo la fugitiva criatura, trepando por su ser desnudo hasta su sonrisa: gigantesca y triangular hacia arriba, levantada en el aire por dos senos globales, fijos antes mis ojos como dos lámparas con luz de aceite blanco y dulces energías. Yo me encomiendo a su estrella morena, a su calidez de piel, e inmóvil bajo mi pecho como un adversario desgraciado, de miembros demasiado espesos y débiles, de ondulación indefensa: o bien girando sobre sí misma como una rueda pálida, dividida de aspas y dedos, rápida, profunda, circular, como una estrella en desorden.
>
> [I weigh each new statue with my arms, and I imbibe her living remedy with masculine thirst and in silence. Stretched out, looking at the fugitive creature from below, scaling her naked being up to her smile: giant and triangular upwards, raised in the air by her two global breasts, still before my eyes like two lamps with white oil light and sweet energies. I entrust myself to her brown star, to the warmth of her skin, and immobile under my chest like a hopeless adversary, with limbs that are too dense and weak, with a defenseless wave: or else turning herself around like a pallid wheel, divided between vanes and fingers, quick, profound, circular like a star in disarray.]

Never before had Neruda written such an explicit narrative account of making love, so audacious with regards to his aristocratic poetic parameters which did not concede any space to the "danceable or amusements" nor to the easy route to an erotic tale. The poetic representation of sexuality was a delicate matter for avant-gardist poets, who risked plunging into the vulgar or

---

10 Eisner, pp. 163–164.

risqué. The Soldier's transgression was the clearest indication of his growing involvement with her:

> Ay, de cada noche que sucede, hay algo de brasa abandonada que se gasta sola,
> y cae envuelta en ruinas, en medio de cosas funerales. Yo asisto comúnmente a esos términos, cubierto de armas inútiles, lleno de objeciones destruidas. Guardo la ropa y los huesos levemente inpregnados de esa materia seminocturna: es un polvo temporal que se me va uniendo, y el dios de la sustitución vela a veces a mi lado, respirando tenazmente, levantando la espada.
>
> [Oh, of every night that elapses, there is something like an abandoned ember which consumes itself, and falls enveloped in ruins, among funereal things. I witness those endings often, covered with useless weapons, full of destroyed objections. I keep my clothes and bones slightly impregnated with that semi-nocturnal matter: it is a temporary dust which becomes part of me, and the god of substitution keeps watch sometimes at my side, breathing tenaciously, raising his sword.]

The key to understanding this enigmatic continuation of the erotic sequence (and the conclusion to the text) are the terms *ruins, destroyed objections, semi-nocturnal matter* and in particular *the god of substitution*.[11] The "fugitive creature" tumbled ("enveloped in ruins, among funereal things") the poet's resistance to substitute his "perturbed origins" with a new founding of his writing. In vain the speaker armed himself with weapons and put forth objections: they were slowly destroyed, night after night, by a new '*diurnality*': "a day of nocturnal and diurnal forms is almost always looming over me." In so doing an irresistible *semi-nocturnal matter* (similar to but opposed to the Night of yesteryear) permeated him and urged him to be born again among the destruction. That Seduction, that plan of attack, was called Josie Bliss.

Archive for the Epithalamion

The jubilant and sunny "Juntos nosotros" [Together]—unique among the poems in *Residence on Earth*—besides switching from prose to verse, spoke

---

11 See: "nada *ha substituido* mis perturbados orígenes" [nothing *has substituted* my perturbed origins], from the poem "Sistema sombrío" [Somber System] written shortly before.

to the formation of the couple, the celebration of living together. "Together" was an epithalamion, nuptial song which sealed the act of Pablo's living with a woman for the first time. The poem took on a three-part structure: a self-portrait of the poet as the cornerstone, situated between two other blocks that traced an image of his beloved, one of them at the beginning of the poem:

> Qué pura eres de sol o de noche caída,
> qué triunfal desmedida tu órbita de blanco,
> y tu pecho de pan, alto de clima,
> tu corona de árboles negros, bienamada,
> y tu nariz de animal solitario, de oveja salvaje,
> que huele a sombra y a precipitada fuga tiránica.
>
> [How pure you are of sun or nightfall, / how immeasurably triumphant your white orbit, / and your lofty breasts' offering, / your crown of black trees, my love, / and your lone animal-like, wild sheep-like, nose, / which smells like a shadow and like a hasty tyrannical flight.]

"It was her, dressed in white"—so Pablo described her in his memoirs, contrasting with her dark hair (*your crown of black trees*), and incarnating a mix of sweetness, fire and fury. Without any explicit reference to the first of these, the next block midway through the poem inscribed an enthusiastic ode to the Self (with resonances of Whitman):

> Ahora, qué armas espléndidas mis manos,
> digna su pala de hueso y su lirio de uñas,
> y el puesto de mi rostro y el arriendo de mi alma,
> están situados en lo justo de la fuerza terrestre.
> Qué pura mi mirada de nocturna influencia,
> caída de ojos oscuros y feroz acicate,
> mi simétrica estatua de piernas gemelas
> que sube hacia estrellas húmedas cada mañana,
> y mi boca de exilio muerde la carne y la uva,
> mis brazos de varón...
>
> [Now, what splendid weapons are my hands, / how worthy their shovel-like bones and lily-like nails, / and the stand of my face and the leasing of my soul / are placed just right among earthly forces. / How pure my gaze of nocturnal influence, / fallen dark eyes and fierce spur, / my symmetrical statue of twin legs / which rise to damp stars every

morning, / and my exiled mouth bites flesh and grape, / my masculine arms...]

This proud and vigorous self-portrait expressed the poet's joy on having found in foreign lands the Lady whose support he needed to resume his poetic mission. Hence the symbolic allusion in the first line to action, to writing: "Now, what splendid weapons my hands." And the following section (two sequences) returned to Josie with Major Art [Arte Mayor] lines that by themselves paid a tribute by placing her on the *prophetic level* in Pablo's writing.

Y tú como un mes de estrella, como un beso fijo,
como estructura de ala, o comienzos de otoño,
niña, mi partidaria, mi amorosa,
la luz hace su lecho bajo tus grandes párpados
dorados como bueyes, y la paloma redonda
hace sus nidos blancos frecuentemente en ti...
  [And you like a month of star, like a fixed kiss, / like the structure of wing, or the beginning of fall, / girl, my partisan, my amorous one, / light makes its bed under your large eyelids / golden like oxen, and the round dove / often makes her white nests in you...]

In Neruda's poetic code the formula *juntos nosotros* [together] was a textual acknowledgment of a serious loving commitment, and its jubilant modality was the sign of the intimate integration or reunification of two realms he never conceived of as divided: love (=dreams) and poetry (=action). Neruda's work prior to this time had not included a poem with the implications this one had. And it would take the appearance of Matilde Urrutia for there to be a new *together* in his future work.

The Archive of Substitution

In 1944 Tomás Lago jotted down Pablo's allusion to his life with Josie Bliss:

I had a life somewhat apart from the English, I only went to their parties once in a while, because there were not many interesting people among them. They were boring and even ignorant. I had moved to another neighborhood which was working-class and included the Burmese. I lived with Josie Bliss, who had been my secretary and with whom I had arguments once in a while.[12]

This evocation—arbitrarily disqualified by Kantor and Eisner—insinuated that a good deal of time had gone by since Álvaro had left, and that period overlapped with Neruda's sending two very important letters—the first to his Chilean friend José Santos González Vera (August 6th) and the other to his Argentine friend Héctor Eandi (September 8th). The latter included originals of three poems: "The Soldier's Night", "Together" and "Sonata and Destructions". After complaining about the climate and his boredom (*"the climate is burning me, I curse my mother and my grandmother, I spend long days talking to my cockatoo, I pay rent for an elephant. The days fall on my head like blows, I do not write, I do not read...an authentic ghost"*), in both letters Neruda declared, nonetheless, that he was coming alive, that there had been a qualitative leap in the quality of his literary work. In short, he had begun to put into place a *substitution* of his foundation, whose triumphant sign *was the title change for the project he had begun in Chile*. Both letters pointed it out in a similar way and with obvious pride. To González Vera he wrote:

> That said, my few poems of late, for almost a year now, have reached a level of great perfection (or imperfection, but within the realm of what I have hoped for). In other words, I have gone beyond the literary limits I never thought I would be capable of surpassing, and to be frank the results have surprised me and consoled me. My new book will be titled *Residence on Earth* consisting of forty poems that I would like to publish in Spain. All have the same movement, the same intensity, and developed in the same region of my head, like persistent waves. You will see how I manage to establish an equidistance between the abstract and the living and what type of sharply suitable language I use.[13]

And to Héctor Eandi he wrote:

> But, really, do you not find yourself surrounded by destructions, deaths, annihilated things? In your work, do you not feel obstructed by difficulties or impossibilities?

---

12 Tomás Lago, *Ojos y oídos. Cerca de Neruda* [Eyes and Ears: By Neruda's Side], p. 60.
13 Neruda, *Obras completas* [Complete Works], V, p.p. 1026–1027.

Right? Well, I have decided to form my strength in this danger, take advantage of this struggle, use these weaknesses. Indeed, this depressing time, fatal for many, is noble matter for me. [...] I have almost finished a book, *Residence on Earth*, and you will see how I am able to isolate my expression, making it vacillate constantly among dangers, and how persistently I make it appear as a solid and uniform substance, as a single force.[14]

These two letters document, for the first time, the title *Residence on Earth* for the book he was working on and which, a few months earlier (in a letter to Yolando Pino Saavedra, December 1927) Neruda had titled *Colección nocturna* [Nocturnal Collection]. And they supplied indirect documentary evidence also that he came up with that splendid new title during the period in which he was most in love with Josie Bliss. The third poem sent with the Eandi letter, "Sonata and Destructions"[15], corresponded to the act of *substitution*, whose formulation was as much elegiac as it was programmatic (an affirmation of the figure of the *witness* or *sentry*). Without Josie Bliss, and the passion she inspired in Neruda (and without her material support, which helped him survive), there is no explanation for the active and enthusiastic rebirth that the *substitution* project entailed. It follows that those letters and the poems I have referred to should be part of the *archival record* or an element of proof to demonstrate that Josie really did exist.

As strange as it might seem, those letters and poems provide proof that the title *Residence on Earth*, today seen as the well-made formulation of Neruda's ingrained materialism, in fact emanated from Josie Bliss. It was the formula with which the bard named her, not daring to call her by her name yet: because within the code of *Dreams*, dependent on the Night-South symbolic system (and on the mythic space of *Cantalao*[16]) which ruled over his prior work and which demanded a sublimation or oblique angle of the erotic, there was no place for Josie Bliss. Then, due to the pressures of falling in love, of

---

14 Neruda, *Obras completas* [Complete Works], V, p. 938.
15 The term *sonata* in the titles of the *Residence* poems alluded to something left behind, but not without suffering.
16 Translator's note: Cantalao is the name of a mythic place which sounds like a Mapuche word, and which was supposedly located in southern Chile. Neruda came up with this invented place in *The Inhabitant and his Hope* (1926). Once he settled in his house in Isla Negra, he bought some adjacent land next to the Pacific Ocean which was designed as a residence for poets and named Cantalao.

passion, Neruda *lowered* his life-poetry from the aristocratic heights of his dreams to the concrete and *earthly* nature of his real circumstances. Accepting those circumstances meant being down to earth, residing in Rangoon with Josie Bliss at the expense of leaving behind *"abandonados dormitorios donde habita la luna, / y arañas de mi propiedad, y destrucciones que me son queridas"* [abandoned bedrooms where the moon dwells, / and spiders that belong to me, and destructions that are dear to me]. A new take off platform for his writing, equivalent to the substitution of the Night-South foundation for the Day-Seduction foundation: "y un día de formas diurnas y nocturnas está casi siempre detenido sobre mí" [and a day of diurnal and nocturnal forms is always hovering over me], he declared during the initial phase documented in "The Soldier's Night".

> Acecho, pues, lo inanimado y lo doliente,
> y el testimonio extraño que sostengo
> con eficiencia cruel y escrito en cenizas,
> es la forma de olvido que prefiero,
> el nombre que doy a la tierra, el valor de mis sueños,
> la cantidad interminable que divido
> con mis ojos de invierno, durante cada día de este mundo.
> [So, I lie in wait of the inanimate and the suffering,
> and the strange testimony which I bear,
> with cruel efficiency and written on ashes,
> it is the form of forgetting I prefer,
> the name I give to the earth, the value of my dreams,
> the endless quantity I divide
> with my wintry eyes, every day of this world.]

This final stanza of "Sonata and Destructions"—which was the poem destined to bring the first compilation of *Residence* to a close, organized in Rangoon—condensed the plan of substitution, of his future poetics. *Acecho, pues, lo inanimado* [So, I lie in wait of the inanimate]: alludes to the surrounding colonial world, *inanimate* because it is immobile, placed on the margins of History by the Indian Empire, as he wrote to Eandi from Batavia. *Suffering*, in the double sense of the suffering of others and the suffering of the self. The *strange testimony which I bear*: Josie's love compensated for having to live in a strange, foreign land that did not stimulate Pablo's *prophetic* propensity. Yet with heroic rigor (*with cruel efficiency*), the poet began to bear witness to what was strange to him and, besides, *written in ashes*, that is, over the destructions of the old foundation.

This *substitution* would later face some severe difficulties (from which the poet would flee), but the revolution it unleashed in Pablo's writing was, nonetheless, irreversible.

The Archive of Production

With the poem "Entierro en el Este" [Burial in the East] Pablo initiated the task of bearing testimony in the domain of *substitution*. He wrote it in August or September in Josie Bliss' house, which I assume was located near the Irrawaddy, where he was able to see the Burmese funeral rites on the shores of the river:

> Yo trabajo de noche, rodeado de ciudad,
> de pescadores, de alfareros, de difuntos quemados
> con azafrán y frutas, envueltos en muselina escarlata:
> bajo mi balcón esos muertos terribles
> pasan sonando cadenas y flautas de cobre...
> Porque una vez doblado el camino, junto al turbio río,
> sus corazones...
> rodarán quemados, con la pierna y el pie hechos fuego,
> y la trémula ceniza caerá sobre el agua,
> flotará como ramo de flores calcinadas...
>
> [I work at night, surrounded by the city, / by fishermen, by potters, by the burnt deceased / with saffron and fruit, enveloped in scarlet colored muslin: / beneath my balcony those terrible dead ones / pass by playing chains and copper flutes... / Because once you turn the corner, next to the murky river, / their hearts... / will roll, burnt, with their legs and feet on fire, / and the trembling ash will fall on the water, / it will float like a bouquet of scorched flowers...]

The poet excluded himself from this rendering, limiting himself to depicting a live and detailed funeral ceremony with the richness of visual and auditory aspects, colors and sounds, the stridency of the flutes, tam-tam and the ash-covered dancers' yelling, thus capturing the movement of a ritual which was as fascinating as it was terrible. It is a poem written with the art of a chronicler, with the duty of he who bears witness, and on the one hand, it differed from the prose-poetic texts of *Anillos* [Rings] and is closest to "Oda de invierno al río Mapocho" [Winter Ode to the Mapocho River] which ten years later inaugurated his writing in *Canto general de Chile* [Canto General of Chile]. Another stylistic debt Neruda owed to Asia, and in this case thanks to Josie Bliss.

But the thematic thrust of "Burial in the East" did not continue. The other product of his new poetry was "El joven monarca" [The Young Monarch], a text that abandoned the collective outlook to return to the personal domain in a different register. Without naming her, Josie Bliss returned to his prose writing, this time as the protagonist of the ongoing domestic and erotic scenario. It was a continuation of "Juntos nosotros" [Together] and a celebration of their consolidated cohabitation.

> Patria limitada por dos largos brazos cálidos, de larga pasión paralela, y un sitio de oros defendidos por sistema y matemática ciencia guerrera. Sí, quiero casarme con las más bella de Mandalay, quiero encomendar mi envoltura terrestre a ese ruido de la mujer cocinando, a ese aleteo de falda y pie desnudo que se mueven y mezclan como viento y hojas.
>
> [Homeland limited by two long and warm arms, with long parallel passion, and her site of gold defended by a system and by a warrior's precise science. Yes, I want to marry the most beautiful woman from Mandalay, I want to entrust my earthly cover to that sound of the woman cooking, that flapping of dress and naked foot that move and intertwine like wind and leaves.]

Applying the term *homeland* to Josie meant seeing in her a space in which he could find his roots. More to the point, and in the same sense, Pablo would call her *patria en que sobrevivo* [the homeland in which I survive] in his next poem, "Diurno doliente" [Daytime Suffering]. That woman who not only drove away solitude and cooked expertly, but also knew how to be an ongoing life and soul of his senses (there is a parallelism explicitly referred to: "two long and warm arms, with long parallel passion, and a place where her site of gold is defended by a system and by a warrior's precise science"). But something was missing in this festive situation and the end of the text insinuates it for the first time:

> Y mi esposa a mi orilla, al lado de mi rumor tan venido de lejos,
> mi esposa birmana, hija del rey.

Su enrollado cabello negro entonces beso, y su pie dulce y perpetuo: y acercada ya la noche, desencadenado su molino, escucho a mi tigre y lloro a mi ausente.

[And my wife on my shore, beside my rumor from afar, / my Burmese wife, daughter of the king. // Her rolled up black hair I then kiss, and her sweet and perpetual foot: / and with night near, its mill unchained, I hear / my tiger and cry for my absent one.]

With this out of tone ending Neruda showed a crack in the *substitution* process. However, this poem in prose was another result of this project, an attempt to make it function on the habitual egocentric plane, but in a strange setting. As noted, our poet's ability to *nerudize* his lived experience, communicate it using his own and recognizable poetic code, rejecting in so doing an attempt to *orientalize* (in Darío's way or any other writers' way)—as in "Burial in the East"—is worthy of admiration.

The Archive of a Crisis

The title of the following poem, "Daytime Suffering", alludes to a crisis in Pablo's life with Josie Bliss. She was the incarnation of the Day, whose positive symbolic valence (which was formerly associated with the Night) was key during the *substitution*. The writing of the poem came after the happy period in which he wrote letters to González Vera and Eandi and included the enclosed poems. This suggests that the dates of composition spanned between the end of September and the beginning of October of 1928. The first few paragraphs of the section dedicated to explaining his flight from Rangoon in his memoirs refer to that period:

> I had problems in my personal life. My sweet Josie Bliss became more intense and passionate until she became sick with jealousy. Had it not been for that, I might have continued by her side indefinitely. I felt a sense of tenderness for her naked feet, the white flowers that shone on her dark hair. But her temperament often led her to a wild boiling point. She was jealous and had an aversion to the letters I received from afar; she would hide my unopened telegrams; she looked at the air I breathed with rancor.
>
> At times I was awakened by a light, a ghost moving outside the mosquito net. It was she, dressed in white, brandishing a long and sharp

indigenous knife. It was she walking around the edge of my bed with half a mind to kill me.[17]

The relationship with Josie underwent a crisis on September 8th, which was when Pablo dated a letter to Eandi. He was still proud of the energy and the valid and broad horizon he was giving his poetic creation. That energy was nurtured by the loving relationship which he suddenly lost, weakening his defenses with regards to the latent assault of tenacious ghosts associated with his recollections, places and experiences in the past, forms and figures that his prophetic ambition unexpectedly returned and that threatened the prevailing calm:

> y en lo fresco que baja del árbol, en la esencia del sol
> que su salud de astro implanta en las flores,
> cuando a mi piel parecida al oro llega el placer,
> tú, fantasma coral con pies de tigre,
> tú, ocasión funeral, reunión ígnea,
> acechando la patria en que sobrevivo
> con tus lanzas lunares que tiemblan un poco.
>
> [and in the freshness beneath the tree, in the sun's essence / which its starry health implants in the flowers, / when pleasure arrives to my golden skin, / you, coral ghost with tiger's feet, / you, funereal occasion, igneous reunion, / threatening the homeland in which I survive / with your lunar lances which tremble a bit.]

The wordsmith knew the ghost, he addressed him with the familar "tú" [you]. Who was that "coral ghost" who during pleasurable days barged in "with tiger's feet", with the same tiger feet evoked at the end of "Young Monarch" (*escucho a mi tigre y llora a mi ausente* [I listen to my tiger and cry over my absent one])? It was, no doubt, the ghost of what had been left behind, the ghost from the past that made its way through the fissure suddenly appearing in his relationship with Josie in his daily life. That fissure offered many faces and nostalgia (hence the ghost was choral, like "*ese coro de sombras*" [that choir of shadows] which appear in "Tango del viudo" [The Widower's Tango]). It also included ferocious demands (*with tiger's feet*) for prophetic action—which the *substitution*, now weakened, was no longer capable

---

17 Neruda, *Confieso que he vivido* [Memoirs], p. 106.

of reaching. Moreover, it included a court of dreams and sorrows that were extinguished (*the funereal occasion*) and the intermittent mixture of creative and passionate fire (*igneous reunion*). The following stanza confirms this hypothetical reading:

> Porque la ventana que el mediodía atraviesa
> tiene un día cualquiera mayor aire en sus alas,
> el frenesí hincha el traje y el sueño el sombrero,
> una abeja extremada arde sin tregua.
> Ahora, qué imprevisto paso hace crujir los caminos?
> Qué vapor de estación lúgubre, qué rostro de cristal,
> y aún más, qué sonido de carro viejo con espigas?
> Ay, una a una, la ola que llora y la sal que se triza,
> y el tiempo del amor celestial que pasa volando,
> han tenido voz de huéspedes y espacio en la espera.
>
> [Because the window through which noon passes / has more air under its wings any day, / delirium fills the suit and dreams the hat, / a bee burns intensely without respite. / Now, what unforeseen step makes the roads crunch? / What vapor from a somber season, what crystal face, / and even more, what sound of an old cart with wheat? / Oh, one by one the wave that cries and the salt that breaks into pieces, / and the time of celestial love that goes flying past, / have had the voice of guests and the space to wait.]

The first four lines allude to a happy period which is condensed in the "*bee* [which] burns intensely without respite," where bee is equated with vital reverberation: "a symbol of the fervor for life, of the loving or Bacchian or Dionysian delirium."[18] The following lines point instead to the wobbly emotional state via memories that invaded and disturbed the space of daily seduction incarnated in Josie Bliss. On the surface these things that seemed insignificant, like the "*vapor from a lugubrious railway station*" (linked to the night train to Santiago, or to José del Carmen Reyes' cargo train), or that "*sound of an old cart with wheat,*" were in fact persistent memories from his childhood: "Frente a mi casa el agua austral cavaba / hondas derrotas, ciénagas de arcillas enlutadas, / que en el verano eran atmósfera amarilla / por donde *las carretas* crujían y lloraban / embarazadas con nueve meses de trigo" [In front of my house the

---

18 Alonso, *Poesía y estilo de Pablo Neruda* [Pablo Neruda's Poetry and Style], p. 217.

southern water dug / deep tracks, mournful clay bogs, / that in the summer were yellow atmosphere / along which the oxcarts crunched and cried / pregnant with nine months of wheat].[19] "A través de la lluvia, veo por la ventana que *una carreta* se ha empantanado en medio de la calle" [Through the rain and the window I see a bogged down *oxcart* in the middle of the street].[20] The formula *salt that breaks into pieces* condenses the negative transition because *salt*, in the symbolic code of *Residence on Earth*, takes on a meaning similar to the expression "salt of life" or the biblical expression "salt of the earth." In other words, it takes on a positive denotation. *Salt that breaks into pieces* was, then, the opening of fissures in his happiness.

The Archive of his Flight

The texts I have analyzed up until now form a parabola of love that Neruda was incapable of writing in narrative form, nor was he interested in doing so. But the texts reinforce the possibility of reading "The Widower's Tango" as the *dénouement* of a very real story. The cryptic form the story takes on makes it all the more real (precisely because his intent is not to captivate or deceive, but rather to hide) and it naturally leads to the separation of the lovers.

By October the relationship with Josie became untenable and Pablo decided to flee without telling her anything, among other things because he feared his lover's fury. From Calcutta, the General Chilean Consul in the region (his immediate superior) let him know about the possibility of a transfer, prompted by Álvaro Hinojosa, who lived in that city and with whom Pablo had reconnected. "Preparé mi viaje en secreto, y un día, abandonando mi ropa y mis libros, salí de la casa como de costumbre y subí al barco que me llevaría lejos. / Dejaba a Josie Bliss, especie de pantera birmana, con el más grande dolor" [I prepared my trip secretly, and one day, I abandoned my clothes and my books and left the house as I used to do and boarded the ship which would take me far away. / I was leaving Josie Bliss, a kind of Burmese panther, with the greatest heartache.][21]

Once on the ship, he began to write "The Widower's Tango", unquestionably one of Neruda's finest poems, if not his greatest. He finished it in

---

19 Neruda, XV, in *Canto general*.
20 Neruda, *Confieso que he vivido* [Memoirs], p. 19.
21 Neruda, *Confieso que he vivido* [Memoirs], p. 19.

Calcutta between November and December 1928. The poem's title had to be *ironic* to counter (via the term *tango*) the impertinent infraction of the avant-garde's aristocratic poetics. By elevating a private cry of love to the highest level of his writing (as the 'popular' Argentine *tango* often does)…, Neruda was committing that transgression. For him the term *widower* cannot be explained unless it is tied to the story the preceding poems traced, and, specifically, the conjugal status that the epithalamion "Together" and the domestic "The Young Monarch" attributed to Josie Bliss ("I want to marry the most beautiful woman of Mandalay").

> Oh Maligna, ya habrás hallado la carta, ya habrás llorado de furia
> y habrás insultado el recuerdo de mi madre
> llamándola perra podrida y madre de perros,
> ya habrás bebido sola, solitaria, el té del atardecer
> mirando mis viejos zapatos vacíos para siempre…
> [Oh, *Maligna*,[22] you will have already found the letter, and you will have cried in fury / and you will have insulted memories of my mother / calling her a rotten dog and a mother of dogs, / you will have already had your afternoon tea, alone / looking at my empty shoes forever…]

The vocative *Oh, Maligna* seems to be a sign of rejection announcing and delineating the separation, but later on it is reiterated in the context of "the greatest heartache," the loss of one's beloved:

> Maligna, la verdad, qué noche tan grande, qué tierra tan sola!
> He llegado otra vez a los dormitorios solitarios,
> a almorzar en los restaurantes comida fría,
> y otra vez tiro al suelo los pantalones y las camisas,
> no hay perchas en mi habitación, ni retratos de nadie en las paredes.
> [*Maligna*, truth be told, how large this night is, how lonely this earth! / Once again I have returned to solitary rooms, / to have a cold lunch in restaurants, / and once again I throw my pants and shirts on the floor, / there are no hangers in my room, nor photos of anybody on the walls.]

Hence, I confirm that the vocative *Maligna* was not, as it might seem at first glance, an aggressive or condemnatory way of concealing the name (or names) of the woman he abandoned, but rather *an affectionate and ironic*

---

22 In this case too *Maligna* is a term of endearment.

nickname, as were the Nerudian nicknames years later for Matilde Urrutia (la *Patoja*, la *Chascona*). The internal contradiction in *Maligna* predicts and condenses the central paradox of the Subject who ferociously suffers the loss he provoked, which is confirmed in fact—despite the lament—with the use of the present tense in the text.

The measure of that loss is weighed by what the Subject would give up to get his *Maligna* back, which the poem organizes hierarchically in three ascending steps: 1) "Cuánta sombra de la que hay en mi alma daría por recobrarte" [How many *shadows* in my soul I would give to have you back!], that is, how much of my nocturnality I would give up; 2) "Daría *este viento del mar gigante* por tu brusca respiración / oída en largas noches sin mezcla de olvido" [How much of *this giant sea's wind* I would give up for your brusque breathing / I heard on long nights with no mixture with oblivion!], that is, the relationship of the Subject with Nature; 3) the third stage carries the ironic nature of the poem to the extreme:

Y por oírte orinar en la oscuridad, en el fondo de la casa,
como vertiendo una miel delgada, trémula, argentina, obstinada,
cuántas veces entregaría este coro de sombras que poseo,
y el ruido de espadas inútiles que se oye en mi alma,
y la paloma de sangre que está solitaria en mi frente...

[And to hear you urinate in the dark, at the back of the house, / as though you were pouring thin, tremulous, silver, obstinate honey, / how many times I would surrender this chorus of shadows I possess, / and the sound of useless swords that can be heard in my soul, / and the bloody dove that lies alone on my forehead...]

Pablo would exchange the most precious aspects of his poetic activity for Josie's most humble physiological activity. Paradoxically, it was an aristocratic route to elude the possibility of showing his emotional heartbreak, wanting to hear her "brusque breathing" again (a sign of a soul who is sleeping) formulated the physical dimension (sensual and sexual) of the loss; wanting to "hear you urinate" expressed their love's tenderness and feelings. All the Subject would give up for her is equal to the essence of his poetic world and his mission, which is summed up eloquently in the final lines of the *tango* ("this chorus of shadows I possess...the sound of useless swords...the bloody dove that lies alone on my forehead"). In other words, the highest value possible.

The Negation of Substitution Archive

Pablo was overjoyed to meet up with Álvaro Hinojosa again in Calcutta, where he was able to observe the great Congress of India which took place there that very December of 1928 (and not 1929, as Neruda mistakenly noted in his memoirs), and able to see the elderly Mahatma Gandhi.

But above all in Calcutta he wrote the significant poem "Arte poética" [Ars Poetica], shortly after completing "The Widower's Tango". This conjecture on my part—given that there are no "archives" or documents to confirm it—became a certainty when I was working on the critical edition of *Residence on Earth*.[23] There was a secret, hidden link that no one had seen and that nonetheless became clear via multiple signs, beginning with the common metric respiration and rhythmic versification in addition to the evident affinity with regards to images and symbols. I would even suggest that Pablo must have deliberately planted those hints leading to the hidden and unstated connection. Both poems use lines pertaining to Major Art, starting with 13 syllables and then turning to 16, 18, 19 syllables. When read aloud the musical and rhythmic agreement between the two texts is evident:

> Entre sombra y espacio, entre guarniciones y doncellas,
> dotado de corazón singular y sueños funestos,
> precipitadamente pálido, marchito en la frente,
> y con luto de viudo furioso por cada día de vida [...]
> como un camarero humillado, como una campana un
>   poco ronca
> como un espejo viejo, como un olor de casa sola
> en la que los huéspedes entran de noche perdidamente ebrios,
> y hay un olor de ropa tirada al suelo, y una ausencia de flores,
> posiblemente de otro modo aún menos melancólico...
>
> [Between shadows and space, between garrisons and damsels, / endowed with a singular heart and terrible dreams, / precipitously pallid, a withered forehead, / and carrying mourning like a furious widower of every day in life [...] / like a humiliated waiter, like a slightly hoarse bell, / like an old mirror, like the smell of a solitary house / which the lodgers enter hopelessly inebriated at night, / and there is a smell of

---

[23] (Madrid: Cátedra, 1987).

clothes thrown on the floor, and an absence of flowers, / maybe in another even less melancholic way...]

This "Ars Poetica" (the first poem so titled in Neruda's work) begins with the self-portrayal of the Subject who has just fled and lost a love, from which there springs the *shadow* and *space* interspersed. Whereas "*between garrisons and damsels*" could refer to the two Chilean rogues' situation: they were surviving in Calcutta like extras in the local film industry, which was already being developed in this period. The formula "*mourning like a furious widower*" is the phrase that most explicitly speaks to the connection between this poem and "The Widower's Tango" (the *widower* plays Josie's *furies*), but "*the smell of a solitary house*" and especially "*the smell of clothes thrown on the floor, and an absence of flowers,*" also where the nostalgia of flowers in Josie's cylindrical hair (see "The Young Monarch") stands in for "there are no hangers... nor photos of anyone on the walls." This painful confession (which takes up two thirds of the poem) diminishes yet it is substantiated in the ironic transitional line, "maybe in another even less melancholic way...," which set things up for the final purposeful sequence.

> pero, la verdad, de pronto, el viento que azota mi pecho,
> las noches de substancia infinita caídas en mi dormitorio,
> el ruido de un día que arde con sacrificio,
> me piden lo profético que hay en mí, con melancolía,
> y un golpe de objetos que llaman sin ser respondidos
> hay, y un movimiento sin tregua, y un nombre confuso.
> [but, frankly, the wind suddenly lashes my chest, / the nights full of infinite substance fall in my bedroom, / the sound of a day which burns with sacrifice, / they ask for the prophetic in me, with melancholy, / and there is a knocking of objects that call without being answered, / and a non-stop movement, and a confusing name.]

The nights without Josie in Calcutta became ever more bitter. And the days even worse, ever more solitary without his *verandah*, without his unforgettable dining room, without the objects he loved and with which he filled the house next to the Irrawaddy. Hence Neruda's need to balance his leaving Ma Nyo Teh with the solemn affirmation of his *prophetic* mission. Examining the poet's path from 1927 until his return to Chile in 1932, I did not find any other reason which would justify his writing "Ars Poetica", a classical and demanding title that a prudent Neruda was careful to avoid up until that point. There is no other "Ars Poetica" in his previous work, although there were moves in the direction of the *ars poetica*, like the fifth of the *Twenty Poems* or the eleventh poem in *Attempt of the Infinite Man*.

While Neruda adjusted the elegy to the now defunct substitution with "Widower's Tango", in the case of "Ars Poetica" he looked to affirm the *negation of substitution*, that is, the principle of the poet's duty (the *prophetic* purpose: "the prophetic in me") at the expense of the pleasure principle (the *erotic* destiny). The powerful title "Ars Poetica"—as well as the title *Residence on Earth*—came about because of Josie Bliss.

More 'Archives' on Josie Bliss

(1932–1935)

"como un párpado atrozmente levantado a la fuerza
estoy mirando"
[like an eyelid atrociously and forcefully lifted
I am watching]
Agua sexual [Sexual Water]

Memory and Eroticism

WHY DID NERUDA DECIDE to end the second volume of *Residence on Earth* [1925–1935] with the poem "Josie Bliss", written in Madrid between February and March of 1935? Why did that poem deserve such a privilege some six years after the poet had seen Josie Bliss for the last time on the docks in Colombo? And more to the point, why did Neruda decide in 1935 to *name* his Burmese lover in 1928 for the first time by giving that title to his hermetic poem?

It bears repeating that the title "Josie Bliss" was an enigma for readers of *Residence on Earth* (save for a few insiders who were the bard's friends) until Neruda revealed the fact in one of his autobiographical chronicles in 1962 in the Brazilian journal *O Cruzeiro International*. Only then did it become common knowledge that Josie Bliss was the *Maligna* in the "Widower's Tango".

All of Neruda's work was, in a certain sense, a difficult exercise in recovering his memories. Until *Residence on Earth 1*, his recollection made great strides in representing his childhood (for example, in the essay "Provincia de la infancia" [Province of my Childhood] 1924), but in that same period memory and sexuality occupied two different spheres. For Pablo explicit eroticism continued to be thematically an ordinary or vulgar matter, missing that 'aristocratic' artistry typical of the poetic avant-garde in the first decades of the 20th century. Therein the irony in the case of the "Widower's Tango", whose title was an attempt to excuse himself in 1928 for the (implicit) infraction of writing a poem that the author knew was intensely erotic and sentimental.

During the crisis at the beginning of 1930, in Wellawatta, Neruda's (poetic and epistolary) writing dealt with sexual matters with an unusual frankness, but without committing it to memory. The poems "Caballero Solo" [Gentleman Alone] and "Ritual de mis piernas" [My Legs' Ritual] implied a *horizontal* acknowledgment of his sexuality, his laying siege to his growing objective of documenting himself.

The months of 1928 in which he lived with Josie Bliss were an extreme and violent manner of discovering his own body, his own physical self, but after a period of sensual and creative elation (whose culminating moment was the invention of the title *Residence on Earth*, as we have seen), the bard ended up rejecting completely the act of internalizing his self-discovery. Indeed, his escape from Rangoon could be interpreted as an unconscious result of the terrible fear toward his own barely glimpsed sexuality (and not, as he contended, toward the kitchen knife Josie Bliss held in her hand). Moreover, this would explain his refusal to accept the passionate Burmese woman into his life again in Wellawatta in 1929, and also, the disastrous decision to get married quickly in Batavia in 1930.

At the beginning of 1934, the three-part erotic work penned in Buenos Aires—"Oda con un lamento" [Ode with a Lament], "Material nupcial" [Nuptial Matter] and, above all, "Agua sexual" [Sexual Water]—represented a qualitative and convergent leap by proposing a first stage of *vertical* recognition of the poet's sexuality, an initial exploration of the enigmas, contradictions, achievements, failures, censorship and oversights in his sexual *history*. Above all, it was a total immersion into the conflictive and dark areas of the Subject's sexual memory without pleasures or delights in the erotic zone. It proceeded in a difficult and painful way: "como un párpado atrozmente leavantado a la fuerza / estoy mirando" [like an eyelid atrociously and forcefully lifted / I am watching] ("Sexual Water"). All this introspective work was the result of a final dark and unconscious goal: to free up access to his memory—that is, access to his writing—regarding the most traumatic of his sexual memories: Josie Bliss.

Archive of the Abandoned Dining Room

New Year's in 1935 caught Pablo's life in the midst of dealing with Malva Marina's irreversible illness and the unhappy marriage to Maruca. Those were sorrows that could only be alleviated by his soirées with Federico and other friends and his affair with Delia del Carril. Nonetheless, from that private tragedy a poem emerged that attempted to breathe some fresh air into the asphyxiating situation via a new immersion into nostalgia: "Melancolía en las familias" [Melancholy in the Families]. Here, Neruda took up the theme of "Sexual Water" again and resumed the submersion into his memories in order to free up the most repressed and frightening of them, and record that in his writing. Here are some of the pertinent passages.

> No es sino el paso de un día hacia otro,
> una sola botella
> andando por los mares,
> y un comedor adonde llegan rosas,
> un comedor abandonado
> como una espina: me refiero
> a una copa trizada, a una cortina, al fondo
> de una sala desierta por donde pasa un río
> arrastrando las piedras. Es una casa
> situada en los cimientos de la lluvia,
> una casa de dos pisos con ventanas obligatorias
> y enredaderas estrictamente fieles.
>
> [It is no more than the passing of one day to the next, / only one bottle / traveling the seas, / and a dining room where roses arrive, / an abandoned dining room / like a thorn: I mean / a shattered glass, a curtain, at the end / of a deserted living room where a river passes by / carrying stones with it. It is a house / situated on the foundation of rain, / a two-story house with mandatory windows / and strictly faithful creepers.]

The poem had begun with these lines: "Conservo un frasco azul, / dentro de él una oreja y un retrato" [I keep a blue jar / and in it an ear and a portrait], where the image of the *jar* tended to circumscribe the space of his memories, a space defined as *blue*: "Blue, for me, is the most beautiful color. It implies human space, like the celestial dome, toward liberty and happiness."[1] The vestiges of a certain character, a prosaic *ear* (voice) to take away from the romantic feeling one might have, and a *portrait*, to evoke a face.

---

1 Neruda, *Confieso que he vivido* [Memoirs], pp. 114–115.

Jar as well as *bottle* are metaphors associated with being imprisoned, suffocating, pressing against the outside. Here the text confers a traditional meaning to the message in *only one bottle traveling the seas,* evoking the unique experience from afar of traveling the immense expanse of the oceans, and pursuing its addressee implacably.

The reiterated image of the *abandoned dining room* refers to a specific scene: Josie Bliss' house in Rangoon in 1928, near the Irrawaddy river, whose living room and dining room were at the center of the couple's daily life with its armchairs, rugs, furniture, plants. There Pablo read and wrote, there the lovers talked and drank glasses of whiskey before eating, there they had their "afternoon tea" ("Widower's Tango") and listened to Paul Robeson records. There, no doubt, they touched each other sensually, there Josie offered Pablo her most refined erotic Oriental knowledge, as the prose in "The Young Monarch" suggests, pretending to defend the delight of her sex (*where the site of gold is defended*) with exciting wisdom, and with a cunning dose of energy (*a warrior's precise science*). And the panther from Rangoon was also a very capable housewife. That unforgettable dining room was the axis of Neruda's first experience living with a woman.

The *abandoned dining room* and the *shattered glass* reemerged together thirty years later, in a poem penned in 1964: "a través del mundo me esperaba. / Yo no llegué jamás, pero en las *copas* / vacías, / en el *comedor* muerto / tal vez se consumía mi silencio, / mis más lejanos pasos" [she waited for me across the world. / And I never arrived, but in the empty / *glasses,* / in the dead *dining room* / maybe my silence, my most distant steps / were consumed ("Amores: Josie Bliss", in *Isla Negra*)]. And the poem "Josie Bliss", which, as we have seen, concluded *Residence on Earth*, had allusions to the "estrellas de cristal desquiciado" [stars made of despairing *crystal*] (the shattered glass), to "*enredaderas* sollozantes" [sobbing creepers] and the "color que el *río* cava" [color that the *river* excavates]. The final stanza of "Melancholy in the Families" put an emphasis on the dining room image:

Pero por sobre todo hay un terrible,
un terrible comedor abandonado,
con las alcuzas rotas
y el vinagre corriendo debajo de las sillas,
un rayo detenido de la luna,
algo oscuro, y me busco

una comparación dentro de mí:
tal vez es una tienda rodeada de mar
y paños rotos goteando salmuera.
Es sólo un comedor abandonado,
y alrededor hay extensiones,
fábricas sumergidas, maderas
que sólo yo conozco,
porque estoy triste y viajo,
y conozco la tierra, y estoy triste.

[But above all there is a terrible, / terrible abandoned dining room, / with broken bottles of olive oil and vinegar flowing beneath the chairs, / arrested moonlight, / something dark, and I look / for a comparison within myself: / it might be a tent surrounded by the sea / and ripped kitchen towels dripping with salt water. / It is only an abandoned dining room, and around it there are expanses, / submerged factories, wood / that only I know, / because I am sad and I travel, / and I know the earth, and I am sad.]

"Melancholy in the Families" was indeed the liberating text which finally unblocked his suffocated memory.

The Archive of the Blue Sonata

The poem "Significa sombras" [It Signifies Shadows], a solemn affirmation of his life and poetic purpose, concluded the first volume of *Residence on Earth*. At the end of the second one, by contrast, Neruda placed a romantic text, "Josie Bliss", destined to rescue—from the perspective of 1935—the sad ending at the docks in Colombo in 1929 of their passionate love story, lived in Rangoon throughout 1928. No poem in the first volume made reference to that farewell. Neruda evoked that episode in the sixth part of his autobiographical chronicles published in the journal *O Cruzeiro International* (1962) and with some modifications, in his memoirs, *Confieso que he vivido* [Memoirs]:

> Something disturbed those days consumed with sun. Unexpectedly, my Burmese lover, the torrential Josie Bliss, appeared in front of my house. She had traveled from her distant country. Since she thought rice only existed in Rangoon, she came carrying a bag of rice, with our favorite

Paul Robeson records and a long rolled up rug. At the front door she began observing and insulting and hassling whoever visited me. Consumed by a jealousy that devoured her, Josie Bliss also threatened to burn my house down. I remember she attacked a sweet, young Eurasian woman who came to visit me.

The Colonial police considered her an uncontrolled presence disturbing the peace on that quiet street. They told me that they would expel her from the country if I did not take her in. I suffered for several days, going back and forth between the tenderness of her unfortunate love and the terror she inspired in me. I could not let her set foot in the house. She was a terrorist lover, capable of doing anything.

Finally, one day she decided to leave. She begged me to accompany her to the ship. When it was about to depart and I had to get off, she left behind those who accompanied her and kissing me in an outburst of suffering and love, she filled my face with tears. Like a ritual, she kissed my arms, my suit, and suddenly, she kissed my shoes without my being able to stop her. When she rose again, her face was covered with the chalk powder from my white shoes. I could not ask her to stay, to get off that ship which would take her away forever. Reason stopped me, but my heart acquired a new scar which has never cured. That turbulent suffering, those terrible tears rolling down her whitened face, are engraved in my memory.[2]

"Josie Bliss", the mysterious, enigmatic poem that concluded *Residence on Earth* in 1935, was the Burmese lover's revenge: it was the poem that resolved the division between sexuality and memory (writing) which up until that point had limited Neruda's poetic potential. After six years, the terrorist lover managed to conquer the poet's intimate resistance and to reclaim the status of the unforgettable Lover in his memory and in his writing. The unequivocal sign of that recovery was the titling of the poem in her name, which appeared for the first time in *Residence on Earth* and with the honors conferred on a title: "Josie Bliss". Because for Neruda, particularly in those years, to title a poem of his with the name of a person who was alive (like the "Ode to Federico García Lorca", also published in 1935) was always a very rare and extremely significant matter.

---

2 Neruda, *Confieso que he vivido* [Memoirs], pp. 114–115.

Naming Josie Bliss meant specifically legitimizing the poet's representation of his erotic impulses per se, without any prophetic pretexts, thereby completing with her full name what he had tried to do on an abstract level in "Nuptial Material" in Buenos Aires. In other words, the decision to name Josie Bliss, the quintessential erotic and anti-prophetic figure, meant sanctioning his own acceptance of his sexual frankness. Consequently, the poem "Josie Bliss" is for me one of the most important "archives" that unquestionably validates the real existence of that woman—especially if we analyze his hermetic writing—without any easy or simple massage of Neruda's ego.

As we have seen, Neruda's road to the elaboration and rendering of a title to that splendid *blue sonata* was dark and difficult. It was scarcely evoked in the version of the memoirs that the biographer Eisner called (showing a lack of knowledge about Neruda's poetry only comparable to Kantor's) "only...an exotic tale." The poem explains the central motive behind the farewell, introducing a reference to the stage of the poet's life in Rangoon in 1928:

> Tal vez sigo existiendo en una calle que el aire hace llorar
> con un determinado lamento lúgubre de tal manera
> que todas las mujeres viste de sordo azul:
> yo existo en ese día repartido,
> existo allí como una piedra pisada por un buey,
> como un testigo sin duda olvidado.
>
> [Perhaps I continue to exist on a street where the air makes one cry / with a determined and somber lament in such a way / that all women dress in a deafening blue: / I exist on that day spread out, / I exist there like a stone that is stepped on by an ox, / like a witness who has undoubtedly been forgotten.]

The last stanza encapsulates the attempt to recuperate the farewell at the ship, beginning with the passionate reiteration of the deictic expression *ahí están* [there are]:

> Ahí están, ahí están
> los besos arrastrados por el polvo junto a un triste navío,
> ahí están las sonrisas desaparecidas, los trajes que una mano
> sacude llamando el alba:
> parece que la boca de la muerte no quiere morder rostros,
> dedos, palabras, ojos:

ahí están otra vez como grandes peces que completan el cielo
con su azul material vagamente invencible.
[There are, there are
the kisses swept along with the dust next to the sad ship,
there are the missing smiles, the suits that one hand
dusts off at the call of dawn:
it seems as though death's mouth does not want to bite faces,
fingers, words, eyes:
there they are again like large fish which complete the sky
with their vaguely invincible blue material.]

BIBLIOGRAPHY

Aleixandre, Vicente. *Los encuentros*. Madrid: Espasa-Calpe, 1985.
Alonso, Amado. *Poesía y estilo de Pablo Neruda*. Segunda edición, definitiva. Buenos Aires: Sudamericana, 1951.
Alpert, Michael. "Los militares, la política y la guerra" en Paul Preston ed. *Revolución y guerra en España 1931-1939*. Madrid: Alianza Editorial, 1986. [English version: *Revolution and War in Spain, 1931-1939*. New York : Routledge, 2001]
Beevor, Antony. *La guerra civil española*. Barcelona: Crítica, 2005. [English version: *The Spanish Civil War*. New York: Penguin Books, 2001]
Bombal, María Luisa. *Obras completas*. Edición de Lucía Guerra. Santiago: Zig-Zag, 2010.
Cardone, Inés María. *Los amores de Neruda*. Santiago: Plaza y Janés, 2003.
Corral, Galo. "Dónde y cómo nació Malva Marina." *Nerudiana* 21-22 (2017).
Curtius, Ernst Robert. *Literatura europea y Edad Media latina*. México: Fondo de Cultura Económica, 1955. [English edition: *European Literature and the Latin Middle Ages*. Trans. Willard R. Trask. New York: Harper Row, 1953]
Dawes, Greg. *Multiforme y comprometido. Neruda después de 1956*. Santiago: RIL Editores, 2014.
De Costa, René. *The Poetry of Pablo Neruda*. Cambridge, MA & London: Harvard University Press, 1979.
_____. "El Neruda de Huidobro" en Hernán Loyola ed., *Neruda en Sássari. Simposio Intercontinental 1984*. Sássari: Seminario di Studi Latinoamericani, 1987.
Délano, Luis Enrique. *Memorias: Aprendiz de escritor / Sobre todo Madrid*. Santiago: RIL Editores, 2004.
Edwards, Jorge. *Adiós, poeta*. Santiago: Penguin Random House, 1990.
Eisner, Mark. *Neruda: The Poet's Calling*. New York: HarperCollins Publishers, 2018.
Falcón, Lola. "Testimonios sobre Delia del Carril/Lola Falcón" en *Boletín Fundación Pablo Neruda*, año III, vol. IV (Primavera 1991).
Feinstein, Adam. *Pablo Neruda: A Passion for Life*. New York: Bloomsbury, 2004.
Fischer, María Luisa. *Neruda: construcción y legados de una figura cultural*. Santiago: Editorial Universitaria, 2008.

Gligo, Ágata. *María Luisa [Bombal]*. Santiago: Editorial Andrés Bello, 1985.
Goic, Cedomil. "Cronología" en Vicente Huidobro, *Obra poética*. Edición crítica de Cedomil Goic. Nanterre / Madrid: Colección Archivos 45, 2003.
González Vera, José Santos. "Testimonio" en *Aurora* 3-4 (1964).
Gutiérrez Revuelta, Pedro. "El galope verde de Pablo Neruda". *Nerudiana*, Sássari (1995).
Hernández, Jesús. *Negro y rojo. Los anarquistas en la revolución española*. México: Imprenta Nuevo Mundo, 1946.
Kantor, Roanne. "Chasing Your (Josie) Bliss: Troubling Critical Afterlife of Pablo Neruda's Burmese Lover". *Transmodernity*, vol. 3, Num. 2 (Spring 2014).
Lago, Tomás. *Ojos y oídos. Cerca de Neruda*. Edición de Hernán Soto. Santiago: LOM Ediciones, 1999.
Larrea, Juan. *Del Surrealismo a Machu Picchu*. México: Editorial Joaquín Mortiz, 1967.
León, María Teresa. *Memorias de la melancolía*. Madrid: Bruguera, 1982.
Lizama, Patricio y María Inés Zaldívar eds. *Bibliografía y antología crítica de las vanguardias literarias: Chile*. Madrid: Iberoamericana Vervuert, 2009.
Losurdo, Domenico. *Stalin. Storia e critica di una leggenda nera*. Roma: Carocci, 2008. [English version: *Stalin: The History and Critique of a Black Legend*. Trans. David Ferreira. Self-published, 2020.]
Loyola, Hernán. *El joven Neruda 1904-1935*. Santiago: Penguin Random House / Lumen, 2014.
_____. *Neruda. La biografía literaria*. Santiago: Seix Barral, 2006.
Medvedev, Roy y Zores Medvedev. *Stalin sconosciuto. Alla luce degli archivi segreti sovietici*. Milano: Feltrinelli, 2006. [*The Unknown Stalin: His Life, Death and Legacy*. New York: Abrams Press, 2003.]
Morla Lynch, Carlos. *España sufre. Diarios de guerra en el Madrid republicano 1936-1939*. Sevilla: Renacimiento, 2008.
Muñoz, Diego. *Memorias. Recuerdos de la bohemia nerudiana*. Santiago: Mosquito Editores / El Juglar Press, 1999.
Neruda, Pablo. *Confieso que he vivido. Memorias*. Santiago: Seix Barral, 2017. [English version: *Memoirs*. Trans. Hadier St. Martin. New York: Farrar, Straus and Giroux, 1977.]
_____. *Epistolario viajero*. Selección, estudio preliminar y notas Abraham Quezada. Santiago: RIL Editores, 2004.
_____. *Estravagario*. Buenos Aires: Losada, 1958. [*Extravagaria*. Trans. Alistair Reid. Austin: University of Texas Press, 1996.]
_____. *Obras completas*. 5 vols. Edición de Hernán Loyola. Barcelona: Galaxia Gutenberg, 1999-2002.
_____. *Poesía completa*. Tomo 1. Edición de Darío Oses. Santiago: Seix Barral, 2018.

_____. *Residencia en la tierra*. Edición crítica de Hernán Loyola. Madrid: Ediciones Cátedra, 1987. [English version: *Residence on Earth*. Trans. Donald D. Walsh. New York: New Directions, 1973.]
Olivares, Edmundo. *Pablo Neruda. Los caminos de Oriente*. Vol 1. Santiago: LOM Ediciones, 2000.
Padura, Leonardo. *El hombre que amaba los perros*. Buenos Aires: Tusquets, 2013.
Peeters, Hagar. *Malva*. Bogotá: Rey Naranjo Editores, 2017.
Reyes, Bernardo. *El enigma de Malva Marina. La hija de Pablo Neruda*. Santiago: RIL Editores, 2007.
_____. *Retrato de familia. Neruda 1904-1920*. San Juan: Editorial de la Universidad de Puerto Rico, 1996.
Sáez, Fernando. *La Hormiga. Biografía de Delia del Carril, mujer de Pablo Neruda*. Santiago: Catalonia, 2004.
Sanhueza, Leonardo ed. *El Bacalao. Diatribas antinerudianas y otros textos*. Barcelona: Ediciones B, 2004.
Saunders, Frances Stonor. *La CIA y la guerra fría cultural*. Madrid: Debate, 2001. [English original: *Who Paid the Piper? The CIA and the Cultural Cold War*. London: Granta Books, 1999.]
Schidlowsky, David. *Las furias y las penas. Pablo Neruda y su tiempo*. 2 tomos. Santiago: RIL Editores, 2008.
Semprún, Jorge. *Autobiografía de Federico Sánchez*. Barcelona: Planeta, 1977.
Teitelboim, Volodia. *Huidobro. La marcha infinita*. Santiago: BAT, 1993.
_____. *Neruda*. Santiago: Sudamericana, 1996. [English version: *Neruda: An Intimate Biography*. Trans. Beverly J. DeLong-Tonelli. Austin: University of Texas Press, 1992]
Uliánova, Olga. "Entre el auge revolucionario y los abismos del sectarismo: el PC chileno y el Buró Sudamericano de la Internacional Comunista en 1932-1933" in Rolando Álvarez et al. eds. *Fragmentos de una historia. El Partido Comunista de Chile en el siglo XX… 1912-1994*. Santiago: Ediciones ICAL, 2008.
Varas, José Miguel. *Tal vez nunca. Crónicas nerudianas*. Santiago: Editorial Universitaria, 2008.
Vial, Sara. *Neruda vuelve a Valparaíso*. Valparaíso: Ediciones Universitarias, 2004.
Woodbridge, Hensley and David Zubatsky. *Pablo Neruda: An Annotated Bibliography of Biographical and Critical Studies*. New York / London: Garland Publishing, 1988.
Yáñez, María Flora. *Historia de mi vida*. Santiago: Nascimento, 1980.
Zerán, Faride. *La guerrilla literaria. Huidobro-De Rokha-Neruda*. Santiago: BAT, 1992.

Hernán Loyola (Talagante, Chile, 1930) graduate the Instituto Pedagógico at the University of Chile in 1954 with a thesis on *Canto general* (1954) by Pablo Neruda, with whom he befriended in 1952, when the poet returned from Europe. He was a professor at his alma mater until November in 1973, when he began his exile in Italy, where reintiated his academic career. Until 2002 he was a full professor in Spanish and Latin American literature at the University of Sássari—a small city in northern Sardigna (where he still lives)—with visiting professorships at the University of Bordeaux and the University of Budapest.

In 1951 Professor Juan Uribe Echevarría encouraged him to dedicate his research to the life and work of Pablo Neruda, poet and senator in exile in Italy at that moment. His books *Ser y morir en Pablo Neruda* [To Be and to Die in Pablo Neruda, 1967], *Neruda. La biografía literaria* [Neruda: The Literary Biography, 2006] and *El joven Neruda* [The Young Neruda, 2014] were the result of his decision to embark in that direction. In between the publication of these books, he published numerous articles in Latin American and European journals, and one hundred pages dedicated to creating an active bibliography of the poet's work (1968 and 1973). He has also published a critical edition on *Residencia en la tierra* [Residence on Earth] (Madrid: Cátedra, 1987) and a new edition of the *Complete Works* (Barcelona: Galaxia Gutenberg, 1999-2002). He is also the editor of three best selling Neruda anthologies: *Antología esencial* [The Essential Anthology] (Buenos Aires: Losada, 1971), the classic *Antología poética* [Poetic Anthology] (Madrid: Alianza Editorial, 1981; with new updated editions in 2000 and 2014), and the recent *Antología general* [General Anthology], published by the Spanish Royal Academy of the Spanish Language (Madrid: 2010). He has been the Editor-in-Chief of the journal Nerudiana—sponsored by the Pablo Neruda Foundation—since 2006.